Finding Real Yoga

Daren Black

Finding Real Yoga

Copyright © 2025 Daren Black
First published in 2025 in the USA by Daren Black

All rights reserved. No part of this publication may be reproduced, distributed, or transmitted in any form or by any means, including photocopying, recording, or other electronic or mechanical methods without the prior written permission of the author, except in the case of brief quotations.

This is a factual, eyewitness account of historical events enriched with original poetry by Daren Black. Most names have been changed to protect privacy. Efforts have been made to ensure that the information listed in this book is true and accurate. The author and publisher do not assume and hereby disclaim any liability to any party for any loss, damage, or disruption caused by errors or omissions, whether such errors or omissions result from negligence, accident, or any other cause. Nothing in this book is intended to diagnose, treat, cure, or prescribe for disease.

Editing and book design by Daren Black.
Cover design by Hector-Webwise.

If you need help with your journey:
PracticalAyurveda.com

Library of Congress Control Number: 2022919946

ISBN 978-1-7350823-0-1 (Paperback)
ISBN 978-1-7350823-1-8 (kindle/ebook)

    1. Autobiography - Spiritual Self-Help 2. Yoga
       3. History - Gurudev Sri Sri 4. Poetry

Table of Contents

SECTION ONE: SPARK IGNITES   1

Chapter One: First Meeting   1
   Blessed Are Those Who Are Confused   6
   Darshan   7
   The Three Gunas   8
   The Sun Blazes   9
   Introduction   10
   Vast Array of Knowledge   14

Chapter Two: First Course   17
   Delivery Vehicles and Emotions   20
   Karma   22
   Be Authentic   24
   Live as Though You Don't Exist   26
   Burn, Vanish and Dissolve   26
   The Present Moment   27
   What Is Real Freedom?   29
   Laughter   31

Chapter Three: First Sudarshan Kriya   33
   Enjoy Each Breath   34
   Chanting OM   35
   The Nearest Wall   42
   Illness and Injury   43
   Ego   47
   Love Is Our True Nature   48
   God, Guru, and Self Are the Same   48
   Late-Night Car Caravan   49
   Secret Hindu Temple   52
   Amazing Meal Cooked by the Master   53
   Gurudev Sri Sri Spoke of Time with Maharishi   54
   The Master Told Me to Teach More Yoga   56
   Spirulina and Chlorella Trip   57

The White Silk Asan	59
Chapter Four: First Advanced Silence Course	*59*
Keeping Silence and Tapas	61
Observing Sensations	67
What Is Yoga?	68
What Is Meditation and What Is not Meditation?	76
Yoga with the Master	82
Fresh Air Increases Prana	82
Creating True Resilience in the Body	85
Facing Challenges on First Silence Course	86
Throwing Thoughts	88
Big Mind	89
Coming out of Trauma	91
Teacher Training Invitation	94
Life Presents	99
Profound Longing	103
In a Fire of Shredded Names	106

SECTION TWO: ACCELERATION — 107

Chapter Five: First Teacher Training	*107*
Singing	116
Praise the Light	124
We All Want to Be	126
Guru Purnima, 1988	129
They Say that the Body Will Die	132
Tears are Cried	135
Ancient Palm Leaf Books	136
Upset Tummy	138
Pain	140
Barely Keeping Things Together	141
You Be My Guidance	143
Chapter Six: Potency of the Sangha	*145*
Path of the Brave	147
Burning Every Day	149
Only the Brave Will Walk This Path	152
Meditating with a Lecture	152
Stop All Exercise	153
Time is that Subtle Thread	156

SECTION THREE: FIND CENTER   157

Chapter Seven: First Los Angeles Art of Living Center   157
  A Very Detached Master   161
  Gurudev Laughs at an Old TV Show   162
  Assignments from the Master   162
  When Will I Be Able to Live?   165
  Editing the Sudarshan Kriya Tape   166
  Silence, an Essential Component of Lectures   167
  The 12 Second Rule   167
  Resistance to Change   170
  Publicity   173
  Surrender   174
  Dealing with Feelings   175
  Love Is Anguish   178
  Religion Versus Saints: Banana Peel or Banana?   179
  We Can Do Nothing   184
  Secret Questions Finally Answered   185
  Mistakes and Acceptance   185
  Be Hopeless   187
  'Positive Thinking' Causes Depression   189

Chapter Eight: Second Teacher Training with Gurudev Sri Sri   191
  Purpose of Knowledge   194
  Basic Course at Casa de Maria   196
  Heavy Duty Blessing   198
  Casa de Maria Advanced Course   205
  Blast Away   209
  Recording Bhajans   210
  The Guru Had Me Keep a Secret   211
  The Karma of Received Instructions   212
  Private Puja   218

Chapter Nine: Guru Purnima 1989   219
  Understanding God   220
  The Guru Blasted Them with Anger   225
  Surprise Adventure in a Foreign Country   229
  Choose One Noble Path   233
  Miraculous Rescue   233
  Wind Takes Me   236
  Blessings   237

Sankalpa	241
Chapter Ten: Airport Tricks	243
First Camp Whittier Advanced Course	246
Answering Questions	249
Disneyland	250
Bhanu's First Vocal Album	251
Choosing a Cook	252
Make Rasayana with Gurudev at 2 AM	253
Run on the Beach with Gurudev	256
Enjoy Something You Don't Like	257
Close Call	260
Snack for One Is a Meal for Another	262
Never Hate Anybody	263
You Are Not Your Emotions	263
Desperately in Need of a Nap	265
Wedding for Chris and Judy Reed	268
All the Past Is Gone	274
What Use Is Poetry?	276
Chapter Eleven: Assistant Teaching with the Master	277
Gratitude and Less Talking	281
Lectured About Clothing Choices	282
Satsang on Our Own	284
Potluck Secret of Mr. X	284
Board of Directors	286
Taking Instructions Only from the Guru	287
Relationships	288
Anger from the Master	289
Newsletters	290

SECTION FOUR: BHAKTI SUTRAS — 295

Chapter Twelve: Opposite Values	295
Using the Land Line Before We Had Cell Phones	300
Bedtime Trick by the Master	302
Love and Longing	307
Lemon Ginger	310
The Third North American Teacher Training Course	311
Loon Lake Guru Purnima 1990	320
Gurudev Enjoys a Canoe Ride	329

Raft Tied to the Shore	331
Special Tears on Guru Purnima	332
Even the Master	334
Not Move at All During Sudarshan Kriya	336
In the Pavilion of Joy	338
Everyone is on Fire	341
Chapter Thirteen: The First Temescal Canyon Advanced Course	*341*
Dancing with the Master Under a Full Moon	343
Be a Tree	344
Refuge and Solace	346

SECTION FIVE: INDIA, 1991 — 347

Chapter Fourteen: First Trip to India	*347*
Amazing Journey in the Tiny School Bus	350
On the One Hand	353
Guru Purnima Blessings	355
Public Talk Given by Gurudev in India	355
Meeting a Shankaracharya	356
Early Morning Meditation with the Master	358
The Original Incense	359
How Gurudev Sri Sri Made Me More Ahimsa	360
Observing Emotional Discomfort	364
Gardening Seva	366
Chapter Fifteen: Saving My Life Again	*368*
Components of Exhalation	373
Cobra Cave Adventure	375
Marriage	377
Ancient Wisdom of Ashtavakra	379
Skill of Handling Silk at the Waterfall	381
Typing a Letter for the Guru	382
Trip to Mysore and Miracle Photo	385
To My Dearest Lord Sri Sri Parameshwari Gurudev	390
Washing Dishes in Noisy Silence	391
Keep Your Smile	393
More Gardening Seva	393
Beware the Exploding Heart	396
Birthing One Smile	397
One Smile	400

Chapter Sixteen: Navaratri, 1991 ... *401*
    Chandi Homa ... 401
    Losing Track of Time ... 403
    Know Only Me ... 405
    Another Opportunity to Be Nobody ... 406
    Creating Advanced Course Teachers ... 407
    Hard to Say Goodbye ... 408
    My Heart Is Soaked ... 409
    Another Lump in my Throat ... 411

SECTION SIX: MOVING FORWARD ... **413**

Chapter Seventeen: Back in California ... *413*
    Where Is True Value? ... 414
    Ganesh, Remover of Obstacles ... 415
    Lord, Let Me Be ... 417
    Gratitude ... 418
    My Heart Holds You Softly ... 419

Treasured Quotes of Gurudev Sri Sri ... **421**

More Poetry by Daren ... **427**
    Celebrate the Exploding Heart ... 427
    My Life Burst into Fullness ... 428

Bibliography: Books and Lectures ... **429**

Bibliography: Articles and Websites ... **430**

Resources ... **433**

About the Author ... **433**

SECTION ONE: SPARK IGNITES

Chapter One: First Meeting

Sitting in bed, I held the plastic phone cable in one hand and the pushbutton phone in the other. I wanted an undisturbed sleep. My final bedtime activity was to unplug the phone. Surprisingly, the phone rang as I squeezed my fingers to unplug the cable. For a blink, I froze.

It was late in March 1988 when a friend of mine called me just half a second before I unplugged my beige, plastic, landline telephone for the night. Given how tired I was, I almost plowed ahead and unplugged the phone without answering the call. Something made me pause and take the call.

"Hello?"
"What are you doing?"
"Going to sleep."
"I want you to meet someone."
"Who is it? When?"
"Now."
"Tonight?!"
"He's really special."
"Let's talk about this tomorrow."
"You just have to meet him. You'll really like him."
"I'm already in bed!"
"He's really special. Just come to meet him."
"This is crazy. I'm tired and aching to fall asleep."
"He would like to meet you."
"Some other time. Who is it?"
"Just come; I know you will appreciate him."
"Who is he?"

"When you meet him, you will know."

"What's his name?"

"I'll give you the address. Just come over."

"What is his name?"

"Write down the address. Do you have a pen? Here's the address."

"Why won't you tell me his name?"

"It's close to you."

"I'm going to sleep! Goodnight!" I said in exasperation as I hung up and simultaneously unplugged the phone.

That was how I refused the meeting when I was first invited to meet spiritual leader Gurudev Sri Sri Ravi Shankar. To deny such a precious opportunity seems inconceivable. The mysterious, frustrating nature of the initial invitation gave no hint that I was turning my back on a supreme embodiment of real yoga. I was in the process of keeping a balance of rest and activity, fundamental in yoga.

A few days later, the same friend called early in the morning. She insisted that it was important that I meet that mysterious person. She was on her way and offered to pick me up.

At that moment, I had nothing important to do. That morning, not having a name for the stranger did not bother me. I could not think of a good reason not to go, so I agreed.

The impact of that first meeting was completely unexpected. At first, it seemed casual and low-key. A course taught by the mystery person had just finished that weekend. Volunteers were packing up in preparation to drive from Los Angeles to San Francisco. The neighborhood where we were meeting in Los Angeles was old and rundown. Perhaps that reinforced the zero expectations I had for this meeting.

Two women told the small group of people who were gathered, "He will meet with you in a few minutes."

In March 1988, most people had not heard of the

swami, Pundit Ravi Shankar. He was then often addressed as "Punditji." Later, he became known as Gurudev Sri Sri.

We were ushered into a tiny bedroom. Dressed all in white, the young master was sitting on the floor immediately inside the door.

A slight wave of uncertainty rippled through me. I felt sorry for him since I had to walk directly in front of him. We barely had room to squeeze past the diminutive swami without stepping on him. My immediate sense was that he deserved a much more honorable seat.

The swami, known later as Gurudev Sri Sri, didn't seem to mind. He radiated a feeling of enjoying a happy adventure. Silently, he greeted me with a sincere smile and radiant eyes. His eyes were filled with joy and kindness.

The young master sat right next to a bed that looked like it was made for a child. The few of us sat in a tight circle on the floor. Luckily, nobody had a big bag with them, since there was barely any room left on the floor. Two people were on my left, and three people were on my right. I was directly facing the mysterious swami.

Due to my previous back and knee injuries, I could not sit cross-legged. My legs were straight in front of me, with my feet pointing at the swami, Ravi Shankar.

He did not say anything about it. Many days later, I heard that it was not considered proper to point one's feet at a saint. It is not just a matter of cultural courtesy. On a subtle level, there is 'exhaust energy' that comes out of most people's feet. In spiritual circles, it is said that the energy of an enlightened person is of such a high vibration that the exhaust energy from their feet can put another person into a state of bliss consciousness.

In spite of my innocent mistake, I ended up having one of the most remarkable experiences of my lifetime.

Remaining seated with relaxed attentiveness, the

youthful Ravi Shankar started on his left and proceeded around the circle. He got everyone's name and briefly said hello. Then he softly uttered, "Let's close our eyes."

I sat waiting for further instruction, wondering if we were going to meditate or do something else.

No more instructions were given. With the door to the room mostly closed and curtains covering the window, it was like sitting in a small, dark hut. In the dim light, I sat, eyes closed, silently waiting. I was impressed that everyone was respectfully motionless. The room was as quiet as an underground cave.

Suddenly, in my mind, I was having a vision of bright light. I noticed that I was pure consciousness, filling the universe with bright light. The light ranged from thick, rich golden to various shades of yellow to pale, transparent white to intensely opaque pearl. Other colors hovered on the periphery. I realized that nothing else existed anywhere other than pure consciousness. Poised within that was my small self, with all of its baggage.

Centered in the middle of that bright light was a dark mass. I realized that I was seeing my own mind, clogging my true self. The dark mass was a mountain of mud, of stresses and impressions from a vast period of time. It seemed overwhelmingly huge. I saw that my mind was full of junk I didn't need. I felt exposed and embarrassed.

Then I was given the understanding, "You can be free of this." The mountain seemed small at that moment, as I unintentionally and suddenly gained a larger perspective.

With deep assurance, I comprehended the truth about the possibility of freedom from the garbage clogging my mind. I saw space surrounding the mountain.

It was profound and straightforward, totally out of the blue. This was a completely unexpected experience.

A compassionate presence that I assumed to originate

from this mysterious saint, yet which was clearly non-localized, was reassuring me that freedom was possible. The sense was not just that it was possible but that it was a certainty. I was told, "You will be free of this."

This was all a silent, clear, spontaneous, internal knowingness, profound yet simple. This experience entirely consumed me. Time was irrelevant.

What the heck!? It was hard to digest. Palpable assurance came from all around me. I understood that I am my true self, pure consciousness. *I am the bright light surrounding everything, not a mountain of mud.*

He quietly suggested that we could slowly open our eyes. Speechless, my experience was crisp and mind-boggling. I was stunned with wonder and felt silent, inside and out, for most of the rest of the day.

This special being seemed to be much more than the name Pundit Ravi Shankar might convey. Puzzled, I knew that he would have a major role to play in helping me remove that mountain of mud. It was sobering to feel that he knew me in a way that I had never known myself. It was embarrassing to think that he could know that I had a mountain of mud stuck in my soul.

At the same time, I trusted the situation. My intention for life was to be as real as possible. It wasn't always easy to be real. It could be frustrating. Sometimes, it seemed impossible to be real. Amazingly, this young master seemed more effortlessly real than most people.

In silence, I filed out of the room. I found myself hovering near the enigmatic young sage. Others chatted and took a couple of photos.

I heard some of the people discussing the planned trip to San Francisco, where the young master would be teaching his next Basic Course. Confused, I was also intrigued.

Blessed Are Those Who Are Confused

(From a talk given in 1988 by Gurudev Sri Sri)

"Blessed are those who are confused.
There is a difference between confusion and doubt.
Confusion arises when a belief system breaks, when some ideas, concepts, or something in your head shatters. That is a sign of growth.
Your progress is measured by your confusion.
Confusion is that shift from head to heart. When your head gets confused and you don't know what to do, then you move towards the unknown. It goes from known to unknown. The first step towards the unknown is confusion. Doubt is from heart to head. Confusion is from head to heart. This is the journey in life.
Blessed are those who are confused, because blessed are those who move from head to heart. Blessed are those who are growing: going beyond concepts, beyond ideas, beyond opinions, into being, their very being.
Doubt is establishing oneself strongly in the intellect. Looking for an answer. When in doubt, you are always looking for an answer.
Intellect divides and dissects. That's what it does: analyze. From there, you drop into your heart. The quality of the heart is that it brings together everything. It brings all parts of you together; it fuses.
Head: analysis. It divides and categorizes. Heart unites.
When people think they know, they are not confused. They are definite about what they know.
In this world, there is nothing that is definite. This world is a place of amusement.
Amusement means nothing definite. Definite means

limited possibilities. Amusement means infinite possibilities, openness, and the unknown."

Darshan

When I met Gurudev, I was a mess. I didn't recognize my own desperation, downward spiral, or failing health. There were some people who thought I was beyond redemption. Giving up was not an option for me. I kept going. Miracles gave me a new life. I want to tell you about it. I need to fill in some foundational understandings first. It will make sense if you keep reading. Let's dive in and keep going.

There is a tradition of going to an enlightened master and sitting near them. Sometimes, the sight of an enlightened master is enough to provoke a personally transformative experience. Some people call viewing or meeting the master "receiving *darshan*."

Darshan is viewing the sacred divine. It could be an image of a deity. There are stories of miracles that have happened when someone was near a saint, or even a statue, or simply thinking of a divine being.

The experience of the state of real yoga, or union, also known as *samadhi*, pure being, supreme self, or pure consciousness, can be shared to some extent. Being near a master, whether or not the master looks at you or speaks to you, can be very uplifting. A true master effortlessly lives real yoga, and conveys the presence of divine energy.

One way to put it is that *sattva*, the quality of purity, harmony, and balance, increases due to the nearness of divine presence. The experience of darshan elevates both sattva, harmony, and energy, or *shakti*.

Darshan enhances the life force, *prana,* or *chi.* Many healings are a result of darshan.

The Three Gunas

Gunas are qualities. Vedic tradition finds three qualities to be fundamental for understanding nature. These three foundational qualities are known as the three gunas: *sattva, rajas,* and *tamas.* The three gunas are active within and around us at all times. The dynamic interplay of the three gunas defines the quality of our mind, body, and energy. Any situation can be analyzed on the basis of three gunas. Understanding something about the nature of these fundamental qualities provides us with a way of making better choices to promote health and harmony in our lives.

Sattva is clarity, purity, and balance. Rajas is kinetic energy. Tamas is inertia. Rajas spurs us to action, and tamas enables us to sleep. Sattva brings harmony, awareness, and peacefulness. You may see it spelled satva, sattva, or satwa.

Yoga and Ayurveda encourage lifestyles that promote sattva, so we can enjoy more harmony and pure consciousness. Rajas leads to both highs and lows. Rajas wants more. Too much rajas leads to aggression and overdoing. Tamas promotes staying in one feeling, place, state, or phase. Excess tamas yields dullness and inertia.

All your experiences affect your balance. Everything you eat or drink and whatever you do affects the balance of the three gunas in your own mind-body system. Each emotion you feel or try to avoid has its own impact.

The Sun Blazes

The sun blazes in my heart eternally.

What kind of contradiction is this?

Where light shines

radiant,

day and night?

Night used to be

full of darkness…

Can we find truth

free of fear and fright?

Things come and go.

Let Divine Radiance

shine forever.

Hold my hand

as you travel

across the eons.

(Poems in this book are originals by Daren Black.)

At the end of my first meeting with Pundit Ravi Shankar, now known as Gurudev Sri Sri, the group lingered outside. There was mention of the drive that they were about to start, from Los Angeles to San Francisco. As he walked slowly, I came close to the young swami. I quietly asked if what I had experienced in that tiny room was from darshan with him. He murmured confirmation. There was more silent, empty space. Then he suggested that I take his Basic Course. Real yoga was calling me.

I was curious and asked, "What is your lineage?"

"The Holy Tradition."

A light went on for me, as this was the lineage of Maharishi Mahesh Yogi and his master, Brahmananda Saraswati.

"That's a great tradition."

From the deep calm of an ocean, he replied, "The greatest."

"And where do your techniques come from?"

"Pure consciousness."

"That's a good source," I observed.

"The best."

That was it. I knew I had to get myself to San Francisco to take the course. Calculations began in my mind to figure out what I would have to do to be able to go.

Introduction

People become seekers for various reasons, though many of such people may not identify themselves as seekers. Many people feel incomplete, want a more meaningful life, or look for something deeper in life. Some people want relief from illness, pain, sadness, and/or hardship. Some people want to celebrate a more expanded reality. All my life, I had been seeking everlasting love, though without much skill. Gurudev Sri Sri has said that chasing money, fame, or relationship is actually a distraction from longing for love.

Spiritual upliftment and moments of expanded awareness can be had through many means. Common methods include meditation, *pranayama* (specific yogic breathing techniques), yoga exercises and positions or *asanas*, performing service (also known as *seva* or karma yoga), chanting mantras, group singing or chanting (also known as *kirtan)*, and discussion or thinking about wisdom.

Many people have had irresistible moments of expanded awareness, or *samadhi*, when everything seemed perfect at that moment. There was a sense of just-right repose and connectedness. Much of the time, most people exist within three distinct functions of the mind: waking, dreaming, or sleeping. There is a fourth state of awareness, which one reaches when the normal modes of the mind are transcended. Usually via meditation. This is a state of yoga or union, known as *turiya*. EEG studies have shown that this fourth state has distinctive brain waves.

One who actively pursues wisdom and the experience of such samadhi moments, or who knows there is something more and is driven to find it, could be called a seeker.

Some people read books and find nuggets of inspiration. Sometimes in a class, uplifting experiences may be had. Better yet, you find a teacher who has had some experience and has attained some expansion of awareness. Even better, and rare, is to meet a teacher who is living with expanded awareness all the time.

Someone with real, continuous depth and stability of samadhi is quite rare. Such a person who effortlessly is constantly in touch with pure consciousness is considered enlightened. There are levels of enlightenment and greater degrees of blossoming in consciousness.

Most rare and most powerful is to meet a fully blossomed saint, trained by their own guru, who carries the wisdom of a lineage of masters. A lineage like that is known as a *sampradaya*. The lineage succession is also referred to as *parampara*. The lineage keeps real yoga alive.

It is truly a rare and profound blessing to be able to spend time with an enlightened master who is the latest representative of a long line of masters. As Gurudev Sri Sri has proven, such a person will effortlessly exhibit important qualities, including equanimity, intelligence, friendliness, pleasant speech, fearlessness, absence of expectations, gentleness, courage, non-attachment, total absence of perversion, and freedom from aversions. All these qualities should be present, or you will end up with a less evolved teacher. Real yoga has many parts. Let's look further.

Real yoga uses mantras. When a person wants a mantra to use for meditation, it is important to receive one from a teacher who is a representative of a tradition. The teacher must be authorized by their master to give out mantras. There is an ancient understanding that, in order to reach the highest, you must receive a mantra via a sampradaya.

Dealing with homelessness and serious illness left me exhausted and desperate. Gurudev saved me. I have been extremely lucky to spend significant time with Gurudev, a living representative of an ancient spiritual tradition. I also spent a little time with Maharishi Mahesh Yogi. Our tradition is known to many as the Holy Tradition.

Most people who knew me before 1988 would undoubtedly have been skeptical that this book could come out of my awareness. If you had asked me to predict what I would be doing after the year 1987, I would not have dreamed of a fraction of the reality of my experience.

If it were not for the saving grace of the Holy Tradition and the real yogi, Gurudev Sri Sri, I would undoubtedly have died many years ago. Besides enabling me to live a healthy life, Gurudev invigorated my life with purpose, value, and the essence of real yoga. Words fail to convey the enormous depth of gratitude that I feel.

Often, in the late 1980's, when the name "Pundit Ravi Shankar" was used, people would assume it was regarding the sitar player. Two tremendously different people had the same name. This often resulted in crazy, humorous incidents. People in many cities would show up for public lectures, assuming that they would be listening to sitar music. Some people signed up for the Basic Course thinking that they would be learning about music from India.

During 1988 through 1994, most people still addressed Gurudev Sri Sri as Pundit Ravi Shankar, or Punditji. During the mid-to-late 1990's, many people began using the term Guruji, or Gurudev, instead of Punditji. After he became known as Sri Sri, the title Punditji was lost.

Gurudev Sri Sri makes no arrogant show of talents, knowledge, or mastery. His simple, open approachability is comforting and winning. Gurudev lives real yoga.

Gurudev's demeanor makes spiritual and yogic attainment seem easy. Possible in the realm of everyday reality. Yet Gurudev's stature of spiritual accomplishment is unfathomably profound and wondrously inspiring.

Gurudev can effortlessly describe details of the laws of nature. He is noted for his ability to share clear, easily understood explanations of both mundane necessities and profound reality. People of all ages find it easy to relate to what Gurudev has to say. His teachings appeal to people of all faiths and backgrounds.

It is just as easy for Gurudev to give lucid commentary

on widely known scripture, such as the *Bible* or *Bhagavad Gita,* or on more obscure texts, such as *Ashtavakra Samhita* or *Soundarya Lahari*. Gurudev's explanations are easy to relate to. One does not need special training to enjoy what Gurudev says.

It has been my personal observation that Gurudev genuinely wants to help as many people as possible. This is obvious to many people around the world. The various organizations that he has established around the world offer a wide variety of courses, which make it possible for people of all ages to gain tools to improve their lives.

From prisoners to presidents, from students to secretaries to security officers to senior management, people from all walks of life find personal relief, wisdom, and techniques of great value in such courses.

Uplifting courses designed by Gurudev Sri Sri are offered around the world by Art of Living, Art Excel, Prison Smart, the International Association for Human Values (IAHV), Vyakti Vikas Kendra (India), Art de Vivre, Apex, TLEX, etc.

Vast Array of Knowledge

There is some notable correlation throughout the wide range of knowledge covered by Gurudev. Many people see this just within the context of a single course.

Gurudev's commentaries provide an abundance of material, making it easy to find helpful, relatable knowledge. In less than 30 years, Gurudev has given commentary on many ancient scriptures, including Narada's *Bhakti Sutras*,

Patanjali's *Yoga Sutras, Yoga Vasishtha, Upanishads, Bhagavad Gita, Shiva Sutras,* Adi Shankara's *Soundarya Lahari,* the *Ashtavakra Samhita,* and *Vigyan Bhairav.* This is a prodigious accomplishment of the highest caliber, making real yoga more attainable for more people.

When a person is satisfied by being stuffed with experience or food, that is a tamasic state of fulfillment. Gurudev says that only by knowing one's inner being can a person enjoy a sattvic state of fulfillment.

Gurudev has made available a mind-blowing abundance of methods and opportunities for a person to blossom in real yoga and experience divine love.

By sharing this collection of real-life events and poems, I pray that people will be helped and inspired. Hopefully, *Finding Real Yoga* gives more than a hint of a tiny taste of the huge reality of supreme consciousness that has been revealed by the divine grace of Gurudev.

Spending time with a master can yield joyful, puzzling, challenging, enlightening, and sometimes ridiculous, shocking, or hilarious experiences.

Masters are often relaxed, kind, generous, and wise people who seem simple and easy. If the time is right, they may answer many questions, accessing knowledge through focused awareness tuned in to the truth.

Real masters are not showoffs who try to impress people with their abilities. True masters are in a flow of pure, divine energy all the time. They effortlessly live real yoga.

Most people have never met a true master. Unfortunately, charlatans and wannabes made some rotten impressions and left a few people with not only an aversion to, but a misunderstanding of what a spiritual master is.

Enlightened beings can be unpredictable. From a space of palpable love and caring, they may do things that seem markedly unusual, chaotic, or nonsensical to help people break through rigid beliefs, concepts, and stuck personal boundaries. Real masters help people connect with their true selves. Ultimately, the master is a profound mystery, just as love, life, and the workings of the universe are mysteries.

For many of my years with Gurudev, I pointedly avoided sharing any of my personal experiences. On various occasions, unplanned poems erupted in my awareness, revealing flavorful, intense experiences. Repeatedly, I have felt an inner prompting to share some of my experiences and poems that illustrate going beyond the struggle for survival.

Reluctantly, I considered putting together a collection of some poems. In this case, a book of poetry did not feel complete on its own. It seemed that sharing some of the adventures I have had would be entertaining as well as instructive. I wanted to share useful wisdom and convey some background on the depth of colors hinted at by poems.

It is important to me that people have an accurate picture of some distinctive events from my early years with Gurudev. Without cell phones, there was a palpable depth of serenity in meetings with the master. Gatherings were more mystical and silent. In that context of purity and wisdom, it was easy for people to be inspired and uplifted.

Gurudev has offered valuable knowledge in tremendous depth and enormous breadth. It is crucial to share this. A living embodiment of Vedic wisdom, Gurudev has a superior ability to express the varieties of timeless wisdom in easy-to-understand English.

This knowledge is as important to me as life itself. I have done my utmost to uphold the purity of the knowledge, the purity of the teaching, and the purity of the lineage of masters. As I have been rescued, I am glad to help others.

Please note that I have done my best to list the factual details of real events with accuracy. Some names have been changed to protect privacy. Offering all this at the lovely feet of my dear Gurudev, I am profoundly grateful. This has truly been a journey of empowerment and discovery with the master. Read further about this uplifting, wild ride.

Chapter Two: First Course

At the beginning of April 1988, a few days after meeting the master, I ended up in San Francisco to attend the "Basic Course." A public lecture had been scheduled for the evening of the day before the course.

Since we arrived at the lecture venue a little early, the master decided to go for a walk while waiting for people to arrive. He invited me to go with him.

How did I get lucky enough to be the only one walking with this mysterious person? Knowing him to be a saint, I wanted to do my utmost to behave appropriately. We walked through an empty, partially lit parking lot and along a pier on the edge of the San Francisco Bay.

I was just some random person struggling to survive. *How can I possibly measure up?* I felt shy and honored to be accepted by this saintly being. My mind was in wonder. I could not have verbalized all these understandings at that moment.

He walked with nothing but his simple white *dhoti*, a wrap-around cloth, over his legs and another white cloth over his white shirt. Nobody else was there. The night was dark in the distance. It felt as peaceful as being in a vast forest overlooked by puffy white clouds in a brilliant sky.

I had been practicing meditation and yoga daily for fifteen years by then, and teaching both when I could. Next to this exalted embodiment of the goal of these practices, I felt like a rank beginner, raw and self-conscious.

During our quiet walk, I had an instinct that this mysterious swami could easily sense any thought or feeling passing through me. *I hope that I do not think about anything that might be embarrassing or disruptive*!

There was also a strong feeling that I was with an old friend who had already been through a lot with me.

On the first morning of the Basic Course, we gathered in a large room on the pier in San Francisco, a popular place for scheduling events. All the windows were open. The temperature was about 50 to 55 degrees F, and there was no heat in the room.

The organizers had informed us that since we would be doing breathing exercises, the windows would be kept open. It was suggested that we bring sweaters, jackets, hats, blankets, etc. so that we could be comfortable. It looked like all of us had followed the suggestion and arrived prepared. Some of us laughed to see happy people in jackets, holding bagged lunches, pillows, blankets, etc. There were lots of smiles and ripples of excitement as we gathered.

Yoga is a tradition with practices designed to increase a person's prana. Several types of yogic breathing practices, known as *pranayama,* will directly increase the prana in people. All the discussions, as well as asanas and pranayama exercises, were conducted in this well-ventilated room. We were getting a wonderful dose of oxygen and fresh prana.

We were told that it is important to have fresh air so that the breathing practices would do what they were intended to do, namely improve health, give us lots of energy, and relieve stress.

Science tells us that when humans breathe, poisonous waste gases are released with every exhalation. Every minute, a person will exhale toxic carbon dioxide, a natural waste product of bodily cellular functions.

The majority of each exhalation is not capable of sustaining human life. Increasing nitrogen or carbon dioxide in the air can make the air unfit to breathe. This is one reason why it is important to have fresh air flowing constantly through the room. Then we are minimizing the inhalation of waste gases from ourselves and others.

The next day, the temperature, though the same, was a complete non-issue. The potency of yogic breathing practices done in the fresh air was distinctly uplifting and refreshing. It was clear that everyone had experienced this. It was vastly better than doing pranayama in a stuffy room with closed windows.

There may have been 19 people attending the course. Oddly, sometimes it felt like many more people were there, and other times, much fewer than that.

At one point, our saintly leader asked me to stand up while everyone else remained seated. He looked at me and declared loud enough for everyone to hear, "So they think you are a madman, so what!?"

I felt impaled on the spot. *How did he know?* was my sudden thought to myself.

I was taken aback both by the words of the master and by my immediate thought in response. I was sensing that, indeed, historically, some people had thought I was a madman! I knew in that moment that I had avoided admitting this to myself. Further, it seemed like I was being given an opportunity to see the issue that had been stuck within me. As well as a fresh ability to let it go and grow far beyond it.

There was no malice from our leader. I sensed that he was waking us up and helping us.

More of my limitations became apparent to me as I spent time with the saint now called Gurudev. When I met him, I had self-doubt that I was not even aware of. In my system, there was a lot of irritation compounded with an aching heart. I also had a burning desire for justice.

I found myself wishing that I would be more like this authentic saint. Real yoga was calling. Over the coming months and years, my awareness of my own limitations expanded. Burning through my limitations accelerated.

Delivery Vehicles and Emotions

Gurudev asked us if it was appropriate to get upset with the postal worker if we received a letter we didn't like. Of course, that sounded ridiculous. Obviously, a postal worker just delivers letters written by others.

Then Gurudev asked us why we got upset with the way other people treated us. They were just delivering some karma that was due to us. It is the law of cause and effect. It could have been one of many people; some x, y, or z person was the one to deliver the karma. They were just taking on the role of a postal worker, delivering some karma.

The first time that Gurudev told us about this, I had a hard time with it. My experiences had taught me to be upset with the person who did something to me that I did not like. But this was just proof of a limited, ignorant way of thinking. It showed that I had buttons that could easily be pushed. Further, even having an intellectual idea of karma doesn't mean that it is easy to act in the best manner.

It makes sense that if a person, Some Name, mistreats others, this Some Name person will then have to be mistreated. That is cause and effect. Some would call it karma. Many seem to assume that there are restrictions and that whoever you mistreat will be the one to deliver the mistreatment back to you somewhere in the future.

Gurudev was opening our eyes to the reality that anyone who is available can deliver a package or letter of karma. It is too huge to figure out every nuance. It makes a lot of sense to do one's best to live up to giving others what one wants to receive.

Many times, during my first two years with Gurudev, he spoke about nature having accepted us. Then he would ask us if we could accept others. I was aware that often my mind would have a hard time letting go of thoughts, such as wishing that certain people would stop doing something that I didn't like. He asked us if it felt good not to accept a situation. I was inspired. I wanted to be able to accept people and situations as they are. We were told that this is indeed possible. Real yoga facilitates this.

If you get upset with someone who does something to you that you don't like, the wise thing is to observe your sensations. Some situations may require a show of force, such as if you see that someone is attempting to steal something. It is important to be in the moment so that you can respond to every situation with full awareness.

Just because someone is rude to you doesn't mean that you should be rude back. If you can digest the rudeness with a smile on your face and not be upset inside, it shows tremendous stability of consciousness. This is real yoga.

At that time in 1988, I would easily get upset. I was still living with PTSD. There was a lot of stress in my system. I wished that I could be as graceful as this real yogi. I realized I had buttons that needed to be disconnected. I had no idea how much it would take to disconnect them.

In ignorance, emotions are like a line scratched into stone; they may last eons. Some people hold on to grudges, and this causes many illnesses. Ayurveda says that most illnesses have an emotional origin.

My mother fed her cancer with her anger. Astonishingly, she even once admitted that she knew she had made herself sick. Significantly, she could only bring herself to speak it out when the two of us were alone in the house. And only when I had my back turned to her.

"Anger is about the past; it has already happened. Is there any use hanging on to the past?" Gurudev often spoke of the importance of living in the moment.

As I started with the master, whom I now call Gurudev, I wanted to be able to have living in the moment as my permanent everyday reality.

As a person cleans stress out of their system, their experience of emotions changes. Reducing ignorance brings one to a point where emotions are like lines in mud. After more purification, it is like a line in sand. After further progress on a path, emotions are like lines drawn in water. For an enlightened person, emotions are like a line in the air that does not leave any impression. That is real yoga.

Karma

The impression of a past action, a current action, and a potential future action. All three of these are karma. Gurudev says, "Karma is action. There are three types of karma. First, potential karma is the tendency in you that will make you act in the future. Second, there is the action that is happening now. Third is the action that has left an impression on you."

Karma is both action and the fruit of action. Karma is the law of cause and effect. "As you sow, so shall you reap" and "what goes around comes around" are alternate ways of expressing the same truth. If you are nice to people, people will be nice to you. If you steal, you will be stolen from. If not at this time, in some future time.

Impressions are part of karma. Whatever habit a person has, that habit creates impressions in the system. Until we erase impressions, they will follow us through our lifetimes.

When you think that some things are bad and other things are good, division happens. Whatever you don't want bothers you. Often, people want some things a certain way. Gurudev encouraged us to understand how we reduce our own joy.

It is ignorant to expect joy from a certain thing. Over and over, Gurudev has emphasized that expectations bring pain when we don't get what we want. Once we have what we want, that also gives us pain due to the fear of losing it. After what we had is gone, the memory brings us pain.

During the first couple of years that I was with Gurudev, several times I heard him say, "If you want to worry, worry big. Worry about what will happen in 5000 years."

Gurudev says that worry is a complete waste of time. He doesn't want people close to him to worry. He says that we should trust that good things are coming to us.

With distinctive style and directness, Gurudev said, "Karma means all the impressions in the subtle body. It determines where you will go in your next life."

Sometimes people will conclude that if they loved a certain person from a previous life, they should be close in this life. On multiple occasions, Gurudev has refuted this. He pointed out that just because we lived in a certain place in a previous life, it doesn't mean we have to live there now. If you were close to a person in a previous life, it doesn't mean you have to be in a relationship with them now.

When a person gets on a path and begins the daily repetition of spiritual practices, there is something truly wonderful and special that happens. Karmas are reduced in duration and intensity. Stored impressions fade away.

This relates to the expression that "the seeds of karma are roasted in the fires of knowledge." This means that some karmas can be eliminated through spiritual practices. There is no mechanical method of calibrating this phenomenon, yet many people have a deep sense of the truth about it.

I know that I would not have lived as long as I have if it were not for massive reductions in karma, the real saving grace of the divine! Real yoga erases stored impressions.

Many wise people have stated that the ways of karma are unfathomable. Karma is incredibly huge, complex, and often quite mysterious. While an astrological chart can hint that various types of karma are likely to affect us at certain times, it is not possible to figure out all the karma that will affect us. Real yoga helps us live life's mysteries with joy.

Be Authentic

In 1988 and 1989, young Master Sri Sri often encouraged us to be authentic. In life, people often adopt false personas. It frequently happens without awareness, and people lose track of themselves. The superficiality of others used to bother me. Gurudev declared that "being spiritual is being fully authentic." He upheld finding real yoga by being authentic.

When I was young, it often puzzled me how to be smooth, sincere, gracious, and authentic all at once. I felt sincere inside but was usually incapable of expressing it.

Many times, even when I acted with a strong positive intention, I put my foot in my mouth. Speaking, especially with more than one person, was often close to impossible for me. Embarrassing moments were frequent, more so when I attempted to be humorous.

I liked it when he encouraged us to be authentic. He told us that when a person sincerely wanted to know the truth, nature would provide the means to do so.

The guru's words triggered some memories. I never liked it when people were phony. A number of times, both early and later in my life, I had been tricked by people.

Meditation has helped me in different ways. Through meditation, I met a whole new community of people. The person who instructed me in meditation embodied a lot of innocence and sweetness.

Unfortunately, as I became more involved in TM, I met a number of meditation teachers who did not have the centeredness and dispassion that I knew were possible. Some of these teachers seemed like immature phonies. It left a bitter taste in my mouth, and I began to doubt whether it would be worthwhile to become a meditation teacher.

A chance meeting with a TM teacher, who had just spent a lot of time with Maharishi on a six-month course, showed me a glimpse of authenticity, enthusiasm, and devotion. Fortunately, that gave me new inspiration to continue on the path.

Interestingly, without anybody saying anything about it, our young Gurudev mentioned that some meditation teachers have big egos. Some teachers go so far as to think that, since they are teachers, they no longer need to meditate. I was grateful that our leader was encouraging us to go for that calm, centered, appealing space of authenticity. Authenticity is essential for those who want to experience the fullness of real yoga.

Live as Though You Don't Exist

Gurudev has a remarkable ability to say things in an unexpected way that grabs attention. Early on, I heard Gurudev say, "Live as though you don't exist." I had never heard this before. It took a long time for me to appreciate the depth of this one simple sentence.

From growing beyond the ego-orientation of "what about me" to living in the eternal now moment and moving with the flow of pure consciousness, there is a vast development and progression of how to "live as though you don't exist." When you live as though you don't exist, you are basing your reality on giving rather than demanding.

In 1989, a little over a year after my first course with Gurudev, someone asked Gurudev about losing an experience of elevated awareness. The person asking the question was concerned about getting back to that state of being. Then someone asked Gurudev if he ever lost an experience or felt upset about not having it. Gurudev replied simply, "I do not exist."

Burn, Vanish and Dissolve

On my first Basic Course in 1988, Gurudev added a surprising dimension when he asserted that yoga gives us the ability to "burn, vanish, and dissolve." Gurudev said that a person is great when they "burn, vanish, and dissolve." His words snapped my mind into an alert, poised state of wonder. If something burns completely, then it will sometimes mostly vanish, but how do you then dissolve after that?

I thought maybe the word order should be changed, but that wouldn't make sense either. Every time he said it, he kept the wording the same. Sooner or later, it would make sense, I hoped.

Thinking about it kept putting me in a state of wonder. Perhaps that was part of its purpose. It didn't seem like anyone had an aha moment with "burn, vanish, dissolve."

It was not until two and a half years later, during the 1990 *Bhakti Sutra* Tour (Bhakti is devotion) that Gurudev revealed some meanings of "burn, vanish, and dissolve." First, the mind is what can "burn, vanish, and dissolve." I realized that I was thinking about the phrase too literally. The key is that there are two main ways to burn, vanish, and dissolve. One is by being a servant to the divine; the other is by holding God as your beloved. Both lead to real yoga and divine love. Both require surrender (see 'Surrender' on page 174). Surrender connects us with unconditional love.

Surrender has been misunderstood in the West. The wise know that higher forms of surrender bring freedom and power. Being a servant to the divine does not mean being a slave. It means you carry the dignity of the divine with you.

To achieve divine love, your mind has to burn, vanish, and dissolve. Some saints held God as their beloved, and some saints felt that they were servants of the divine. Both approaches are valid, and they both require surrender.

The Present Moment

One aspect of the value of real yoga is its ability to help people be fully present in the moment. The present moment is not a miniscule point. On that first course in 1988, Gurudev assured us that "the present moment is deep and vast." Diving into this idea felt warm and huge.

Another key point Gurudev often made was that "the present moment is inevitable." This particular wording helps to get a person's attention. It is clear that we cannot change the past. There is no way to magically erase whatever experience you happen to be in the middle of. It is already happening. The present moment is inevitable.

Knowing this helps us to relax. When we are relaxed and centered, not dwelling on the past or future, it is easier to come up with an appropriate response. When we respond with awareness, there is less chance of regretting our present actions in the future. What a relief!

Gurudev insisted that most people are reacting more than they are responding. We are like vending machines. With the vending machine, when someone presses a certain button, they get a soda or an orange. When someone presses the right button of yours, you get angry. Press the right button sequence, and someone will be sad or embarrassed.

It took some time for me to be aware of and acknowledge that I had inner buttons and that I had a lot of irritation in my system. The irritation was buried in layers of frozen shock. At times, during the mid-1980s, when I wasn't mired in anguish or shock, I was ready for a fight. One day I realized that that was an unhealthy mindset.

It is important to disconnect all the inner buttons. This is one way of characterizing some of the benefits of the daily practice of meditation and yogic breathing exercises. When the stresses and patterns have been cleaned out of our system, someone can say something insulting, and we can choose a response rather than blowing up on autopilot.

Whatever happens to us is meant to happen. This is

a little hard for some people to accept. "went further, stretching minds even more by saying that anything that happens in the universe has an effect on us.

Gurudev emphasized that our every experience, whether pleasant or unpleasant, has contributed to our growth. When a person is in the middle of reacting to an incident, it can seem impossible to see any good in the situation. Real yoga raised my ability to choose how to act.

It is true that when people have not had any problems, they tend to be a little weak. Many times, Gurudev has claimed that every problem has strengthened us. When we are able to look at the bigger picture of reality, then it becomes easier to see how situations have made us stronger. Gurudev asserted that everyone in the group contributes to our growth in one way or another.

What Is Real Freedom?

Often, Gurudev will speak about freedom. Most people have a restricted idea of freedom. How free are you if you are usually angry? How free is a person who is afraid? How free is a person who is so excited or driven that they can't stop what they are doing? Some people skip meals or even postpone using a toilet, till they hit the proverbial wall and collapse. Are you free if you need a coffee to get going or some intoxicating substance to unwind? Are you free if you are so burned out that all you can do is be a blob holding a remote control on a sofa?

In the USA and other Westernized countries, we have myths and illusions of freedom. Is a person free if the only major choice they make is the type of electronic distraction they will engage in? Are you free if some corporation gets laws passed such that you must buy their products?

Are you free if you end up arguing with friends about the latest political distraction while actual decisions are made with zero voter influence behind closed doors?

You may have heard someone say, "It's a free country!" This is sometimes a rationale used by someone who wants to get away with something or by an insecure or guilty person who seeks to avoid being questioned.

Real freedom is a lack of inner triggers or buttons. True freedom means being free of old programs and patterns. Suppose someone yells at you. You are free if you can choose a response without resorting to a knee-jerk habitual reaction. Personal experience showed me this is possible.

Real freedom is being centered on your true self. True freedom is the goal of real yoga. The goal is to live in a non-stop, permanent state of enlightenment. Once you achieve freedom, you will do good things in any given situation. With real freedom, your choices will be life-supporting for the greatest good of all beings. Freedom is our true nature. Freedom is the nature of the higher self, not the ego.

Many times, Gurudev has maintained that taking life as a game gives freedom. How we play is more important than the result. We can take life less seriously.

Gurudev made it strikingly clear by reminding us we are all going to die. Everything that lives on this planet will die. This knowledge can help people be more relaxed in the moment.

Many people act like they are going to live forever. That leads to problems. Several times, I caught myself doing things that seemed to stem from the idea that I would live forever. It happened unconsciously. It surprised me.

As stated many times by Gurudev, "Discipline

protects freedom. Freedom without discipline is like a country without a defense."

Laughter

Gurudev pointed out that many people have to have a joke or see something awkward happen to someone else in order to laugh. Yet laughter is a natural part of us; we had it before we even started speaking.

Gurudev underscored that the greatest gift to humanity is laughter. Humans are blessed to be able to laugh.

At the point in my life when I first met Gurudev, I was not laughing easily or often. Some part of me recognized this, and I had a sense of feeling a bit crippled.

We should be able to laugh freely for no special reason. Too often, we lose our ability to laugh without being prompted.

I am grateful that it is much easier for me to laugh now.

Gurudev asserted that the people creating the images of Jesus were showing their own feelings by making images of Jesus look sad.

I felt some inner joy when he commented, "God hides in laughter."

I think he shocked a few people when Gurudev claimed, "Laughter is the greatest prayer!"

Gurudev mentioned Buddha. He asked us if we had all seen a Buddha statue with a big belly. He maintained that the big belly that Buddha is given is a sign of laughter and of being happy. Instead of postponing living, we should be able to laugh easily, for no reason. And find joy in the moment.

Gurudev told us that we should laugh like children. Laughing with every cell of our body is valuable. This is quite attractive. When I first heard him insist that there was nothing worth grumbling about, it was hard for me to accept. I wondered about this.

Our spiritual practices should make us lively. Spiritual practice should not make us dull.

Laughter makes us lively and centers us in the present moment.

The goal is to be centered in the present moment, to be total, 100% where you are right now, all the time. As a daily reality, I certainly wanted this.

It took a lot for me to get to the point where I felt more alive than ever. If I can do it, then many people can do it.

Keep going. Don't give up. Keep reading, and we will cover details that will help along the journey.

Gurudev said, "To me, being spiritual means laughing from the inner core of yourself."

Often, wherever Gurudev travels, people sitting with him will feel lighter and happier. People have seen how laughter spreads in groups when Gurudev is present. This is part of what kept bringing me back for more. It feels wonderful to laugh.

Real yoga includes being able to laugh freely. Real yoga includes being fully present in the now moment. It brings relief and comfort.

Gurudev said it very well, "Wanting perfection is in the nature of human beings and the way to achieve it is yoga."

Note that we mean the full package of yoga, not just physical exercises.

Real yoga enables you to take care of yourself in an intelligent, constructive way. In your journey deeper into love it is important to take care of yourself and those around you. Please reach out to me if you need support or guidance.

Chapter Three: First Sudarshan Kriya

Sudarshan Kriya (also known as Sudarshan Kriya Yoga, SKY breath meditation, or SKY breathing) is a powerful yogic breathing technique. In April 1988, I sat for my first SKY session. I was about ten feet away from the swami, who is now known as Gurudev. At times, it seemed like the practice was lasting for hours, when only a few minutes had passed. It felt natural and refreshing, yet there were moments when I wanted it to hurry and finish. Maybe large chunks of stress were gushing out of my nostrils right then. Not wanting to inhale other people's stress, I was grateful that we had all the windows open with a good flow of fresh air.

For several years prior to starting Gurudev's breathing techniques, I had been experiencing deep peacefulness in my meditations. Yet the peacefulness would not last all day. Gurudev addressed this phenomenon. He said that it was a common experience among meditators who did not do yogic breathing practices. Pranayama and Sudarshan Kriya are powerful breathing techniques that promote peacefulness and happiness. These breathing techniques are a way of cleansing many types of emotional patterns, whether the person is aware of the patterns or not.

Meditation certainly helps eliminate stress. Some stresses are more easily addressed by breathing techniques. The breath is a link between the body and the mind. The breath is a way to manage emotions.

The distinction between squared breathing and circular breathing intrigued me. Much of the time, when most people breathe, they inhale and pause, then exhale and pause. This is what you can call a square type of breathing. The inhale makes the left side of the square, the pause makes the top side, the exhale makes the right side, and the pause after exhaling makes the bottom of the square.

In Sudarshan Kriya, we breathe in circles. When we breathe in circles, we start exhaling right after inhaling and begin inhaling immediately after exhaling. Not pausing between inhalation and exhalation allows air to flow continuously through the nose. The square becomes a circle. This allows better oxygenation and brings more prana into our system. This promotes improved health and bodily functioning, and stress gets released faster.

Enjoy Each Breath

Most people are usually not aware of their breathing. Over and over, people have heard Gurudev say that different rhythms of the breath correspond to different moods or emotions.

Many people breathe using only a small part of their lungs. When you consciously breathe more fully, you can train your body to use more of your own lung capacity. This increases oxygenation, reduces stress, and improves energy.

I enjoy putting awareness into the simple act of breathing. Observing the breath is a powerful technique. Just as you can slow down and enjoy every bite of food that you eat, you can focus on and enjoy your breathing. You can enjoy your breath even when exerting yourself and breathing intensely. By focusing some awareness on our own breathing, we can reduce stress and gain more energy and alertness. This is a part of real yoga.

Breathing through the mouth increases stress hormone levels in the blood. This accelerates aging.

Yoga and Ayurveda encourage breathing through the nose most of the time. Through conscious effort, you can train yourself to breathe through your nose even during hard exercise. This will give you more energy and less stress.

Chanting OM

We were all seated in position to start the Sudarshan Kriya. Then Gurudev had us chant OM, the original sacred sound, three times out loud. He revealed that OM is the original sound of the universe. *Yoga Vasishtha* is a sacred text that says that the first vibration in the universe is OM. (Multiple translations of the ancient *Yoga Vasishtha* are available.) OM is common to many religions; e.g., you can find distorted forms, such as "amen," in modern religion.

To get along with other people and function in society, it is fundamentally important to chant OM out loud. Gurudev emphasized this point. We never do silent repetitions of OM. Maharishi also emphasized this point, as did Maharishi's master, Brahmananda Saraswati. Generally, you can use a compound mantra, such as OM namah shivaya, both silently and out loud. When using OM by itself, it should always be spoken out loud.

Many people enjoy chanting OM regularly. When you chant OM, to get the most out of it, it is important to put your full attention on it. Keep your eyes closed and sit in stillness while you chant out loud. Let yourself dissolve into the sound. Watch the fading out of the final sound, and you may feel a shift in your awareness. This is part of real yoga.

On subsequent occasions, Gurudev talked about

Patanjali. Patanjali was a profoundly skilled yogi. Patanjali gave a complete, scientific understanding of the details of the art and science of real yoga in the ancient text, Patanjali's *Yoga Sutras.* (There are many versions available by different authors.) A sutra is a condensed seed containing many levels of knowledge. The full meaning of any sutra is only available to those with highly developed consciousness.

Patanjali noted, *"Tasya vaachakaha pranavaha,"* meaning, as Gurudev explained, that the *pranava*, praise of the divine, OM, is the sound we can use to address the totality of consciousness. Patanjali also said, *"Tajjapastadartha bhaavanam."* Gurudev interpreted that this means that chanting OM brings the feeling of unconditional love and totality of being, reminding us of the Lord of Creation.

No recordings were used in April 1988 on my first Basic Course in San Francisco. Gurudev guided us with his own voice.

During Sudarshan Kriya, SKY, we are breathing in circles. Until we are cued for exhalation, we have to keep inhaling. Until we are given the signal for inhalation, we keep exhaling. During SKY, there is often a silent space after the signal to exhale. We have to keep exhaling during the silence until the inhale is signaled. Likewise, we have to keep inhaling through the silence until the exhale is signaled.

SKY breathing is an amazingly powerful technique, especially when you do it with fresh air. SKY reduces the *tamasic* energies of dullness, sadness, lethargy, and resistance to change. At the same time, the *rajasic* energies of impatience, frustration, agitation, and aggression are also reduced. The practitioner is left in a sattvic state of balance, harmony, peacefulness, and awareness. SKY helps to bring an imbalanced body-mind complex into better homeostasis.

Gurudev encouraged us to give the breathing our

100%, meaning to put our full focus on what we were doing and drop other thoughts. We get more out of SKY breathing when we are not lazy or halfhearted about it. We were told to put all our thoughts and emotions into the breath. At the same time, we were instructed to relax the body. The breathing does not require straining, jerking, pumping, or clenching of muscles. Giving your 100% does not mean using more muscular force than is necessary to sit up straight and breathe with the rhythm.

We learn from Ayurveda that toxins in the body will influence thoughts and emotions. Toxins will cause a person to have a desire to do things that will keep the toxins inside.

Many times, it happens that a person decides to live a healthier life. For example, to stop bad habits, eat better quality food, get meals on time, get up near sunrise, go to bed earlier, drink more water, do yoga regularly, reduce eating sweets, eat organic food, do pranayama and meditation every day, etc. Yet they sometimes find themselves being drawn to do the opposite of what they had decided to do. A random thought will occur that pushes them to do something other than what they know is best.

Stress stored in the body is a type of toxin. There can be many kinds of toxins, whether from poorly digested food, toxic products, late nights, intense emotional experiences, chemical exposure, suppressed emotions, poor eating habits, shallow breathing, synthetic fragrance, insufficient sleep, iced drinks, insufficient drinking of water, etc.

Any individual toxin or combination of toxins can affect our thinking and feelings. An urge to do something you know to be harmful or bad usually arises from toxins in the body. Thus, it is vital to follow wisdom rather than just random feelings. Hold on to this tip from real yoga.

Emotions may be stored almost anywhere in the body. We can release stuck emotions using the breath.

As the mind-body system is purified, there will be fewer toxins in the system, and intuition will develop and strengthen. This can start right away. Depending on the amount of toxins and when you begin, it might take several to many years of dedication and focused effort.

Living a sattvic life of balance will yield more sattvic thoughts and desires. For most people, many of the toxins in the body have an emotional component.

Unfortunately, simply eating organic, vegetarian plant-based food on a regular schedule and taking herbs is not enough to purge all toxins. Toxins themselves try to stop people from doing things that remove toxins. Some yogic breathing practice and meditation performed daily are essential for people to bring harmony and smoothness to their minds and emotions. Yoga asanas help the body to be in ideal health. Ayurvedic methods of oil application can make a huge difference in the process of self-improvement.

During both of my first two sessions of SKY breathing, there came a point when I felt a significant change or difference in the quality of the space near me in the room. I wondered what was causing this difference. I kept breathing with my eyes closed. I felt calm and let my attention be on the space around me. I could not figure out what I was feeling, but I knew something was happening. Curious, I quickly peeped out of one slightly open eyelid.

His feet gave him away. There he was! Gurudev was standing right in front of me!

The first time it happened, I noticed that he was gently moving his hand up and down, mirroring the inhalation and exhalation. It actually felt easier to keep breathing in circles with this mostly unseen, subtle assistance. I felt grateful that he was checking on me. The second time it happened, it was less mysterious yet definitely uplifting.

SKY breathing is a method of rapidly relieving

emotional toxins. Sometimes there can be such an accumulation of stress, blocking the proper movement of prana in the body, that people may feel a slight tingling. This sometimes happens during the first sessions that they learn SKY. SKY moves the prana dramatically through the body and mind.

Most people have a habit of avoiding any unpleasant sensation, whether by scratching or moving the body, eating, watching videos, or whatever. We were instructed to observe any sensations we experienced during the breathing, whether they were pleasant or unpleasant. This alert observation, without judgment or reaction, facilitates the dissolution of stresses and their release out of the body.

Sometimes people will feel cold while doing yogic breathing practices, even if the room temperature is a comfortable 70 to 80 degrees F. This is natural since the air element, *vayu,* or wind, is cooling. Breathing practices increase coolness. For each session of breathing, Gurudev guided, "If you feel cold, don't mind, just feel cold." With that little nugget of wisdom, the mind can relax.

When you keep grumbling about what you don't like, it disempowers the mind. Everyone was bundled up, well-insulated in long sleeves and sweaters or jackets and/or a blanket. We were being practical. It was not serious; we weren't being asked to walk through snow barefoot, sit on slabs of ice in our underwear, or do anything ridiculous.

If you can address a situation without compromising others' health and safety, taking corrective action calmly provides comfort and smooth feelings. By accepting a tiny discomfort, you can often transcend it. Gurudev added that every uncomfortable situation we have experienced has made us stronger.

During the course, there was a period of *shavasana,* lying on the back with arms straight at our sides. Before lying down, I instinctively wanted to be closer to the master. He sat on the stage without a chair. I adjusted my blanket so I could put my head near Gurudev's seat. Then my head was about four feet away from him as I lay on my back with my feet pointing away from him.

I could not say how long we were lying down. That moment seemed safe and comfortable. I went into a profoundly deep state of rest.

When I heard an instruction to turn to my side, I felt a need to orient myself. It took some effort to crack an eye open for a mere fraction of a second. Confusingly, with the first peep of my eyes, the scene was that of a bright blue wall right next to my head. I lay there a little longer with my eyes closed. I was trying to figure out how there could be a bright blue wall right next to my head. It didn't make sense. I knew that I would have felt myself being moved if someone had attempted to move me. The walls of the room were a drab, washed-out pale green, at least eight feet away from me.

When I fully opened my eyes as I sat up, I realized that the blue wall was a silken garment on a big woman. She had decided that she just had to sit between my head and Gurudev. There was a lot of open space all around the master; no other person was sitting near him. Planting her large girth in that exact spot, only a mere couple of inches from my head, was peculiar. It seemed like a physical way of telling me in no uncertain terms, "He's mine!" or "Me first!" or "You shouldn't be here!" Or, what?? It was confusing. I wasn't sure what was going on.

It was a little disheartening to see this behavior coming from a follower of the master. The breathing practices had already blown my mind. I felt a palpable question mark, so puzzled was I at that moment.

People sometimes expect perfect behavior from those around them, especially when on a spiritual path. This invariably results in disappointment. Followers on a path are on the path because they are not enlightened. Many people on a path would like to get enlightened. Expectations of perfection from others will lead to problems. Sometimes people have asked Gurudev why he allows people who behave badly to be in the Art of Living. Many times, he has repeated that the path is here for everyone to grow.

Gurudev says that there are no bad people. This is a perspective coming from unconditional love. Often, he has insisted that inside a culprit is a victim who needs help. One of the points repeatedly emphasized is to accept people, things, and situations as they are. "We have said to accept others as they are. I myself have to live with that."

Gurudev has said, "If you are miserable, you do yoga to get out of your misery. Yoga makes you ready. This is the first step. The second step is, if you are restless or unhappy, yoga brings you equanimity. It first relieves you from misery and then brings equanimity. At the third step, it helps you attain skills that you do not have."

This a wonderful possibility of real yoga! Complete yoga, not just exercise for the body.

Gurudev advises us to look deeper. "Yoga is not just doing some exercises. It has been mistaken to be just asanas. Yoga is the expansion of consciousness. It is the connection to who we are."

Real yoga rescues. Yoga uplifts. Yoga transforms. Yoga saves lives. I am living proof. It is a miracle that I am alive. Real yoga helped me to keep going. No matter how horrible things are, you have to keep going. Never give up.

Looking back, it is easy to note that people start on their path carrying whatever patterns are inside their system. I myself had stubborn behaviors I needed to lose.

Enlightenment is extremely rare. A long while later, I wrote the following poem reflecting my thoughts.

The Nearest Wall

The nearest wall

you can reduce in size.

Allowing new sparkles

to greet your eyes.

This is the wall of ego

so mysteriously erected,

to protect your fragile center

from being detected.

There is calmness and strength,

when connected you feel,

with life and earth,

genuineness and freedom are real.

It may seem scary to some

who would rather have power.

But letting go of control over others

will make you feel cleaner,

cleaner than you can ever get

in a shower.

On that April 1988 course, after we concluded the first session of SKY breath meditation, we headed outside to eat lunch. I felt a little dazed. I also felt relaxed, refreshed, and rejuvenated. It seemed like some real healing had happened! A personal feeling of serenity began to sprout.

Illness and Injury

In college, I was on a dining hall meal plan from 1972 to 1973 that went along with dormitory living. The food was mostly greasy, based on meat, eggs, white bread, semolina pasta, potatoes, canned fruit, and a few heavily cooked, frozen, or canned vegetables. When my acne became worse due to the dining hall slop that I had to eat, I felt trapped. After taking a few yoga classes, the thought kept coming to me to be a vegetarian. At that time, in the early 1970s, vegetarianism was considered peculiar and strongly disapproved of in most meat-centric Western countries.

I did not consciously know any vegetarians. It was only later that I found out that my yoga teacher and a few of his fellow devotees at the Integral Yoga Institute were vegetarians. The Integral Yoga Institute was founded in the

United States by a yogi from India known as Swami Satchidananda.

Becoming a vegetarian struck me as an important thing to do. At the time, I could not articulate why. It was gut sense. I felt an inner knowingness. Gradually, my acne began to disappear when I stopped eating eggs and meat. I felt lighter. Unfortunately, there was not much else to eat in a university dining hall in 1973! Deleting all types of meat and eggs left me with few options for most meals. I could not afford to buy meals at the campus restaurant.

None of my family members were vegetarians. When I told my mother, "I'm eating only vegetarian food," she got angry. She snapped at me, "You were a heavy meat eater!"

Not only did I stop eating meat, but I also thought I should stop eating dairy. For about the first year of being vegetarian, I was mostly vegan, though I had never heard the word "vegan." At that time, Western society was extremely skeptical, unsupportive of, and often overtly negative about both yoga and vegetarianism. Even though meditation is part of yoga, during the 1970s in the USA, meditation gained more acceptance than yoga.

Multiple uses of pharmaceutical drugs to treat my childhood illnesses had left my body with deficiencies, allergies, and weak organs. After eight years, the haphazard, uneducated, whole food-deficient, fresh vegetable-deficient approach I took to being vegetarian increased my deficiencies and weaknesses. My health was declining. Stressful situations made things worse. By the time I met Gurudev, I had already experienced many problems and had ended up with several simultaneous illnesses.

When I met Gurudev in 1988, some of the simultaneous illnesses I had included colitis, brain injury, chronic fatigue, candida, allergies, hypoglycemia, kidney pain, irritable bowel, and parasites. I was mostly hungry, almost all the time. I could eat two huge plates of food and be ravenous less than two hours later.

Allopathic and chiropractic doctors told me I had to eat meat every three hours, a disgusting regimen. I despised having to eat meat, yet I wanted to live. Living at that time seemed to require eating a lot of non-vegetarian food. Hemp seed might have been a lifesaver for me, but it was not available. Even after eating meat every three hours, I would need snacks in between. Usually, I had to have something in my stomach almost every hour. I felt trapped.

If I ate yogurt or drank hot milk, due to my illnesses, it took a full week, sometimes even two weeks, to recover. Because of these issues, I didn't eat any cheese at all for ten years. I did not eat ice cream for 19 years.

Pumpkin seeds were unknown to me. If I missed a single meal, the effect would be dramatic. Sometimes people would ask if I had lost weight, and indeed, I often noticeably lost weight in a single day. If I did not eat frequently throughout the day, I would lose weight. It was humiliating and strange. From 1979 to 1988, I felt weaker and weaker.

Because of my finances before I met Gurudev, I often did not have money available for herbs or health supplements. The various doctors and health practitioners that I saw were only able to help me regain small portions of my health.

After multiple accidents, I had chronic pain, unstable joints, and weak ligaments. Sitting for longer than 30 minutes was painful. I could not sit cross-legged for meditation; my legs had to be straight in front of me. My feet and knees had to be supported, so that my toes would point straight up.

In 2005, a doctor confirmed I still had parasites in my body and brain. Some came from travels in Asia. The worst parasites, in my brain, stemmed from years before I met

Gurudev. It was pointed out that one of the reasons I was not feeling well was a long list of allergies to various substances, including motor oil. (This explained to me why I had come to hate driving a car.)

Parasites in the human body often trigger allergies to various substances. It took many sequences of detox and parasite cleanses to rid my system of these issues. The parasites in my brain created tremendous fatigue and degraded my learning skills and physical endurance. Various herbs were crucial to my recovery.

Before my first course with Gurudev, I heard we were not supposed to eat from the beginning of class at 9 a.m. until the lunch break. Lunch would possibly be as late as about 1:30 p.m. I wasn't sure how I could go without food for that long. I decided to stuff myself, eat as much as possible for breakfast, and hope that I would be okay.

That first time I did SKY, in April 1988, I ate a gargantuan meal for breakfast. An hour later, I did not feel overly full. The day of the first Sudarshan Kriya, after eating as much as I possibly could, I was ready to begin.

After my first experience with SKY, it was gratifying to feel that the breathing practices had given me some relief. It was amazing. I was not entirely overwhelmed by sharp hunger by the time we had lunch. I felt positive that my health would get a lot stronger using these techniques.

Looking back, I feel the extreme good fortune of being able to live a healthy life. Miraculously, I have maintained a stable weight on three meals a day as a strict vegetarian for over 30 years. Divine grace has given me a new life that used to be far beyond my reach.

It is a miracle. I am more alive than ever and am able to be helpful to others. The divine grace of real yoga made this possible. Gurudev's blessings have been instrumental for enormous transformations in my life. I feel very lucky.

Ego

In our first two years together, I heard Gurudev speak about ego on many occasions. He said that ego creates a sense of separation between ourselves and others.

Gurudev explained, "Likes and dislikes belong to the ego. Ego is a layer on the being; a limited identity of likes and dislikes."

Gurudev also revealed that "people with the greatest show on the outside have little inside."

According to Gurudev, Buddha said that the ego can easily bring hell to a person.

Whether you think you are good and special or especially bad, both are signs of ego. People often get caught in the trap of trying to get rid of their ego. Gurudev cautioned that this creates more problems. By doing the breathing practices, we naturally reduce the negative effects of ego.

"If the ego is there, let it be there. The ego will remain there in either one of the three forms: sattvic, rajasic, or tamasic. It is the sattvic ego through which you can see this. A sattvic ego is one where there is no hatred or aversion towards anybody."

"When one gets a glimpse of the space that is beyond the ego, which is the same everywhere, then how can anyone hate or dislike anything? The aversion simply vanishes when you realize that all these bodies are just a wave of one huge life force."

The many techniques and components of real yoga help to reduce the rajasic and tamasic forms of the ego. This makes it easier to experience unconditional love. For me, I was able to understand this in my own life after gaining the perspective of many years on the path.

Love Is Our True Nature

Repeatedly, Gurudev has claimed that love is our true nature. He made the distinction that by doing spiritual practices, we are not growing love, which was not there. The love is already there within us, and we just need to uncover it.

"Love based on judgment is not coming from depth." In several different times and places, Gurudev emphasized that there are no demands in unconditional love.

People search for love in many ways. Some people are looking only outside themselves. That was me for many years. Some people are searching inside themselves by going within. Either way, everyone wants love.

Gurudev maintained that any technique that we use will serve us fully only if there is love behind it. Otherwise, the techniques are barren and dry. Love supports our growth.

Gurudev explained that love is the essence, the reality. It is not seeking and finding it; it is purifying within and increasing sattva in ourselves enough that we can perceive the fullness of the reality of consciousness.

God, Guru, and Self Are the Same

Sometimes when people would ask Gurudev about God, Gurudev would reply that God, the guru, and your true self are the same thing. When I first heard this, it just seemed too vast for me to fully appreciate it. For some people, this statement may seem too mystical or mysterious. It requires a significant depth of experience for a person to feel comfortable with this idea of God, the higher self, and the guru being the same. I wanted to experience it fully, not just appreciate it intellectually.

To help explain or create more comfort with this idea, Gurudev would sometimes say, "Don't think I am just this body." One time, when he suggested this, it seemed he twinkled with a grin. He enjoyed watching us in various degrees of wonder or confusion as we tried to digest these understandings. At other times, he would have a serious look and seem intent on shattering our limited preconceptions.

Late-Night Car Caravan

In many countries, it has often happened that there will be a caravan of cars following the car that the master is riding in. On several occasions, when I was in such a caravan, I observed the lead car stopping, and one of the people riding with Gurudev would say that we stopped because Gurudev mentioned that someone in one of the other cars was hungry or needed a bathroom break. This happened many times in various countries, when none of us had cell phones.

During the April 1988 weekend of my first course, for sleeping, I was camping on the floor of a house with a group of other people. There was only one car, so we had to travel as a group. By 10 p.m., I was tired and achy, ready for bed. The driver of the car happened to be a woman who preferred dealing with women. I had observed that if I asked her directly if she was ready to leave, even if she were, with keys in hand, about to leave, she would then delay at least another twenty or thirty minutes. I learned to avoid making requests of her.

Around the guru, sometimes plans are made quite abruptly. One night, I was hoping to head back to the house to sleep. A woman told me that the driver would only be ready to leave after about fifteen minutes. Suddenly, there was a rush of people leaving the house.

"What's happening?" I asked as people were running past me.

Over a shoulder, someone blurted out, "We're going for a car ride with Gurudev!"

I walked out of the house, wondering what I should do. I noticed that the lady who had claimed that she would not be ready to leave for another fifteen minutes was already sitting in her car, with female passengers loaded and doors closed, ready to go. It was clear that no additional occupants would be welcomed. I didn't know which car I would ride in. As I was standing there in a moment of indecision, someone leading the last two people came rushing out of the house. While she was running to a car, she blurted out, "Come ride with us!" I ran. I was confused. *How did I end up being the last person to get into a car?*

We had four cars. I was in the third car. Quickly, we headed out. My driver was not sure of the exact destination. Possible destinations included a mystery person, Mount Tamalpais, or just a drive in the Berkeley hills. There was some scenic spot elsewhere in the Bay Area, which was also a possible destination. It seemed random. One must let go of aversions to disorganized spontaneity around masters.

Keep in mind that this was before we had GPS or cell phones. To make sure we all wound up in the same place, the cars needed to maintain visual sight of the leader. Despite the vague nature of this expedition, there was a general air of giddy playfulness. Being in the car with the master is a great blessing and a chance for some serious darshan. It seemed vaguely possible that even being in a caravan behind the car Gurudev was riding in might have some benefits for the participants.

The comfort of simply lying down on the floor seemed more appealing to me at that moment, due to the need to sleep and the aches and pains in my body. I kept my mouth shut and figured that whatever happened, I would just go along for the ride. I knew there was some subtle benefit, even if I was physically separate from the Guru.

Yet, at first, my mind was calculating: *10:30 at night, at least a one-hour drive each way, plus who knows how much time once we reach whatever the final destination might be.* I told myself, *Groan, it will likely be at least one o'clock in the morning before you are even starting back toward the place where you sleep.* My mind was tangled in this thinking during the entire passage across the Bay.

We finished crossing a bridge over the San Francisco Bay. I felt like I was trapped in a strange black-and-white movie. Finally, I relaxed and figured there was no alternative but to enjoy being there. We were driving along a quiet, dark street that was usually extremely busy during the day.

Without warning, the lead car made a U-turn. With varying degrees of skill, the cars following the lead car made U-turns. We ended up driving back to the starting point.

"What happened?"

"I don't know; maybe Gurudev has something else in mind."

As people got out of the cars, somebody from the lead car came up to our car and told us, "Gurudev said someone was tired and needed to rest, so we had to turn around and come back."

Gurudev looked over the roof of a car at me and called out to me, in front of the whole group, "You are tired; you should go and rest." It was surprising, impressive, a little embarrassing, and touching for the sincere care. Gurudev acted out of unconditional love to care for my urgent need.

It was interesting to note that the moment that I relaxed and accepted the situation, immediately after that, the lead car made the U-turn. Acceptance. That put me on the way towards getting to bed at an earlier time.

One afternoon, we met at a private home for meditation. We were just a handful of people. One lady wore a stiff lace garment over her top. Her every little movement was broadcast as the lace made swishy noises. This lady sat just a foot away from the master. All through the meditation, she was moving and swaying in her little seated dance, providing a soundtrack of rustle and swish.

Gurudev seemed peaceful, relaxed, and dispassionate. Feeling tense, my mind was caught up in distraction and judgment. I realized I was letting myself be distracted. I told myself not to be bothered by the noise. Right before the end of the meditation, I finally started to feel settled.

Another time in the same room, we sat with Gurudev while an adept chanter played the harmonium and sang the *Shiva Mahimna,* an ancient, sacred text. Gurudev went into a deep, blissful state and several times made long, deep "Mmmmmm!" sounds of appreciation and rapture.

Secret Hindu Temple

We went to a small Hindu temple in San Francisco. I heard that since the temple was not open to the public, we had to have permission to see the temple. Someone had called ahead and made an appointment. I could see no signs on the outside of the building. It seemed like a secret temple.

Beaming with joy, Gurudev liked this temple. Smiling broadly, he revealed that "proper *puja* locks the prana in." (Puja is a ceremony of gratitude that helps open awareness to divine energy.) This was a Hindu temple with Caucasian priests. The lead priest stretched out on the floor and did a full prostration at Gurudev's feet.

Amazing Meal Cooked by the Master

One day we were in a car driving through San Francisco, and Gurudev was sitting right in front of me. Out of the blue, he offered, "I can cook a meal for us."

The driver gushed, "Oh, that would be really sweet!"

I was surprised and, with more disbelief than I felt, blurted out, "You can cook?" Such a look Gurudev gave me. It showed surprise, repudiation, a bit of scorn, and even pity. I felt stupid and was sorry that I had disappointed him. I was only beginning to learn to get used to surprises from this modest and charming saint.

When we reached the house, Gurudev appointed one lady as the kitchen helper. Everyone else was to stay out of the kitchen. Most of the items in the refrigerator were taken out. Cupboards were raided. Many different possible ingredients were spread out to choose from.

I noticed that among the many kinds of vegetables, there was an apple and a cauliflower. Before I left the kitchen, I brought up the understanding that generally, it is better to eat fruits and vegetables apart from each other.

Gurudev maintained that sometimes certain ones can go together if you do it properly and use just a small amount of fruit. He proceeded to put together a truly remarkable meal.

The scents drifting through the house were subtle yet enticing. When we were served, we each got a moderate amount on a simple paper plate.

These were recipes I had never before experienced and which I have not since seen duplicated. The food felt like a treasure. Everything about it seemed perfect.

People took those plates with a lot of enthusiasm. After taking a first bite, conversation dissolved as everyone went into a silent place with their plate of food. We all found our own seats. We tucked ourselves into various nooks, corners, and alcoves to be totally at one with this amazing food.

I treasured each bite. Wonderful flavors and textures melted in my mouth. There was such smoothness permeating my cells as to promote a deep meditative stillness inside. I yearned for that plate of food to last as long as possible. There was an atmosphere of stillness after that meal.

Gurudev Sri Sri Spoke of Time with Maharishi

In 1988, when a handful of us sat down with Gurudev, he shared a few powerful memories. We called him Punditji in 1988. He spoke with deep respect and reverence about Maharishi. He remarked that Maharishi "was completely self-referral," meaning established in true self. We froze in rapt attention.

Throughout the ages, many devotees used the term

"Gurudev" as the name for their guru. Maharishi referred to his own master, Brahmananda Saraswati, as Gurudev. Maharishi insisted that no one should address him as Gurudev. He wanted to be known only as Maharishi.

Known today as Gurudev Sri Sri, Punditji revealed that Maharishi's instructions could be surprising. Maharishi might focus on a small detail of a minor daily activity or start planning a gigantic project involving thousands of people.

Punditji shared a small incident that illustrates how a master may give seemingly arbitrary instructions to cultivate a flexible mind. Punditji told us that one day he put on a dhoti that was decorated with a red border. When Punditji entered Maharishi's room, Maharishi commented, "What about the dhoti with the green border? That green border is so nice." Punditji went back to his room to change into the dhoti with the green border. Punditji shared his thought process with us: "I was thinking, red border, green border, it doesn't really make much difference. But if it pleases him, that is good."

Punditji shared that Maharishi kept him endlessly busy all day and sometimes long into the night. Maharishi demonstrated acute awareness of what was happening with Punditji. Maharishi called Punditji on the phone first thing promptly, as soon as Punditji awoke in the morning.

With a sheepish giggle, Punditji quietly shared, "Maharishi would call me right after I woke up. On some mornings, after many late nights, I would keep myself completely still when I woke up to try and get a few more minutes of rest. But Maharishi always knew when I was awake, and the call would come." It was charming to see Punditji smiling wistfully about that funny memory. We could tell that Punditji appreciated and was quite fond of Maharishi's idiosyncrasies.

The love between them was impressive and uplifting.

Punditji told us about a time when Maharishi had sent him to work out some details for an event in India. There were some conflicts and misunderstandings in the area where the event was scheduled to happen. As organizations grow, more people are needed for administrative functions. Masters become removed from day-to-day details happening in different cities. Politics within the groups often intensify. The conflict escalated to such an extent that people gathered for a protest, holding signs and shouting. Punditji vividly described the angry protest, saying that some people even yelled, "Kill Punditji!" He didn't know what he would do, but he went in surrender and faith because Maharishi had told him to go.

Punditji related that, "Somehow I spoke to them, they calmed down, and everyone ended up happy."

After a poignant pause, Punditji, now known as Gurudev Sri Sri, softly revealed, wistfully, "All I wanted was to share Maharishi's knowledge." Perched motionless in reverence, the few of us hearing this felt reluctance or difficulty speaking. The profound bond of love between Maharishi and Gurudev Sri Sri was obvious and inspirational. We all went deep within our own reflections.

The Master Told Me to Teach More Yoga

While going up a steep hill one day, the car approached a stop sign. Gurudev whipped around in his seat in front of me. With blazing potency, he sternly stared into my eyes. With no warning, he emphatically declared, "You should be teaching more yoga! You'll be teaching all over!"

Surprised to the point of speechlessness yet pleased by the vote of confidence, I barely managed to get my mouth to move and say, "Okay." Gurudev's approval was a jolt of divine grace. Many times, since then, I have felt gratitude for the attention and support of the master.

Until then, in 1988, yoga had not gained widespread popularity in the mainstream USA. In the 1970s and early 1980s, meditation was gaining acceptance in the US more rapidly than yoga. Interestingly, I observed that after Gurudev's command and blessing for me to teach yoga, each following year, the growth in the popularity of yoga accelerated exponentially.

Spirulina and Chlorella Trip

One morning, we made a car trip to San Rafael with Gurudev. Chandrika, Claire, Janael, and I, at that time in 1988, were all plagued by blood sugar imbalances, such as hypoglycemia. Researchers had found that taking chlorella and/or spirulina has a stabilizing effect on blood sugar. Someone had heard about a business in San Rafael that distributed spirulina and chlorella products, and she wanted to go there and possibly make a purchase. Gurudev agreed to go to see the place. We all ended up riding with Gurudev in one car to see the spirulina business.

On the way there, I sat right behind Gurudev. After a while, my awareness was dominated by the intensity of the physical pain I was feeling. The usual agony of my daily life. The initial causes were five serious bicycle accidents, including being hit by a car while riding a bicycle. Foolishly,

I had not allowed my body time to heal after the accidents. I had told myself to keep going, keep exercising no matter what. There were a few other car accidents on top of that, which had happened before I met Gurudev. I assumed that eventually I would somehow heal, which turned out to be a big mistake. It is important to rest for several weeks and months immediately after having torn muscles and ligaments, or the injured person is likely to end up with more severe problems and chronic injuries, as I did.

Holding on to the headrest on his seat, I leaned close to his right shoulder and asked Gurudev, "Will I ever be free of this pain?"

His reply was simple and reassuring: "Ah, keep doing the breathing, and it will go."

After we reached the spirulina business, Gurudev sat in the lobby. There was a kind of tropical decoration theme, with green walls and some pale pieces of bamboo contrasting with darker, thicker wood beams overhead. There were no other people, just our own group sitting in the lobby by ourselves.

Copies of product information sheets and price lists were out on the counter, and some of us started reading. The discussion started with one person asking Gurudev which product would be best for them: spirulina, chlorella, or a combination. He ended up telling each one of us what would be best for us. It was obvious that we were there to be with Gurudev. I was happy that the store remained empty for our private impromptu hangout. Only one person ended up actually buying any products.

The White Silk Asan

Saints often have a wool or silk cloth that they sit on. Many people notice that natural fiber is better against the skin than synthetic. Enlightened beings are sensitive to the energies in substances and situations. For the enlightened, there is value in having a slight protective shield between them and whatever they are sitting on. Silk and wool also help hold the positive energy that radiates from the body of an enlightened being. The cloth they sit on is called an *asan*, meaning a seat.

In 1988, Gurudev traveled with a piece of white silk. This would be draped over whatever chair or car seat he sat on. The day that we drove to San Rafael, I was enjoying the pattern of the design of leaves and flowers, white on white, that decorated the silk.

It is always a privilege to carry the asan. Often, it takes alertness and perfect timing to be the one to pull the asan off the chair after the master stands up. When I carried the asan, I felt good energy radiating from the cloth.

After a couple of years, Gurudev started using orange wool shawls to sit on instead of white silk.

Chapter Four: First Advanced Silence Course

During the second weekend of April 1988, one week after my first Basic Course with Gurudev Sri Sri, I went for my first silent Advanced Course. The group of about 12 or 14 people met in the high desert near Apple Valley, California. I wasn't sure what to expect. I was eager to dive more deeply into time with Gurudev and experience whatever he was going to teach us. Once again, for my final meal before leaving for the course, I stuffed myself with as much as I could eat.

Gurudev met us right away when we arrived. A Hindu priest accompanied him. Gurudev had a big grin. He told us that they had done a puja and purified the grounds. They were flicking puja water around the premises. Gurudev invited us to drink some jeera water (cumin seed infusion), which was in a pitcher on an old wooden picnic table in the dining area.

A person walked around the property at 5:30 a.m., waking people by ringing a bell. We had a roommate who woke us up earlier. I was housed in a dorm room with three other men. There was a small bathroom farthest from the entry. My bed was the closest to the entry. A professor occupied the bed next to the bathroom.

The professor was always the first one in the bathroom. He could easily have slipped in quietly and allowed the rest of us to sleep. However, he enjoyed slamming the bathroom door with a shockingly loud bang.

Buck was in the bed next to mine. In response to the loud slamming door, Buck and I woke with a start. Abruptly, we sat up, groggy and weaving, looking at each other, bleary-eyed, with our mouths hanging open. The second morning was the same. A loud slam woke us as we groaned. Only Buck and I popped up like jack-in-the-boxes sitting on the beds, looking at each other like dazed kids.

On the third day, we both held back and didn't bounce up quite as high. By the fourth day, we managed to keep the bounce minimal while grunting, grimacing, and rolling over.

The shock seemed to stimulate the bladder. It was a challenging exercise in accepting the present moment: to wait for the toilet to be free after a premature awakening.

At one point, the other roommate yelped incoherently

and threw himself onto his bed in upset, but mostly we kept good silence and endured the bizarre door-banging ritual.

Keeping Silence and Tapas

Keeping silence is a powerful technique. Silence can help promote the refinement of awareness. Talking takes a lot of energy. By not talking, we have more energy for personal growth and healing emotions.

Keeping silence for two or three days can have a meaningful effect on one's awareness. Keeping silence while engaged in a program of extra meditation and daily Sanskrit chanting provides a profound acceleration of personal progress. Awkward at first, it can become cozy.

Silence is a type of *tapas*: penance, endurance, or forbearance. Tapas, or tapa, is cooking, getting cooked, following discipline, and enduring. Tapas is a fundamental component of yoga. Real yoga gives us a greater ability to withstand opposites and maintain our cheerfulness, regardless of outer happenings.

Considered one of the most important of the earlier known teachers of yoga, Rishi Patanjali gave out his *Yoga Sutras* many hundreds of years ago. The time period of Patanjali may have been much earlier than what history edited and censored by colonials tells us.

One of Patanjali's sutras says, *"Tapaha swaadhyaaya ishvara pranidhaanani kriya yogah."* This means that the yoga of action, Kriya Yoga, consists of forbearance, self-study, and being devoted to the divine. Tapas can be sattvic, rajasic, or tamasic. These three gradations apply to each:

tapas of the mind, tapas of the body, and tapas of speech.

Patanjali stated, "*Manaha prasaadaha sowmyataam mounam aatma vinigraha.*" Gurudev explained that the first part of mental tapas is to maintain contentment and pleasantness in the mind. The first step can be as simple as deciding within oneself to be happy.

One goal of ayurveda and yoga is contentment. True contentment resonates throughout the system, down to the cellular level. Even while busy, it is possible to be calm and composed. This is fundamental to real yoga.

One's mind needs to learn how to be silent, not constantly full of noise. You grow into staying centered. You bring your mind back to your true self, again and again. Put all these together, and you have mental tapas.

To gain real yoga, tapas of the body consists of following your disciplines and healthy habits, such as bathing, brushing teeth, doing pranayama and asanas, drinking water throughout the day, getting meals on time, going for walks, etc. It is important to have control over the body and the senses. We do not, for example, eat any random thing at any time of day or night. Nor do we watch TV or YouTube for hours and hours or zone out late at night on a computer. This goes hand in hand with the idea of following wisdom rather than following feelings. The person who wants to be a yogi or yogini has to make a sincere effort to make wise choices.

Gurudev explained, "Tapas in Sanskrit implies accepting and enduring discomfort with a purpose. Perfection or success in any task is possible only with tapas."

Several times I have heard master Gurudev say that "Pranayama is the greatest tapas."

You may have heard of people who stood on one leg for a year and called it tapas. It is tamasic tapas because there is no tangible purpose other than a display of dim-witted egotism. That can be called demonic tapas or *rakshasi* tapas.

Think how much could have been accomplished if those people had planted trees every day. What if they taught pranayama to school children instead of wasting time and energy standing on one leg, fooling themselves?

I find traveling on a plane to be one of my least favorite forms of tapas. Looking into that type of tapas is a way of seeing proof of the master's divine nature.

Year after year, Gurudev kept flying around the world, flight after flight after flight. Often, he would take several flights each week. In different years, more than once, I have heard Gurudev tell a group that he had taken forty flights in thirty days. Such intense travel accelerates aging.

In later years, he would spend only one to two or three days in any given city. When he stays for a week in a given place, it will often be to direct courses at an ashram or a big venue for a special program. That would not necessarily happen every month.

People who travel with Gurudev have to be rotated out every few weeks for fresh participants. Nobody else can maintain his relentless pace. I don't have proof, but I would be surprised if Gurudev does not hold, by a vast margin, the world's record for the greatest amount of time spent flying in a plane. Thinking about such mastery of this advanced level of tapas leaves me awestruck.

Tapas in speech means to speak the truth, yet in such a way that our words are sweet and not destructive. Our "modern" society could use more of this.

Yoga says that it is important to express the truth in a considerate way. This understanding has been promoted many times in many places around the world, yet just knowing does not make it easy to do.

Much of "modern academic schooling" promotes so-called critical thinking, which is often done with a negative focus, opposite to yoga. Modern "journalism" promotes readership by publishing opposing opinions, even when many opinions have zero factual basis. At some point, after spending time with the master, I realized that I was trained to be good at finding flaws, yet I primarily wanted to express positivity and gratitude.

First comes awareness that one is doing something one doesn't want to do, then the ability to do the positive increases. I have gone through this countless times. It works.

This doesn't mean one becomes all wishy-washy and goody-goody. Sometimes it is important to be blunt or do something quickly, e.g., to prevent a person from getting injured. Thank goodness for all the techniques that give us the possibility of breaking free of old habits.

Tapas, or tapa, is frying or cooking. Getting well and thoroughly cooked, by the grace of the divine, can be said to be a type of burning. When you study yourself deeply, you can vanish into your big self. Devotion to the divine is essentially dissolving in love. It took me many long years to make the connection on my own and see that Gurudev's "burn, vanish, and dissolve" is another way of saying *"tapaha swaadhyaaya ishvara pranidhaan."*

Silence is a routine component of many meditation retreats. For some people, the discipline of silence is extremely intense, especially if a person has not had experience with silence or being alone. A wide variety of emotions may surface at any time.

To keep good silence, not only is it important to refrain from speaking any words, but one also does not read anything (other than course signs and instructions). Nor does one watch or listen to any recordings (unless they are part of the course). To communicate, one may use a minimum of written notes. This requires self-discipline and bravery. I have witnessed a few people who became quite rattled and would go to absurd extremes to avoid silence.

On that April 1988 Advanced Course, we were asked to keep strict silence, starting with the yoga asanas the first morning. That course was blanketed in timeless silence.

Keeping silence helps a person get more out of meditation. Talking actually requires a lot of energy. By staying silent, we conserve a lot of energy. That extra energy can be used by the human system for deeper healing and faster progress on the spiritual path.

At first, keeping my silence took a strong effort. I found myself wanting to say something here or there and would catch myself about to blurt something out.

The intention to get the most out of the time motivated me to make a serious effort. Even though Gurudev advised that it could be a joyful silence, I felt I had to be serious. It took a strong effort to keep my mouth from blurting out words here and there. After a few courses, silence became second nature. I still take it seriously, even though I feel joy in being in silence. Silence feels pleasant and comfortable to me now; it is easy to drop into silence at any time.

"Silence means being with the truth," according to Gurudev. From one perspective, what is true is whatever is right now. The past is not the truth; it is gone. The future has yet to happen. In Sanskrit, *sat* means truth and existence. Anything that is not here right now is not the truth. Gurudev claimed, "The purpose of silence is to be with the truth."

Our daylight comes from the sun, that is the truth. Gravity keeps you on this planet. That is the truth. In terms of ultimate reality, what is true is that which never changes. The eternal consciousness is the only thing that does not change. Our physical reality is always changing.

Gurudev said that "being in silence is being alone." This is a new understanding of *being alone*. Most people keep themselves endlessly busy. Prolonged calmness in silence seems to bother many people. Most people are never really alone, even when nobody else is in the room.

Many people will keep some noise going: music, messages, emails, news, videos, TV, etc. Most people are uncomfortable being alone with themselves without distractions. Silence is an opportunity to simplify and reduce mental activities. Real yoga includes deliberate silence.

Being alone with yourself, yet being in a group, is a skill. Some people think that to truly meditate and achieve on a path, they must run away and be a hermit in the mountains. There is no proof of attainment by hiding in a cave. Strength is being with others while still being alone.

Silence is not lonely. Being in silence is being in love. One's ego creates the other, creating separation and duality.

When you get close and intimate, the other dissolves, and you are one. When you are one, you are alone and present with emptiness inside.

Animals live in the present moment, not thinking about tomorrow. People think about tomorrow. Gurudev said that the ego is in relation to others. The ego creates attachment and fear. The ego shrinks if we are truly alone.

I guessed he was stretching people's minds and blowing away concepts with his "be alone" suggestion. It seemed intriguing to me to be alone in silence.

Gurudev affirmed that "every moment of silence is precious." He claimed we could be in love all the time with no complaint. Strength is being in the midst of people and feeling alone, not lonely. We can smile within the cells of our body. With real yoga, we love our breath.

Boredom is not something outside you. Boredom is inside you. If you are centered in the moment, you will not be bored. Real yoga conquers boredom. Every moment, we can be aware. Our breathing can occupy our full awareness.

Being physically isolated by yourself is not proof of being with your true self. Similarly, as Gurudev pointed out, a lack of opportunity to commit a crime is not proof of being a good person. Gurudev insisted that running away from this world is an insult to God. Being with others in society and still being alone is tapas. It brings freedom.

Gurudev advised, "Being alone is joy. Smile, be joyful in every moment." He defined *kaivalya* as "being alone."

Observing Sensations

On silent retreats, there will usually be a time for *seva*, or service activity. Various chores, which must be done for the course to be successful, will be completed quickly when many hands pitch in. On that silent Advanced Course in April 1988, we had some simple kitchen jobs as seva. Washing and chopping vegetables, washing dishes, and washing pots and pans were the main chores.

It bothered me that the volunteer who was in charge of the kitchen felt free to talk casually while we were working in the kitchen. His talking to me made my first silence course more challenging. It seemed that strict silence made him uncomfortable. Maybe his own personal issues caused him to avoid silence. Even if I ignored him, he would talk to me and try to have a conversation with me.

On a path, at any time, some physical or emotional sensations may come. During meditation and activity, there may be pleasant or unpleasant sensations. If you observe unpleasant sensations, they will fade, assuming you do not currently have a serious injury. You will not know the truth if you avoid observing the sensations in your own body.

The more you have an aversion to unpleasant sensations, the longer they will stay. Emotions will bring sensations. Before you react, watch the sensations in the body. Detachment is watching the sensations in the body and letting them fade and fall away. This is real yoga.

Suppose you get hit and have pain. If you get mad, tense up, or wish the pain were not there, it will feel worse. Trying not to feel the pain makes it last longer. You may give yourself an additional headache by not accepting the pain. If you relax and allow the pain to be, going inside with your awareness and feeling it fully, it will fade as fast as the severity of the injury in your unique body allows.

You can observe anger without expressing it. It is important to watch what we judge as bad thoughts. Gurudev revealed that when you have an aversion to bad thoughts, it creates another impression. Each impression is yet more baggage clogging our consciousness. The complete system of yoga aims to remove all impressions.

What Is Yoga?

Most people living in modern culture approach yoga only as a type of exercise. In January 1973, this was true for me. I was lucky to begin taking yoga classes in college. Initially, it was just a way of getting some exercise. From the twice-a-week class, I felt wonderful benefits, better than just physical exercise. I felt much more alive. I began doing the *asanas* (yogic exercises) on my own every day.

Some yoga classes have pranayama and/or meditation,

but generally, only in simplistic, limited, and minimal amounts. Most of the names of the various styles of yoga that have become available since 1995 didn't exist before 1988. While Hatha Yoga historically includes pranayama and meditation practices as fundamental components of its path, many people today think Hatha Yoga is just a style of physical asana exercises.

It has been said that there are asanas for every type of incarnation a soul could have, whether insect, bird, snake, cat, dog, cow, fish, etc. Some have claimed that mastery over an asana will supposedly give one freedom from the necessity of incarnating in the corresponding type of life form.

Shiva is sometimes reputed to have been the original yogi. Gurudev has repeatedly said that Shiva is a name for the eternal, innocent, pure consciousness, not an actual person. The consciousness contains everything.

Yoga is one of the six key systems of Indian philosophy, known as *Darshana*, *Shad Darshana,* or *Shad Darshan*, meaning six types of inner and outer vision. The six systems of Indian philosophy are *Sankhya, Nyaya, Vaisheshika, Mimansa, Yoga,* and *Vedanta*. These are teachings that help us understand experience from a perspective that promotes personal evolution towards self-realization or enlightenment.

Patanjali's sutras on yoga are widely recognized as deeply authoritative. Rishi Patanjali gave the following as the definition of yoga: *"yogashchittavrittinirodhah."* This means that real yoga happens when the movements or modulations of the mind have stopped. When the mind is still, one can more easily experience pure consciousness.

Patanjali goes further to explain that yoga is the state when we see our self as it truly is without identifying with any of what we know as normal states of mind, or *vrittis*. The vrittis are: correct knowledge, wrong knowledge, fantasy or imagination, sleep, and memory. These are considered to be the five modes, states, or modulations of the mind.

Most of the time, for most people, they are lost in whatever mode the mind is functioning in. Being established in real yoga, a person will not lose their experience of their true self while the mind perceives the world.

Gurudev Sri Sri has brought great clarity and revolutionary understanding to Raj Yoga, the royal path of Patanjali. Raj Yoga is known as an eight-sided gem, *Ashtanga*, or an eight-limbed path. Note that Patanjali's understanding of yoga as a science is much broader than the physical style of asanas being taught in many cities called "Ashtanga Yoga." The eight fundamental categories of **Raj Yoga** are:

Yama – Restraints or values regarding dealing with the world:
   ahimsa - non-violence in body, mind, and feelings.
   satya - present truth, tapped into eternal infinity.
   asteya - non-theft, physically and mentally.
   brahmacharya - moving with pure consciousness (Brahmin). Unmoved by sensual cravings.
   aparigraha - non-accumulation physically, mentally, and emotionally.

Niyama - Duties, requirements, methods of managing oneself:
   shaucha - cleanliness of body, mind, and speech.
   santosha – contentment.
   tapas - austerity, spiritual effort, forbearance.
   swadhyaya – self-study, awareness.
   Ishvara pranidhaan - devotion to the Divine.

Asana - Positions of the body; physical exercises.

Pranayama - Breathing exercises, various types of breathing techniques.

Pratyahara - Withdrawing the senses from scenery.
Dharana – Keeping the mind on a special space.
Dhyana – Meditation, smooth flow of awareness.
Samadhi - Joyful state of harmony and blissful experience of the moment.

Likening samadhi's effect on the mind to the effect of refrigeration for food, Gurudev explained, "Samadhi is a state where the mind freezes. The refrigeration of your life. The secret of youthfulness, the secret of bubbling enthusiasm, and the secret of renewal of life is samadhi, steadiness."

There are different types of samadhi. It can happen with the eyes open or closed. Equanimity with rational awareness is *savitarka* samadhi. There are more varieties of samadhi with the eyes closed. In one kind of eyes-closed samadhi, there is just the awareness of 'I am', without any experience of who I am or where I am.

Samadhi is a way of living as though you don't exist. Samadhi happens when the mind and senses are steady.

The complete science of real yoga is a means of improving a person's life. For most types of personal problems, yoga and the sister art of ayurveda have solutions.

Ayurveda and yoga provide many means of attaining experiences that have been out of our reach. Anyone who applies themselves to incorporating even part of the fullness of yoga into their life can become a better person.

People who meditate, do pranayama, practice complete yoga, chant, sing, dance, laugh, and serve others will, at various times, experience some pure consciousness. It is the same, whether you call it big mind, higher self, pure love, God, infinity, Purusha, pure being, or pure consciousness. Many people do things on a regular basis to improve their lives, remove obstacles, and expand awareness. From ancient times, this has been called *abhyasa*, or practice.

Abhyasa is something promoting sattva that you do repeatedly, with respect and full awareness, to align yourself with the present moment. Abhyasa is being centered in the present moment. Abhyasa includes using a mantra and/or some combination of the eight limbs of yoga: yama, niyama, asana, pranayama, pratyahara, dharana, dhyana, and samadhi. Daily abhyasa gives a great start to my mornings.

Gurudev reminded us that, "Amidst all concepts about enlightenment, we forget the essence, dispassion, and being centered. Being centered despite everything and living in the world." He says that abhyasa, daily practice, and *vairagya*, dispassion, are essential for progressing in yoga.

Desire means wanting. Desire means that you feel an insufficiency. Desire is different from intention. Desire makes a person weak, according to Gurudev. After some years of regular abhyasa, I had fewer desires. This happens naturally. Gurudev reminds us that if you are trying to get rid of desires, that is another desire itself. He emphasized, "Some people are on this trip to destroy their desires. They are beating around the bush. Nothing happens to them. This principle should be very well understood."

A person's life can evaporate in desire. Only too easily, with choices bombarding us. With real yoga we become able to disentangle ourselves from scenery, including our own mind, and repose in the seer, true self.

Gurudev made a clear distinction: "Vairagya is putting a stop to the craving for happiness. This does not mean that you have to be miserable. It does not say you should not enjoy. But if you can retrieve your mind from the craving for joy, you can meditate."

Raj Yoga has been around for many hundreds and thousands of years. Yogis have known about the importance of cleanliness for thousands of years. So-called "modern society" only began promoting personal hygiene in the late

1800's. Many thousands of people died from dangerous diseases that were caused mainly by filth. As washing of hands and use of public sanitation became the norm in Western society, the death rates due to significant deadly illnesses dropped dramatically. People who have pursued a complete path of yoga, not just asanas, have, in general, enjoyed better health. The complete path yields real yoga.

As Gurudev told us, it is not necessary to master one limb of yoga before working on another. Some have contended that one must master the limbs of yoga sequentially. There may have been some people who did that, yet it is easy to see that this is a belief and not a necessity. You can work on all limbs daily, as many do.

For example, there are many people skilled in asana who know little to nothing about yama or niyama. Many students do not practice all the limbs. The more one uses all the limbs of yoga, the faster the progress.

Yoga increases skill in action. If you are becoming less skilled in life, perhaps you are not actually doing yoga, or your yoga is incomplete. As I learned, a true master can take people much further than a book or even a good teacher.

Gurudev explained it clearly: "Three gunas come in cycles in our lives: sattva, rajas, and tamas. When sattva comes, there is alertness, knowledge, interest, joy, and happiness. When rajo guna comes, there are more desires, feverishness, restlessness, sadness, etc. When tamo guna comes, there is delusion, attachment, lack of knowledge, lethargy, etc. These three phases come into life in cycles. But one who is centered will watch, witness, and just move through them very naturally and easily, without being averse to any."

Ignorance is called *avidya*, meaning lack of knowledge. Most people don't notice their own ignorance; they are caught in the momentum of it. When you notice that you have a bad habit and you want to get out of it, then you are aware of your own ignorance. Repeatedly, Gurudev has cautioned that acting as if or thinking that impermanent things are permanent is part of ignorance.

Thinking that only you are correct and others are mostly or always wrong is ego, and that is also part of ignorance. Ignorant people are caught up in the outer forms of things. That was a major problem for me when I was young. Gurudev said that when a person is not aware that they are being judgmental, then they are more attached to it.

Making it seem easy, Gurudev advised, "When you become aware that you are judging, then you can drop it."

Cravings and aversions are part of ignorance. When I started with Gurudev, I was always trying to be perfect. Gurudev said, "What happens when there is aversion? You promote it. You stay with whatever you are averse to. You continue to crave whatever it is that you want. You allow the craving to continue. Therefore, moving through the gunas without craving or aversion is a real skill. And that is yoga."

Gurudev went deep into Patanjali's sutras. "*Yoga karmasu kaushalam.* The skill in action is yoga. The word yoga means skill. Skill to live your life, to manage your mind, to deal with your emotions, to be with people, to be in love, and not let that love turn into hatred. In this world, everyone loves, but that love does not stay the same for long. Soon, it turns into hatred, sometimes almost immediately. But yoga is that skill, that preservative, that maintains love as love all the time."

When you put it this way, who wouldn't want more skills in life? Real yoga is a path to increasing awareness. It requires taking time to make our awareness simple, so we can simply be with whatever is happening in the moment. Gurudev pointed out that one way to lose awareness of yourself is to keep yourself endlessly busy.

Yoga means being able to maintain awareness while being busy. Yoga requires taking time on a daily basis to recalibrate ourselves. Without this, I would not be here.

Recalibration of yourself with the techniques of yoga can yield significant acceleration on a spiritual path. This is what saved my life. Real yoga includes all of its components: mantras, yama, niyama, asana, pranayama, pratyahara, dharana, dhyana, and samadhi. Daily recalibration of yourself through yoga increases mental awareness while promoting better physical health. I enjoy enormous relief.

Sometimes, some indifference may come up. A person may lose motivation or not feel like doing anything. During the early years, Gurudev revealed that yoga asanas help reduce indifference. Long, deep breaths remove lethargy.

One of Patanjali's sutras that reveals how to perform asana is "*sthira sukham asanam*." Gurudev explained that the proper meaning of this sutra is that correct asana "is steady, comfortable, and dropping the effort." When you hold a pose, it is important to relax into the pose and let go of effort.

Yoga asanas help us to be in touch with the present moment. This has been my daily experience. I had heard some people say that the purpose of yoga asanas is to enable a person to sit still for longer periods of meditation. Gurudev later confirmed this as one purpose of asanas.

At the same time, asanas help to bring awareness inward. Asanas help keep us youthful. Asanas promote the process of stress release. Breathing practices and meditation increase and accelerate the release of stress. Sanskrit chanting adds clarity and bliss. A complete package of practices, such as those taught in the Art of Living, can give a person rapid progress on the path to real yoga.

If love is not involved, repetition can lead to boredom.

The boredom is in the person. Boredom is not an external fact. Daily practice, or abhyasa, may stir up feelings of boredom. It is important to continue daily practice to break through, conquer boredom, and grow past that stage. Then you no longer have to be a victim of boredom.

What Is Meditation and What Is not Meditation?

Meditation is a means of achieving a deeply refreshing rest in a short amount of time. Meditation is resting with awareness, as differentiated from sleep, which is resting without awareness, an unconscious rest.

Inspiring many people to meditate, Gurudev is a supreme expert on meditation. Gurudev says that meditation is essential for anyone who wants to get things done. Gurudev has guided people in meditation in hundreds of cities around the world. He says, "Meditation is a journey from sound to silence." Listening to music is not meditation.

Meditation is accomplished by effortlessly bringing the mind into the present moment. There are various methods to do this. Observing the breath, observing the body, and repeating a mantra are some key techniques. The most refreshing meditations will be effortless in the sense that no concentration, strain, or forcing are required.

The effort to meditate is in the preparation: finding an appropriate place to sit, turning off devices, sitting down, and keeping the eyes closed. Once you have settled comfortably in your seat, you start the process and let go.

It is important to understand what meditation actually

is. You may have heard people say things such as, "Running is my meditation," "Surfing is my meditation," "I get into a meditation when I go on the computer," or "My meditation happens when I work on my car."

Getting focused and in your zone during an activity is not truly meditation. Experiences of centeredness and flow happen more easily and often as a result of meditation.

When a person exercises, the body releases endorphins. Endorphins have actions similar to those of opiates; they reduce pain. Endorphins are manufactured naturally within the body, and they make us feel good. This gives rise to what is known as "runner's high." Meditation means a state of mind in which we go beyond the normal activity of the mind. An endorphin high is not a sure sign of meditation.

Tension in people will usually correlate with constricted blood vessels. Some people resort to using substances as a shortcut to feeling better. Drugs, alcohol, marijuana, smoking, etc. produce a brief state of apparent relaxation. This is because blood vessels will relax from the stimulus of the intoxicant. But after the intoxication wears off, the blood vessels return to being constricted.

After intoxication from substances wears off, the blood vessels will often be more constricted than they were before the intoxication. People who use intoxicating substances on a regular basis experience increased cravings, delusions, addictions, poor health, and weakness. They end up feeling much worse in the long run and going deeper into states of ignorance.

Meditation produces a relaxation of blood vessels that can last for hours. The elevation and relaxation that people feel from meditation become cumulative and progressive when meditation is done on a regular, daily basis.

Recreational drugs generally provide both an initial,

stimulating, or rajasic effect and a subsequent dulling or tamasic effect. After intoxicants wear off, they leave a person with increased dullness and reduced functionality.

Meditation and yogic breathing practices reduce rajas and tamas and elevate the mind to a state of greater sattva.

According to ayurveda, alcohol, cigarettes, marijuana, and drugs significantly reduce and block a person's ability to digest emotions. In bold contrast, meditation and yogic breathing practices directly enhance emotional processing and increase emotional centeredness.

You can be focused, calm, steady, and undistracted in your activity, but that is not meditation. For many, these positive qualities are a result of successful meditation. You may be having some periods of samadhi in your activity. Yet activity is not meditation. Meditation is sitting down, having your eyes closed, going inward, and relaxing into being.

Wallace (1970) found that based on oxygen consumption and heart rate, meditation can give us a rest that is deeper than the deepest sleep. Meditation is not just a little more refreshing than deep sleep; it is sometimes twice as deep as deep sleep. And significantly more restful. This is a major reason why deep impressions and stresses that don't get cleansed through sleep can be released by meditation.

Dhyana is a dispassionate, transcending type of meditation. Sometimes mantra repetition is used, known as *japa*. In the West, many people have mistakenly thought japa was only external. These days, most people think japa is only rapid, external repetition of the mantra.

The word japa has been used to mean any repetition of a mantra, whether totally internal and silent, *manasa*, whispered, *upaanshu*, or out loud, *vaikhari*. One approach to japa is to repeat a mantra for a set period of time or a specific number of times, such as 108 repetitions.

Different levels of effort may be used in japa, from a

mild effort when it is spoken to an effortless effort when it is internal. Japa can bring waves of ecstasy. Japa can clear negativity and is sometimes used to remove obstacles seen in an astrological chart. Japa is a valuable technique.

Some people say they meditate on harmony or love. They keep their minds focused on their chosen ideals. This is actually a type of concentration and not meditation. It keeps the mind in surface layers of thought and activity.

In meditation, we let go and experience whatever naturally happens as we relax into our true nature. After a relaxed meditation, we typically feel more tranquil, and it is easier to focus and concentrate. Naturally, we will be more peaceful and more loving. Many have experienced this.

To dive to the deepest, quietest levels of consciousness, it is important to relax and allow the process to unfold. The experience of millions of meditators was scientifically validated by Travis & Shear (2010). They showed that effortless, silent repetition of a mantra is the most efficient vehicle for an individual to gain the deepest meditations on their own.

Using a mantra silently, in an effortless way, can provide what is known as an automatic self-transcending technique. We are not counting the repetitions of the mantra. The pace is relaxed and easy. When we notice thoughts, we stay relaxed and easily return to the mantra.

Due to various conditions of the body, such as health reasons or fatigue, we may naturally lose awareness in meditation. This is the body getting what it needs. It is best accepted without judgment.

Meditation can give the deepest rest possible. When the metabolism slows down in meditation, the body cools off. You may feel cold. That is why many people of different traditions wrap themselves in a shawl when they sit for their practices, even if they feel warm before sitting.

It often happens that people will go deep in meditation and not feel deep because they have some alertness. Habituation to lack of awareness in sleep makes it hard to get past this type of doubt. Studies have shown that meditators can have significant reductions in metabolism while feeling alert. You can have thoughts and still be in a very deep state. It is imperative to come out of meditation slowly, no matter how shallow or deep you think you went.

For most people, the single most important point for getting benefits from meditation is to come out of it slowly. Sometimes, even when they are open to inner, personal change, people are in a rush, so they get up quickly from meditation. This can cause energy loss, impatience, headaches, disorientation, or irritability.

If you do everything correctly, results will come. Be sure you are sitting comfortably with a mostly empty stomach (such as before a meal), eyes closed, relaxing, and not exerting effort. But those results can be broken or shattered by coming out of meditation quickly.

Meditation is a profoundly restful state, which may not be perceived as such since the mind can be alert while meditation is happening. Most people are used to being unconscious when resting. With awareness in meditation, the mind tells itself it is not deep. Incorrectly, a person may figure that it would be no big deal to open their eyes, stand up, and walk away. This would be a huge mistake.

To stop meditation, it is critical to keep the eyes closed and gradually transition to the normal waking state. It helps a lot to do some pranayama, such as alternate nostril breathing, called *nadi shodan*, to make the transition smooth.

Many people find that having a clock or watch right in front of them is essential. Otherwise, it is easy to feel like five minutes have gone by when only forty seconds have passed. To end meditation, three to five minutes of alternate nostril pranayama before opening the eyes feels soothing and strengthening. This solidifies the benefits of meditation.

Gurudev clarified, "Without dispassion, your meditation is no good. It is of no use. It cannot provide you the rest that you are longing for."

Gurudev says, for good meditation, drop wanting, needing, and doing as you close your eyes. The key is effortlessness, not imagination. Imagination requires effort. Completely letting go feels natural and wonderful.

Sahaj Samadhi is a very effective, powerful meditation technique, taught by the Art of Living Foundation. Mantra based, Sahaj Samadhi is simple and easy to learn.

The ultimate goal of meditation is to be in samadhi, a state of blissfulness, peacefulness, and serenity. In the *Yoga Sutras*, Patanjali says that many years of practice are necessary to train the mind to be able to exist in a non-stop, continuous, permanent state of blissful awareness. This goes hand in hand with the removal of samskaras and karmas, a major achievement of real yoga.

With a fresh perspective, Gurudev puts it this way: "Samadhi is a state where you feel like you could stay like this for a million years."

Atma is the individual self. *Paramatma* is the big self, the supreme being, the Lord. Patanjali says that the Lord is free of misery and karma. The Lord has no cravings or aversions. It is profound to experience that your true self and the Lord are one and the same. When you live that experience all the time, that is enlightenment.

Gurudev put it in an unexpected way that got my attention. Gurudev proclaimed, "Enlightenment is no explanation and no complaint."

I once asked Gurudev if being in crowded, polluted cities had any effect on his level of consciousness. He responded that it was insignificant.

Yoga with the Master

In April 1988, we did yoga asanas with Gurudev at 6 a.m. All the windows were open, with an ambient temperature of approximately 50 degrees F and no heater. Even with my sweatshirt on, it felt too cold to me, and I got angry. When I walked into the room, I paused briefly, then marched over to close a window.

One of the assistants, B, blocked me and announced, "The windows have to stay open." I complained that it was too cold. B gestured at Gurudev and casually said, "Talk to the Master." His French-Canadian street-pronunciation made the word "the" sound like "da." "Tock to da Master."

Blissfully relaxed, Gurudev calmly explained, "We need the windows open for the prana."

A light went off in my head. It is a key revelation. Simple and important. The point of yoga is to give a person more prana, not to leave them drained. Sure enough, the asanas in the fresh air gave me calm exhilaration. By the third day, we were used to it and didn't mind the cold air.

Illness is an obstacle to yoga. This is specifically mentioned in Patanjali's *Yoga Sutras*. Stale, oxygen-deficient air due to a lack of fresh air flow breeds illness. Stale air is an obstruction to health and yoga.

Fresh Air Increases Prana

People in society sometimes forget the basic principles of science. Science tells us that in a closed room, with every single breath, oxygen decreases and carbon dioxide, nitrogen, methane, and other waste gases increase. The average exhalation contains only approximately 16% oxygen. Humans need at least 19.5% oxygen in the air to be healthy. Groups of people executing pranayama, yoga asanas, or other breathing practices use air much more rapidly than groups of people sitting at a computer.

The healthier a person is, the easier they will tolerate wider ranges of temperature. Warmer garments can be put on. Each person can gauge what layers they need for comfort. As the body gets warmer during asanas, layers of clothing can be taken off. Unless a person has an illness, the heat generated by movement should be enough. In a frozen season below the freezing point of water, heat is, of course, essential for most people.

Some people say that it is important to heat the room before doing yoga asanas so that your muscles will be loose. This thinking is actually based on a misunderstanding. In a moderate climate, for healthy people, the heat within the muscle should be self-generated. If it is colder than about 45 to 50 degrees F, a little external heat can be appropriate.

The colder it is outside, the smaller the opening of the windows is needed to maintain a flow of fresh air. If a room is artificially heated, then the entire body is heated. When people are healthy and the room temperature is over 50 degrees F, it is usually not necessary to add heat.

While it is, of course, healthy to sweat, Ayurveda says that it is better to avoid heating the head. For Ayurvedic steam treatments, the head of the person will be kept outside the heated container. A person who heats their head on a regular basis will experience fire issues such as skin rash, graying of hair, frustration, hair loss, eczema, impatience, skin breakouts, irritation, and/or anger.

Heat application for the body is better for those who have more moist, cold conditions in their body and mind.

Thus, according to Ayurveda, the ideal candidate for performing yoga asanas in a heated room would be a cold, lazy, fat, slow, thick, and sluggish person with a dominance of water and earth elements in their system.

To cleanse toxins, heat can be applied to the body in a container without heating the head. People with more fire element tend to get impatient, frustrated, angry, or irritable easily. They are better off not being subjected to additional external heat in a closed room, especially when ambient temperatures are already over 60 degrees F.

For dehydrated people with more cool dryness in the body, some heat may initially feel good since it counteracts coolness. Heated air is rapidly drying. Ayurveda says that anxiety, worry, fear, constipation, and panic relate to dryness. People with these conditions need to avoid hot yoga. Sweating increases internal dryness. Yoga in a heated room is sometimes initially comforting. It will eventually promote anxiety, forgetfulness, tight muscles, dryness, uncertainty, skin irritation, panic, doubt, respiratory irritation, fear, constipation, irregularity, and/or worry, etc. Especially if hot yoga is done repeatedly.

Layers of clothing are the best way to apply personal heat for yoga. Then fresh air flow, higher oxygen levels, and better prana can be maintained. Garments can easily be added or removed. This provides personal temperature adjustments that will not interfere with the health of others.

Heat or coolness can be generated by thought. Some yoga adepts develop body control to an advanced level. Then they can sit in the snow with little clothing and no ill effect. Such powers, or *siddhis*, are byproducts of the development of consciousness. To avoid landing short of enlightenment, siddhis should never be sought as the goal. Showing off is ego. Showing off is not a part of real yoga. Real yoga, as I learned, offers development for the whole person.

Creating True Resilience in the Body

For thousands of years, many yogis have lived in more simple conditions close to nature. This provides plentiful fresh air all year. Yoga, done with abundant fresh air flowing, is most conducive to the development of better health and higher consciousness.

People who keep their windows open all the time, year-round, find that their health, mood, and clarity improve. Aging slows down. Progress on the path is much more rapid with fresh prana. It is common knowledge that fresh air reduces illness. Personal heat doesn't need closed windows.

We have thermostats and metabolic regulation built into our bodies. Gurudev talked about how, when we live in closer connection to the natural climate around us, our body's ability to regulate itself is stronger.

Gurudev declared, "Your body has its own air-conditioning system. But if you turn on the external air conditioner all the time, then you are destroying the self-modulating system of the body."

At the same time, it is important to be practical; if a person is cold, they can put on as many garments as needed to feel comfortable. In colder weather, the window opening needed for air flow is smaller.

I used to be bothered by slight temperature changes. In several classes that I took before I met the master, I can remember opening and closing windows during a single class to try to regulate the temperature. After meeting Gurudev and making a point every day to keep more windows open for a flow of fresh air, I noticed that my body gradually became less sensitive to temperature fluctuations.

Many yoga studios have followed the example of certain studios with closed environments. Before yoga was popular in the US, certain no-air-flow studios charged high prices and made a lot of money. After 1989, as yoga grew in popularity through the 1990s and 2000s, more studios started keeping windows closed. Yoga classes became associated with wearing minimal amounts of skimpy clothing since many yoga studios were hot and had no fresh air. Just because you can produce a fad in the market does not make you an expert on yoga.

While yoga is not against having a good-looking body, the purpose of yoga is not to display minimally dressed bodies in a low oxygen, hot environment. Glamor-driven Western culture has distorted yoga into cultish, sweaty athletics performed in overheated rooms with low-oxygen and little prana. Yoga will increase physical, mental, and emotional health, but only if done with fresh air.

Gurudev clarified, "I have nothing against air conditioners but making sure that the fresh prana comes and your body temperature agrees with the environment will make a difference. Then, you gain the ability to be in a cold place without having to wear too many warm clothes. Or to be in a hot place and not feel suffocated."

Facing Challenges on First Silence Course

For the April 1988 Advanced Course, we were instructed to avoid eating heavy meals so that we could be alert for prolonged meditations. Doctors had advised me to keep fruit consumption extremely minimal, as in no more than one piece of fruit per week. They also advised that I always have something more solid with the fruit.

Breakfast consisted of nothing but one piece of fruit for each participant. Lunch on the first day was one bowl of tepid, watery soup with only a handful of tiny bits of vegetables distributed through the whole cooking pot. Given my health conditions, I wondered whether I would make it to the end of the course with such minimal meals.

As a tribute to the healing power of what we were doing, by the time I finished that first silence course and went home, I felt strong enough that I naturally ate less food than before the course. Spontaneously, my body gravitated toward being vegetarian, and I was able to sustain it for a couple of weeks. This was miraculous, given the severity of what I had been dealing with.

While meditating, one lets go of bodily concerns, and my body made that painfully difficult. Due to my musculoskeletal injuries that had never completely healed, I had chronic daily pain. It was dangerous for me to sit cross-legged since that could make my sacroiliac joint pop open. Doctors had told me to sit on a firm, flat floor with lumbar support, with my legs straight in front of me. Feet and knees had to be separately propped up to maintain good alignment.

After 20 minutes of sitting, my lower back, hips, and legs would start cramping, and pain would intensify. I would be forced to change my position, and if I continued to sit, I would have to keep changing positions at least every 8 to 10 minutes. This would make courses with multiple daily meditation periods seriously challenging and frustrating.

Ironically, Gurudev revealed that both intense pain and intense pleasure will bring awareness to the present moment. The goal is to be centered on the moment all the time, regardless of what is going on.

In order to give myself more sitting ability, I took to standing during all the discussion and lecture periods. I figured that if I ate all my meals standing up, I would also have more ability to sit for meditation. Thus, for all meals, I held a plate and stood off to the side, with a view in front of me. For the next year, I would make a point of standing during lectures at Gurudev's Advanced Courses so that I would have more capacity to sit for meditation.

A guy who had been in India the previous year as a teenager came up to me at the end of the course. He asked me if I was following some special yogic discipline. He thought the practice of standing while eating might be part of some esoteric teaching. He seemed disappointed when I told him the truth about my pain management practice.

On that first Advanced Course, we spent many hours observing the breath in meditations with Gurudev. It felt like we did the maximum possible amount of meditation.

Meditation with a group usually ends with Gurudev chanting in Sanskrit. Over the years, I have heard many different chants at the end of meditations. The chanting feels good and makes a wonderful ending transition.

Throwing Thoughts

Being angry about something that happened in the past or worrying about what will happen in the future reduces our ability to enjoy the present. I used to waste many hours thinking about the past and future. This flip-flop between the past and the future is a deeply ingrained habit for most people. The breathing practices flush out the charge in many memories and eliminate a lot of these useless mental patterns.

Adding another fun trick, Gurudev had us do a

simple exercise to help train the mind. We sat and imagined some buckets in front of us. One bucket on the right for the future, left for the past, and center for the present. When in doubt, you can use the center one for miscellaneous if you want. Then, as each thought comes into your mind, you toss the thought into the corresponding bucket.

The first time you do this, have your eyes closed. After that, you can do this with your eyes open or closed.

It is an entertaining game. Many people are impressed that they have a lot of thoughts about the past and the future. It can be surprising for some people who have been out of touch with themselves.

Throwing away thoughts helps reduce mental chatter. It creates more inner silence. After doing this, I noticed that my mind was more settled and less scattered.

Throwing away thoughts can be used at any time in our daily lives. Any thought that bugs you, you can just toss out of your mind. Many times, the master has emphasized that it is disempowering to go on and on, chewing on the same thought. I encourage everyone to throw away any bothersome, repetitive thoughts.

Big Mind

On that April 1988 Advanced Course, Gurudev spoke at length about the big mind. Keeping silence helps cultivate big mind awareness. The big mind is also known as pure awareness or pure consciousness.

A master is immersed in big mind all the time. As a student grows into the big mind, they can still get confused about whether what they think is coming from the big mind or the small mind. The sutras of ancient texts only reveal their full meaning to someone established in big mind.

Most people experience reality in their normal waking state of awareness. Like me when I met Gurudev, most people are stuck with their small minds. Their thinking and actions are chosen, colored, moved, and swayed by ego, patterns, desires, fears, upsets, and impressions from the past. Yoga and ayurveda refer to impressions as *samskaras*. Desires often stem from patterns, tendencies, and habits known as *vasanas*. Samskaras and vasanas reduce our ability to experience real yoga.

The small mind will not allow you to be fully centered in the present moment. Your small mind does not allow you to be 100%. Part of you is elsewhere. Some people get occasional glimpses of big mind reality. Fewer will regularly do something to cultivate big mind awareness.

People often notice that when they bring some of this value of the big mind or pure consciousness into their lives, they feel better, happier, healthier, and uplifted. There are many means of increasing the value of consciousness in life.

It has been said that an enlightened master has realized the big self, true self, or pure consciousness. Another way of saying this is that an enlightened master is continuously in the big mind and has personal awareness of real yoga or pure being. Not just awareness, but the continuous presence of infinity. True self, pure consciousness, Purusha, God, Chaitanya, infinity, Paramatman, and big mind are terms that have been used to label the same thing.

Yoga Vasishtha explains that it is not possible to teach the true nature of the infinite consciousness; you can attain it only through direct experience.

Yoga Vasishtha also asserts that studying scriptures will not give a person direct experience of the true self.

Direct experience of the true self requires that the disciple surrender, follow the instructions of the master and study sacred wisdom. Any one of these alone is usually not enough to gain enlightenment. All of these components must come together in order for a person to achieve enlightenment.

One reason that some people who meditate have less experience with big mind is that they come out of meditation too quickly. Coming out of meditation slowly and not making an effort during meditation are important keys to successful meditation.

For most people, three minutes is usually the minimum for a transition with eyes closed, after stopping the mantra or other process of meditation, in order to get all the benefits.

Coming out of Trauma

The more time that I spent with Gurudev, the more I wanted to spend time with him. It is clear that he genuinely cares about all those around him and is able to uplift many different types of people.

Gurudev's authenticity as a true master was astounding to me. My life experiences had taught me that few people were trustworthy. I didn't like having that understanding, yet the reality was that most people seemed to lose their humanity under just a little pressure, or no pressure at all. I wanted to trust people, yet repeatedly I was confronted with strong reasons not to trust them.

While it is true that my experiences were due to my own karmas, knowing this did not stabilize trust. To meet someone truly noble to their core and beyond, like Gurudev, seemed miraculous. Ancient wisdom says that getting a chance to be in the presence of a saint, an enlightened master, is one of the rarest of rare things a human can experience.

Gurudev laid it out clearly: "The greatest pain in life is the shaken trust. The second greatest pain is shaken love. What is needed is to have the trust re-established." By doing the courses and maintaining daily practice, we can do this.

On Christmas day in 1978, my first wife informed me that she wanted a divorce. You could say that we rushed into marriage too quickly. You could also say that we were not skilled at communication.

After that, my grandmother told me, "Sometimes a kick is as good as a boost." At the time, I decided that I was a person with a lot of problems. I started reading a lot of self-help books. Much later, it became clear that I had to be on another track, in another location, in order to be able to meet Gurudev. My real destiny was waiting, hidden.

Reading books can be inspiring. Yet in spite of how many notes you take, how many underlines you make, how many times you read the same passages, and how many post-notes you put on the mirror, when you get upset, the emotions often quickly and easily override the intellect.

By 1988, when I met Gurudev, I had a lot of irritation and frustration in my system. My psychology was still in survival mode, in large part due to my having been essentially homeless for almost three years.

There were many periods, from late 1981 through mid-1984, when I was sleeping on one or another of a random sequence of living room floors. The floor camping periods usually lasted from just two to three days up to two or more weeks. There were a couple of places where I was able to stay for a longer period of time. Sometimes I was allowed to leave stuff while I was gone during the day. Such as a small bag with a rolled sleeping bag and clothing. Some people wanted all traces of me removed every morning.

Those were haunting, challenging times, when sometimes I did not know in the morning where I would be sleeping at night. Technically, I was homeless for most of that period. The people who allowed me to camp on their floors were guardian angels, to whom I will be forever grateful.

Due to the intensity and demand of the day-to-day struggles, I never seemed to have ability, time, or sufficient means to adequately thank those who helped me. During those days, I was often in a state of overwhelm and shock. Repeatedly, it felt awful to have to seek out yet one more place to stay. My ability to express myself diminished. Sheer survival was a bleak, humiliating reality.

I had no credit card or bank account. I ate a sparse diet of the least expensive food I could buy. Some days, I was not sure when or if I would eat. One day, I noticed that all I had in my possession was one subway token and not a single dollar more. My supply of food was gone, except for half a stick of butter. *This isn't working.*

Humiliation, loneliness, and aching emptiness threaded through many days and nights. The stress added to the illnesses brewing in my system. I was not taking any health supplements. Amazingly, I never ended up sleeping on the street. Fierce courage surged like a tide.

I did not give in to fear. I focused on my next step. *What now? What can I do?* I kept going. I did not give up. Meditating on a regular, daily basis kept me alive and off the street. I am certain of it. *No matter what, keep going.*

Gurudev maintained that the shaking of trust even happened to Jesus "at the last moment, but only for a moment."

Gurudev pointed out that, in comparison with Jesus, usually, only small things have shaken our faith.

Teacher Training Invitation

A private meeting with Gurudev was granted to each course participant at the conclusion of the April 1988 silent Advanced Course. When I sat with him in his room, he was warmly welcoming. He surprised me by saying, "We need teachers of this knowledge. We are having teacher training this summer in Canada."

My first thought was, *what would Maharishi think?* I was thinking of Maharishi Mahesh Yogi, known as Maharishi, whom I felt devotion for, though I did not usually think of him as my guru.

In June of 1973, I learned the Transcendental Meditation Technique (TM) from a teacher who lived in my college dorm. Less than a month later, all my acne was gone.

I was diligent about meditating every day for twenty minutes, twice a day. In later years, when there was uncertainty about living quarters and relationships, meditation kept me from completely falling apart.

In 1975, I had friends who were dedicated to meditating. We attended weekend retreats called Residence Courses, which included extra periods of meditation. Some friends wanted to become teachers of TM, yet I was put off by the behavior of a few of the local teachers.

Disillusioned, I thought that becoming a meditation teacher had not cured certain people of their arrogance or bad habits, so what was the use?

A teacher who had completed a six-month program with Maharishi crossed my path. Here was a person who radiated good energy and real inspiration. A brief time spent with that man at the TM center actually promoted my thinking that I would like to be a teacher of meditation.

With a casual attitude, in the summer of 1975, I drove

across the US to a month-long meditation retreat in Upstate New York. By the end of that course, I was determined to become a TM teacher. It seemed that the fastest way to accomplish that was to sign up and work on staff at Maharishi International University, MIU, in Fairfield, Iowa. I drove from New York to Iowa.

In 1975, even though I only got to stand in some lines, as Maharishi walked in front of me, I felt blessedly lucky. Just a moment of being near Maharishi felt magical.

As a member of the MIU kitchen staff, I attended a meeting in the early fall of 1975 that was for the university staff to meet with Maharishi. We were in an old gymnasium, the Fieldhouse, sitting on wooden bleachers.

High up, I was sitting with other kitchen staff packed side by side. After enjoying 25 minutes of Maharishi, I started to have the thought that I should go outside.

Go outside? For what? I wondered, pondered, and finally figured it meant to go outside and stand and wait for Maharishi. It was puzzling me. *Where was this thought coming from?* My feet were a good ten to twelve feet above the floor. People were packed in close on all sides of me. *How could I possibly get to the stage and then out the door?*

Go outside. The thought kept coming, as if I were being told. I knew to go to the right side of the stage without knowing why.

Why me? Why now? I wondered briefly.

The thought to go could not be ignored. It was a sure thing that if I just stood up and tried to go through the crowd to the exit, it would disturb a lot of people. It would be a disaster; I would be stopped. Where I sat was diagonally, nearly all the way across the room from the exit.

When I looked down, I saw the only way out that wouldn't create a disturbance. That was, while bending my body like a well-cooked noodle, to slip through the boards of the bleachers. Then I would have to hang by my fingers above the floor and silently drop. Taking a deep breath, I prayed nobody would notice my disappearance.

It was still at least three feet from my feet to the floor, with my body stretched out full length, as I hung by my fingers off the bleachers. My body swayed back and forth. I wasn't sure how quietly I could drop. A loud thud could ruin the whole project. Holding on, I willed the swaying to stop.

I let go and fell, doing my best to be as quiet as possible. Landing on tiptoes, I kept my body limp as it folded up at high speed until I planted my fingertips on the floor. Nobody seemed to notice my amazingly quiet drop.

Under the bleachers, the floor was clear. I took a deep breath. I hastily walked around the edge of the back of the room to get to the side. Everyone remained entirely focused on Maharishi. The awareness hit me that I would have to walk casually, as if it were perfectly normal and necessary, and somehow get past everyone. Including people known to be picky: the guys in suits and women in formal dress.

There I was in my rumpled and used, all-white kitchen uniform, trying to blend in. It was as if everyone were hypnotized; not a single person seemed to notice me.

Maharishi kept talking and, thankfully, seemed to ignore me. I walked all the way along the sides of many rows of chairs. It felt like a dream. I walked past groups of staff, past department heads, past the guests in chairs, past university security and administration, past well-dressed VIP's, past the front of the audience, past the stage, past the senior teacher door-monitors in their three-piece suits, and through the two sets of open doors.

At that moment, I discovered a surprise, gleaming in the sun. The limo that Maharishi would ride in was waiting, perfectly parked. Maharishi had only to walk about twelve or fifteen feet straight out of the building to the car. I was the only person between the car and the building. I felt surprised and lucky. A deep breath of relief gave way to a large wave of contentment.

If I had delayed another minute, I would have missed out and probably been stopped. I took a stance next to the car door that was open for Maharishi. I had my back toward the wall and my left side close to the car. Putting my hands together in a prayer position, I waited.

After a few moments, people started lining up to my right and across from me. Quickly, the row was at least three, and then four or five people deep opposite me. Maharishi's energy perked up my awareness. I could sense his approach before Maharishi himself emerged from the building.

As Maharishi was about to come into view, a thought bubbled up: *Here is the most powerful person in the world!* Waves of joy welled up inside me. Nothing else mattered. I felt ecstatic.

The only thing I could think of was Maharishi slowly coming closer. Step by step. He was about to walk right in front of me. Fantastic! It was the last thing I was aware of.

I was standing in samadhi for over 20 minutes before Jerry Jarvis stuck his smiling face right next to mine and snapped me out of it by saying, "Feeling good, are we?"

They had taken Maharishi in the car and dropped Maharishi off. Maharishi must have sent Jerry back by himself so he could bring that young man, me, back to earth. It was the same shiny black car, and the entire area was devoid of people! It was a real surprise.

The doors to the Fieldhouse were closed. Jerry and I were completely by ourselves as I came out of my state of samadhi. It was astonishing that everyone was gone. Silent serenity prevailed.

The mind-boggling event soothed and uplifted me. My mind could not put any words together. Not having anything to say, I just looked at Jerry for a moment. Then he turned back to the car. On my own, I started walking away in my little bubble of bliss.

In 1977, I became a TM teacher, taking intensive training in Vittel, France. My TM Teacher Training Course was the first TTC at which Maharishi did not personally spend any time. Yet I still felt devoted to Maharishi.

By the time I became a teacher of the TM technique, its popularity had crested. There were already large numbers of TM teachers in the US, so there was competition for the people signing up to learn. My dream of teaching a lot of people how to meditate fizzled out pretty quickly.

At the end of Gurudev's April 1988 silent Advanced Course, Gurudev declared that teachers were needed. When he sent his gaze deep into my being, I was wondering how Maharishi would feel about this TTC. Gurudev's invitation felt good and auspicious, and a little tingle of excitement was kindled.

It turns out that Maharishi was actually my *Paramguru*, the guru of my guru, though I didn't appreciate that at the time. I had met a number of famous TM teachers who had spent a lot of time with Maharishi. It became obvious to me that I had never met anyone whose being was as deeply saturated with love and devotion for Maharishi as that of Gurudev's.

Life opened doors for me that I never imagined I would see. Via poetry, I attempted to express that miracle.

Life Presents

Life presents

a little doorway.

"Oh, it's open!"

You just happened

to notice.

You step through

and discover…

that you have changed!

Things seem different.

At some point

you might pause,

and think that,

maybe going back

might make things

the same

as they used to be.

However,

there is no going back.

You realize that

changes are within you

and around you.

It can't be undone.

After the end of the April 1988 Advanced Course, Gurudev was taken to Santa Monica. I was in one of the cars in the caravan. We stopped at the home of devotees living in Apple Valley. We enjoyed some spicy Indian food. While we were there, I was mulling over a question I wanted to ask Gurudev.

I wanted some clear direction from a real master to help me make a decision about how to move forward in my life. My life seemed empty, lacking a deeper purpose and meaning. I was tired of struggling. My mind had been going back and forth, thinking about the idea of becoming a chiropractor.

The thought of going back to school seemed like misery to me then, yet I also thought that I would enjoy being a chiropractor and that it would lend some authority to my talents. Gathering my resolve, I asked Gurudev if it was a good idea for me to go to chiropractic school. I wanted bravery, since I was inwardly preparing myself to follow his hoped-for instructions.

With characteristic unpredictability, his reply was simple: "It's all in the big mind."

As I asked my question, he seemed relaxed and peaceful. After he had made his terse reply, he had a slight grin. He made it clear that the discussion was over by turning away.

At the time, I had mixed feelings about this enigmatic response. A familiar hint of despair came up, as I figured at that moment that he was just brushing me off with minimal attention and a cute little phrase. I was disappointed, as I had hoped for some specific, clear guidelines.

My mind was a small whirlwind: *Does this mean that I should wait until I feel strong intuition? Hope to magically find my answer with big mind? Hope he might explain another time? Or give up, just keep blundering along?*

I was not sure, and it didn't feel right to press Gurudev for more information. He clearly didn't want to say anything else about it, and I respected that.

Feeling foolish and deflated, I lapsed back into my state of uncertainty. It seemed doubtful that I would get a big mind insight that would make it clear what to do. A familiar sense of bleakness and confusion rippled through me.

Often, the master will communicate through minimal glances and gestures. Gurudev may use no words. Or even sounds instead of words. I was still getting used to being around the master. I was not yet in tune with him enough to catch all the nuances of his meanings contained within his minimalistic communications.

Looking back, one can see some deeper meaning, for all knowledge of every possible kind is in the big mind, the supreme consciousness. Everything is contained within the big mind. Many wise teachers have said that all knowledge is in *akasha*, or space. Real yoga opens up that vista.

In one sense, Gurudev was telling me that everything I will need to know is in the big mind. It was several years later before I recognized how his simple statement was perfect for me. Cleansing and tuning myself to be able to tap easily into the big mind with clarity has been paramount.

After that April 1988 Advanced Course, Gurudev stayed at the home of the well-known astrologer, Chakrapani, who was at that time living in Santa Monica.

In the evening, we had a *satsang*. Satsang means to sit in company with the truth. The group included many people who had not taken any courses with Gurudev. Gurudev spoke about some of the practices being taught on his Basic Course. He invited people who had taken the course to share their experiences with the group.

Even though I was feeling awkward and embarrassed, I realized that it would be worthwhile to share some of my good experiences. Because Gurudev called on me, I found myself standing up and pushing through my self-consciousness. Sharing my experiences with a group of strangers had not been easy for me prior to that moment. This one small incident was an indication of the kindness of the master in helping me take a step out of my limitations.

Diving deeper into yoga enables a person to eliminate the roots of feelings of awkwardness and embarrassment. With real yoga, you can be centered in many different types of situations. With real yoga, you can feel calm and happy without needing to fake it.

Profound Longing

The next morning, I had a puzzling dream in which I was watching someone from a distance. The person was sobbing with grief. I felt concern for this person, who was crying intensely. Wondering why they were crying, I decided to move closer to them.

As I began to shift from standing to walking, I realized that the person who was crying was me! At the same moment, I popped inside the body of my crying self.

I was crying in the dream, and I did not know why. Then I woke up with real tears coming out of my physical eyes! It was strange. I still didn't know why I was crying. Talk about surrealism.

My mind was puzzling over the experience of seeing myself as another person, watching that person cry, and then actually being that person. Like witnessing from fifty feet away and magically, abruptly getting sucked into the middle of the experience. Who then wakes up actually crying after crying in a dream, without knowing why they are crying?

Why am I crying?

As I was waking up, I desperately wanted to know. It was clear that the tears were genuine, not just a dream happening. Must there not be a huge reason to provoke tears both inside a dream and outside the dream?

For a fraction of a moment, I started to calm down, then the awareness struck with painful clarity: *He's leaving!*

Tears began to flow again. I felt surprised and frustrated. The intense anguish and vulnerability were unexpected.

What is this? Why is this happening?

I was in a daze. Honestly, on that morning, I did not welcome this experience and judged it as foolish. Trying to grasp a sense of normalcy and calm, I got myself into my morning routine. The aching inside would not go away.

I had arranged to ride with some others to the house where Gurudev was staying. Impatiently, I watched the time go by.

When the others arrived, the word from the house was that we had to wait longer before going over to see Gurudev at Chakrapani's home.

Together, we did some *sadhana*; yogic breathing practices, and meditation. Sadhana is an interesting word, meaning true wealth. (The love and wisdom we gain in life are the only types of wealth we take with us when we die.)

Someone attempted to reassure me that it was actually a beautiful experience that I was having, though I did not see the beauty. It seemed like a long, surreal dream.

Feeling without speaking, I wondered if anyone had ever had such an experience before. It didn't matter. The immediacy and potency of my own experience were more than enough.

I could barely talk. When we arrived at Chakrapani's house, I did not feel like socializing at all.

I was grateful when I could simply be seated in the living room and wait to meet Gurudev. After some time, Gurudev came out.

I tried to speak, which only made me burst into tears again. There was no way I could even get a word out. It was surprising and embarrassing. I just sat on the floor and waited for it to pass.

Each of several attempts to begin to speak would bring more tears. Gurudev simply sat calmly and quietly.

A couple of other people then arrived. They sat across the room on my right, directly in front of Gurudev, while I was just to the right of the front of the chair where Gurudev sat. The new people had a short conversation with Gurudev.

It was superficial chitchat. Soon, they left.

Gurudev stood up and gently encouraged me by saying, "Suitcase needs to be packed; come."

Feeling grateful that he was including me, I followed Gurudev to his small guestroom.

While Gurudev started packing his suitcase, he asked me, "So, what is your plan?"

I didn't know how to answer. Taking myself by surprise, I admitted, "I can't bear the thought of you leaving."

"Don't think that I am ever gone."

These words placed an invisible bandage on my heart. I reassured myself that I would pull myself together and be fine. My mind could barely articulate the wonder of how it could be possible.

I wanted a deeper sense of *knowing* that it must be true. Then my mind came up with some doubts about his statement. In an effort to soothe myself, I focused on just relaxing and observing.

Gurudev kept me sitting there. Watching a couple of other people come to have a few brief words with Gurudev only added to the surreal nature of the morning.

Gurudev was equally loving with a man who was angry and using foul language and a lady who was soft and grateful. When the man was confrontational and blaming Gurudev, Gurudev reached over and gently touched that man on the cheek.

Ultimately, Gurudev was tucked into a small Mercedes sedan. A few people were riding to the airport with him. Gurudev waved goodbye to me through his window.

As the car pulled away from the curb, the tears came out again. At that moment, it was difficult for me to accept the intensity of my feelings for this peaceful saint.

Poetry gave me a way to describe inner intensity.

In a Fire of Shredded Names

In a fire of shredded names

I burn,

rotating on an unknown axis

never seen.

Memories pop into my mind....

I didn't ask for them.

Yet there they were,

adding fuel to scorch

the edges of my heart.

Can you smell the smoke?

Does it happen to you, too?

If we meet, will we be able

to identify each other

by our crispy,

toasted edges?

SECTION TWO: ACCELERATION

Chapter Five: First Teacher Training

After that April 1988 Advanced Course, Buck and I kept in touch. A few times we met, spent time together, and did sadhana together.

Buck was an electrical engineer who was fascinated with stereo systems and audio recording equipment. He would frequently start talking about various pieces of audio equipment. A lot of the information was new to me.

I appreciated the large speakers that Buck built. These were the best-sounding speakers I had ever encountered. Even so, sometimes I wondered why I was getting involved in long, detailed discussions about sound equipment. Out of the blue, Buck would just start rattling off details and comparing various types of equipment. It was about a year later before I saw how these conversations turned out to be divine steps in the unfolding of my path.

In early June of 1988, I traveled to Montreal, Canada. I took a plane flight from Los Angeles to New York, then traveled on a bus across the border. The bus stopped at the US/Canadian border. The driver, moving rapidly, mumbled something like, "Blah blah kleh office gimble, blah dibble dib, mbahga blahla slayo, seats!" as he rushed off the bus.

It was an air-conditioned bus with all windows sealed. During the drive, one passenger smoked a cigarette and ruined the air. The smoke lingered. Stiff and tired, I was dying for fresh air. It was my first experience crossing the border on a bus. I was not familiar with the protocol.

All the other passengers stared blankly, motionless, like lifeless mannequins. They remained seated as I stood. I walked to the door and stepped out, right next to the bus.

If I stand right next to the bus at the bottom of the entry steps, then surely nobody will mind. Even though I was still within one foot of the bottom of the bus stairs, I was wrong. An angry guard asked me what I was doing. My honest answer was not good enough. I was marched into the station and placed in a small chair across a table from another officer.

The hostile interrogation officer spoke to me with distrust. Rapid-fire questions tried to establish me as a criminal element. If I had not had the phone number of the house where I would be staying in Montreal, they would have automatically sent me back to the USA.

The next stroke of luck was that someone at the house recognized my name and told the officer over the phone that I was expected. Finally, the officer relaxed a little and shared that the Canadian Border Patrol was being vigilant since there was a big rock concert in Montreal. They were expecting trouble. They sent me on my way with a warning.

Vicky met me at the bus station in Montreal. She was holding up a picture of Gurudev. The dim light of a single bulb that cast a sickly glow made the station look run-down and full of shadows. In that stark setting, we could as well have been in some other country 40 years earlier.

The photo of Gurudev immediately brought a sense of safety and security. That was how we identified each other. Vicky is an artist and has since published some highly entertaining books. That night, she stood silently with a mildly quizzical look on her face. I was happy and relieved to be met late at night by a sweet, compassionate, and friendly person.

The picture of Gurudev sparked a feeling of being blanketed in divine grace. Here was a sweet secret we shared that was profound enough that all the gritty travel and border guard station experiences faded into insignificance.

While Vicky drove, I grazed on snacks from my backpack and relaxed. Giddy with relief over approaching the end of this strange journey, I was happy that a gentle, caring person was kind enough to escort me.

In Montreal, a big three-story house was the center for the "I and i Awareness Foundation." This was the name of the Canadian organization before it became the Art of Living. A basement room was my sleeping area. The next day, I found out where Gurudev's room was. I moved my sleeping bag across the basement room, putting it under Gurudev's room. I slept directly beneath the spot where Gurudev had his sleeping and sitting pad on the floor above.

For a couple of days, Gurudev gave lectures and held evening satsangs at various locations around Montreal. During most lectures, I would stand up to make it easier to sit for meditation.

In those days, I had a lot of doubt and judgment about myself. I felt that being sensitive made life more difficult. I made no mention of this to Gurudev. Yet, in every talk at that time, Gurudev spoke about the value of being sensitive. He made the point that being sensitive is what allows a person to experience love, beauty, and higher consciousness. A dull, unaware person will not get enlightened. This knowledge was soothing to me.

Gurudev often answers unasked questions. Many people notice that their secret concerns are addressed when Gurudev speaks. "I felt like he was talking right to me!" is a common sentiment when people gather to hear Gurudev talk. The amazing thing is that this happens for many people at the same time in any single gathering.

There was a huge amount of fatigue in my system. During one of my first satsangs in Montreal, I felt myself aching with discomfort. My body was slumping into sleep. My head kept nodding. I was overwhelmed by tiredness. It was embarrassing and seemed beyond my control. This was in contrast to an air of relaxed alertness in all the people around me. It seemed like the only proper way to be in the gathering was to be respectfully seated in an upright position. There must have been desperation in my eyes when I opened them to find Gurudev looking right at me. He motioned with his hand for me to lie down.

Feeling a rush of gratitude, I promptly passed into a refreshing, deep *shavasana,* or yogic rest pose, of oblivion. It was an extremely unusual event, earning me a nasty look from an enthusiastic singer sitting next to me. She may have missed Gurudev giving me the instruction to lie down. In some cases, it is not considered proper to lie down during Sanskrit chanting. The master granted me welcome relief without my even asking for such unusual treatment.

Most of the public talks that Gurudev gave in those days had titles advertised ahead of time. Such titles included:

Can You Laugh Like Me?
What Attracts Us to Spirituality?
Meet the Alien Called Guru.

Most of these titles ended up being used in more than one country. One talk, in particular, had alternate titles: *Learn to Be a Fool,* or *Can You Live Like a Fool?* This is in contrast to later years, when many public talks were given without any title or planned subject.

An Advanced Course was scheduled over a long weekend at a rented facility, called Val Moran, outside Montreal. I asked Gurudev if I could ride in the car with him to get to the course. I was happy when he consented. A few other people, all women, had also requested to ride with Gurudev.

There was a heavy-set woman who presumed to always sit right behind Gurudev in whatever car Gurudev happened to be riding in. Each day, every time Gurudev went somewhere in a car, that lady would insist on sitting behind him. The day we were leaving Montreal to go to the Advanced Course, she gave me an angry, dirty look, as if it were all my fault that she would not be in the car with Gurudev. Three other women were also passengers in the car.

During that drive out of Montreal to get to the course site, my almost ever-present fatigue caught up with me. I couldn't keep my eyes open, and my head kept bobbing. The next thing I knew, I found my chin on my chest, and I was waking up. I felt a little better, yet I was still tired. Gurudev turned his head to look at me. "You had a nice nap?" He was sincerely sweet about it.

Unfortunately, some grumpiness was in me, and I immediately regretted it when I replied, "Yes, but I'm still tired." I sounded ungrateful, and I sensed that Gurudev seemed disappointed by that.

With sudden awareness, it occurred to me that he had given me a blessing of rest, and instead of responding with gratitude, I had focused on the negative. His attention went elsewhere, and I felt regret, wishing to do better at being graceful and grateful.

At the end of the Advanced Course, I again had the thought that it would be nice to be in the car with Gurudev. I dared to express it to that lady. She glared and belittled me, saying, "You had your time with the Guru!"

For the Advanced Course, the buildings were basic and simple. Ongoing construction on some buildings was skeletal, unfinished, and bare wood. Nails were sticking out in many places. Some rooms smelled of sawdust. It didn't matter; we were all excited to be there in Val Moran.

Right before going to the hall for the evening talk, some of us were standing around outside the dormitory buildings. We waited for Gurudev to come out of his room.

Gurudev slowly strolled in front of me. I was taken by surprise when I thought I saw faint images of naked, overweight people walking by. It was strange that there were these odd, random thoughts popping up. Especially when Gurudev was right there. It didn't make sense. It was as if I had seen some fat, naked ghosts marching by. I had done nothing to instigate this, nor did I want it, yet there it was.

Shortly after, we were all gathered in the comfortable meeting hall. Gurudev reassured us that if we had a thought that bothered us, "You can just think that some angel has brought that thought. Some angels are playing, and it is their fault that we had some silly or crazy thoughts." It seemed miraculous that he felt the situation and addressed it without anyone telling him about it.

At that Advanced Course, on the first day for breakfast, there was oatmeal, fruit, bread, butter, and peanut butter. I was glad to have more than just fruit. The following morning, only the fruit was there. Gurudev admonished us that too many people had eaten such a heavy breakfast that they were not able to go into meditation.

Deep peace prevailed in the surrounding forest. Soft bird calls accented the quiet. We were instructed to spend time in nature. Many forest trails were available.

Gurudev warned us that looking at other people could give us thoughts. For the sake of keeping good silence, we were told to avoid looking at other people. All formalities could be dropped while keeping strict silence.

Gurudev had us sit in silence in the hall and listen for a sound. "Hear the sound?" he asked us. He then told us we could listen to the sound when we were alone in the trees.

One afternoon, I was enjoying walking along a trail in a densely wooded section. As I thought to listen for the sound, I took a step into a clearing. At the same moment, from the far side, a lady who was coming through the trees towards me also stepped into the clearing. We both froze, like deer or rabbits. We must simultaneously have remembered the instruction not to look at people. In synchrony, we looked away from each other and kept far apart as we moved around opposite sides of the clearing.

Gurudev told us that what we were gaining from this course was real wealth. What we gained from the course we can never lose. Despite the chaos in the world, we can find some peace. Despite the noise, we can find some silence.

At the end of the course, some of us returned to the house in Montreal. We were excited to dive into the TTC. Each day, the schedule was different.

The bathroom that I was allowed to use had a tiny window that had been painted shut. I tried to open it to air it out. Many layers of paint, with a final coat of thick purple paint, sealed all edges. The window wouldn't budge.

Due to the number of people in the house, there was a lot of competition for the bathroom. It stayed in a perpetual state of dampness, so I would leave the door open for a few minutes to air it out. While I understood the Feng Shui and Vastu value of keeping bathroom doors closed, mold grows easily in moist places. Mold can be a big problem. I would time myself to go back after fifteen minutes to close the door. Each time, I would find the bathroom door had been closed before I got there. Later on, when I shortened the time to ten minutes, I still found the bathroom door already closed. Reducing the time to five minutes, I again found the bathroom door closed. Even with only a three- or two-minute gap, I invariably returned to find the door already closed. It was as if invisible bathroom police were patrolling the halls. They would immediately close any open doors. While I was there, that little bathroom never fully dried out.

When I was in Gurudev's room, I noticed that he had papers, letters, and envelopes in various disorderly, random piles. I thought it would be helpful if he had some kind of portable file container to help organize papers. I asked house residents where to find the nearest stationery store. At first, they thought I wanted something for myself, and they were happy to help. But they were curious about why I would need to go there. They said that there were extra notebooks at the house, in case I needed a notebook.

When I shared that I wanted to help Gurudev organize his papers with some kind of portable filing system, I was told that Gurudev would definitely not want to do that. I had a hard time accepting that. Perhaps because I felt like I wanted to contribute in some way. Then I realized that if he wanted to use a system like that, he would probably already have started.

Indeed, Gurudev made a point of breaking boundaries by pitting order against disorder. One day, he shared with us that when he had been alone in his room, he had been eating some nuts out of the shell. As he held the shells in his hand, he was wondering where to put them. He said that he thought about putting them in a bag but decided against that. He then deliberately tossed the shells on the floor.

He got animated as he told us, "I just threw them! I scattered them and left them there!" His eyes were wide and bright as he spoke. He seemed proud, as if he had done something both difficult and genuinely good. The group was skeptically quiet. Many people didn't get his deliberate disorderliness or see any goodness in it. They thought it was crazy that Gurudev consciously chose to be messy when that just created more work.

I could feel the confusion, disappointment, and judgment in the group. Gurudev attempted to explain that most of the time, we just do things without being aware of what we are doing. It is valuable to be fully present and to have 100% awareness in each moment, whatever we do.

Some of the group may have appreciated the wisdom that Gurudev was sharing. It mostly seemed to go over their heads. Or annoy them. Not appreciating the mess-making was getting in the way.

Some eyebrows remained raised. As one lady was walking away, she was saying that even if she were focused on the moment, when she made a mess, she would still have to clean it up. Then she pointed out the irony that Gurudev might enjoy making a mess, "but we are the ones who will have to clean it up!"

During the TTC meetings, we discussed various aspects of the course and practiced how to teach. One point that got repeated was to keep bringing awareness to the breath, both during and outside of breathing practices.

We were told that additional sessions of pranayama could be done if we were feeling tired in the middle of the day.

We were advised to enjoy the breath. Just as you might slowly sip a drink to get the most enjoyment, you can sip the air and enjoy breathing. Gurudev emphasized using our full attention whenever we did any breathing practice. When you focus only on what you are doing, you get more out of it.

One exercise we did while sitting with Gurudev was to sit with a partner and just open our awareness, tuning in to that person. I sat with a lady whom I did not know. The word "archive" popped into my awareness. When I told the lady about this, she got excited. With a big smile, she told me that that was her job; she worked as an archivist.

After spending ten days in the Montreal house with the TTC course, I began to feel saturated with Gurudev's energy. With no cell phones or digital devices, the depth of focus was great. When we sat together in small groups, just a slight movement by Gurudev might cause a small rustle of fabric that could change the texture of the space. I was getting well-cooked. I felt fortunate to be there. It was hard to comprehend the miracles that had put me with a real master of the highest caliber.

Singing

During evening gatherings with Gurudev, it is customary that the chanting of *bhajans* is a primary activity. Bhajans are repetitive, call-and-response chants usually sung in Sanskrit, an ancient language. Bhajans may be followed or preceded by some discussion of knowledge. All of this is often interspersed with innocent laughter.

Gurudev pointed out, "When you sit in bhajans, your entire body gets soaked with energy, and transformation takes place."

By chanting in the old language of Sanskrit, we can activate ancient portions of our consciousness. Gurudev also maintained that it is not that one language is higher or lower. Each language has value. It is just that the utility of chanting resides in Sanskrit. It is more powerful to chant in Sanskrit since it is incredibly ancient. Real yoga includes chanting.

Bhajans are composed mainly of mantras, names, and praises of divine beings. Mantras are positive sounds that carry energy in their vibration. The meaning is not important, as the transformative power of the mantra comes from the vibration of the sound. The potency of the bhajan is enhanced by the clarity and innocence of the singer.

Many who don't know the meanings of bhajans have felt the positive energy of chanting. Some people enjoy intellectual satisfaction from knowing the translations of some bhajans. Gurudev made it clear that memorizing meanings is not important for getting value out of chanting.

Some teachers say that if you focus on the meaning, it helps you grow in devotion. Knowing the meaning adds enjoyment on an intellectual level when a person is not chanting. During the chanting, it is important to let go and dissolve into the sound. If you stay in your intellect during the chanting, it can block ecstatic transformation.

What I have noticed is that sometimes when people translate bhajans, they add meanings that aren't specifically there. For instance, take the bhajan, *Radhe Govind*. *Radhe* is longing. *Govinda* is love. Radha was a lady whose devotion to Krishna was absolute. Krishna was also known as Govinda. Whether one is devoted or not to Krishna and/or Radha, singing this can be beautiful. It is not necessary to hold a picture in your mind of Radha or Krishna doing any specific thing.

This bhajan also refers to the eternal principle of love and longing. Many times, Gurudev has mentioned that, where there is love, there will be longing. If longing is not there, it is not really love. At the same time, a person can have a powerful experience without knowing any of this. If you enjoy the meaning, fine. If you are not concerned with meaning, that is also fine. The real power lies in going beyond and transcending name and form.

According to Gurudev, "Singing helps to bring serenity. Singing is simply merging into the sound, floating on its waves with a sense of contentment and meditativeness."

Bhajans bring in a lot of positive energy, promote sattva, and are distinctly uplifting. The chanting brings harmony to individual minds as well as to a group of people. A powerful expansion of awareness is possible.

Singing helps us move from our heads, which have

concepts and conflicts, to our hearts. In our hearts, we can be free from conflicts.

The use of chemical intoxicants, such as alcohol, smoking, or drugs, creates dullness and illness and promotes illusion. Chanting has no negative effects. Ayurveda says that intoxicants, whether alcohol, marijuana, drugs, or smoking tobacco, all inhibit emotional processing. Many people want to avoid the discomfort of painful emotions. Some try to escape the pain by using substances to alter their experience. By blocking the emotions, the stress just goes deeper into the system.

Minor upsetting situations can provoke emotions. Some physical sensations will accompany emotions. If the person puts all their attention on the sensations, they can clear the emotion out of their system. By breathing deeply while simply observing the sensations, some emotions can be cleared out of the system in minutes. Fear of emotion causes many people to hold on to things for long periods of time. One might incorrectly assume that it cannot be faced. By not allowing the system to digest the discomfort, that discomfort gets stuck in the human system. Possibly for many years, or, some say, even lifetimes. As, day after day, undigested situations build up, a person ends up with many layers of garbage under the proverbial rug.

At the time I first met Gurudev, I had oceans of shiploads of layers of multiple types of discomfort. Many of those discomforts themselves undoubtedly contributed to my feeling awkward, inhibited, and shut down.

By the time I reached the age of 12, the scornful attitudes of my parents towards me provoked more and more anger. Rebellious behavior was a way of expressing my anger. Simultaneously, my sister's health was deteriorating from cystic fibrosis during her last two years of life. Stress and tension increased in the house.

As a 12-year-old, it became important for me to be self-reliant. I realized that reading newspapers and watching TV was a waste of my time, so I strictly avoided them. There were no cell phones or computers available in those days.

My parents had little energy to deal with me or my brother. I had been quite well-behaved in school up to that point. It was a huge contrast for me to begin getting into trouble. I was not truly bad, but I was quite miserable. While other kids broke things, I never actually wanted to hurt anyone or anything. Yet I kept ending up in the wrong place at the wrong time. A "friend" would want to do something bad. I would hang out with them. Then I would get caught and blamed.

After multiple incidents, the administration of my junior high school informed me that I had set a record in the history of my school. Out of all the students ever there, I got suspended the greatest number of times in two semesters. They gave me an ultimatum that any further trouble would result in permanent expulsion from the school.

It occurred to me that all the trouble I had gotten into was a negative way of asking for attention. I was tired of it. I decided that it was a waste of time. I stopped engaging in such stupid behavior.

My daily meditations had worked on these and other stressful experiences by the time I met Gurudev. Yet the mountain of mud still needed some serious bulldozing.

Chanting mantras and bhajans, especially with eyes closed, helps to release and digest stuck emotions. I was incredibly fortunate to be led to Gurudev. Gurudev made available to me the fullness of this path. We are very lucky that chanting in Sanskrit is a major feature of the path.

Chanting integrates the personality. Gurudev revealed that chanting even removes toxins from the brain.

With Gurudev, there is no rigid schedule for satsang. We might sit in silence for ten minutes or more. We might start with some discussion. Regardless, it is great to be there.

When I first attended these satsangs, I was not singing any bhajans. I couldn't bring myself to chant anything. One person who noticed gently tried to encourage me. After seeing multiple gatherings come and go with my mouth closed, that same person got a little heated and told me firmly that chanting is important.

Bhajans invoke pure energies that help people develop better qualities. The mantras are powerful tools for change. I was told that I'd be better off if I chanted the mantras.

It didn't matter what I was told; I could not get myself to sing! I was stuck with my mouth closed. Gurudev himself just sat patiently, the perfect master, including and welcoming without being pushy or aggressive.

Some people feel more comfortable with specific guidelines for singing. Gurudev emphasized that it is best to sit in silence for about half a minute after each bhajan and let the vibration soak in before beginning the next chant.

In many groups, it happens that the silence between bhajans is shortened. Sometimes to fractions of seconds when singers are too feverishly eager to begin leading before someone else starts. Competition to lead chanting reduces the sattvic effect. Another point for singing bhajans that Gurudev mentioned is to sing the last verse once to end the bhajan.

As Gurudev put it, "You are music yourself. You are an unsung song. You are silence singing. To get to that depth, it is good to sing. If you feel like dancing, get up and dance. Involve yourself fully with your mind and body. That becomes ecstasy."

One day during a break in the TTC, in June of 1988, I wandered into the small, front living room of the house in

Montreal. The evening satsangs would sometimes fill that room to bursting, often with about 20 to 30 people.

It puzzled me that we would use that little front room for satsangs when we could easily use the significantly bigger room where we met for TTC. To be lucky enough to get a seat at satsang one usually had to arrive early. Latecomers would be clustered in the doorway, especially on the night that had the largest attendance, which was 40 people. It seemed obvious to me, yet we were not using the larger room. I brought it up with one of the residents.

I was told that they wanted to have the door to the street open in case people in the neighborhood felt drawn to wander in. If the satsang met in the larger room, then someone would have to miss the satsang in order to sit at the front door of the house and greet any strangers that might show up. Nobody was willing to miss the satsang. Leaving the front door open with signs posted to direct the way to the satsang was not considered acceptable.

Divya was the only one in the little front room that afternoon. Sitting on the polished wood floor, she was working on a song on her guitar. After a pause out of curiosity, I was about to head elsewhere and looked away.

"Daren, I'm having trouble with the chorus."

Wondering what she was talking about, I looked at her.

"I'm trying to figure out how to play this; it's a new song. If I just had someone to sing the chorus, I think I could get it."

My first thought was that she needed someone else, since I never sang songs. I was ready to go find someone for her. Silently, I turned away from her, about to leave.

"Would you just repeat this line for me, and then I'm sure I can get it?"

Feeling that it would be unreasonable to refuse, yet in a state of dread, I sat down. I tried to assure myself that it would only be a moment. Divya spoke the English words and asked me to repeat them. She played some chords and sang some other words, then gave me my cue. I would sing the line every time she nodded at me.

My body and my mind felt awkwardly cramped. I was overwhelmed. *How did I get stuck here? My singing must be bad.* I was grateful that we were alone and that it was over quickly. I don't think I could have done it if someone else had been present. It was even difficult to think about it.

Spoken communication had always been challenging for me. In college, I decided that I had some type of speech impediment. I could have pages of notes for discussion and, in some groups, not bring myself to speak even a single word. Speaking improved a tiny bit after TM Teacher Training. During the time that I was homeless, it became more difficult to express myself with clarity.

Divya was appreciative. "Thank you; that was really helpful." I quickly left the room. I was relieved it was over, yet still uncomfortable and glad to do something else.

That night, around fifteen or more people were in the room. I sat on the floor, with Gurudev close to me on my right. Divya had her guitar and looked up at me. Everyone else was silent as Divya encouraged, in a crystal-clear voice, "Let's sing this together, Daren."

Like a deer in headlights, I froze. I was certain that everyone in the room could hear what Divya had said. My guts contracted. I felt small and afraid. Part of me wanted to run away or disappear.

It struck me that, without thinking about it, mysteriously we had ended up sitting in the same positions on the floor that Divya and I had been in for the rehearsal.

That realization promoted more awareness. I felt trapped. I pictured myself walking out quickly. Leaving the room was appealing but would have been ludicrous. There seemed to be no way out of this except to go ahead and sing.

She started playing the guitar. I took a deep breath, and I ended up singing the chorus as a solo. I wanted to be invisible. We made it through the whole song without incident. Gurudev sitting immediately on my right undoubtedly helped make this miracle successful.

When I was little, I liked to sing. While my mother played piano, I sang songs with my sister and mother.

I remembered that when I was small, I had been in a children's choir. We had performed on the auditorium stage in a school performance. After the performance in school, some older kid yelled at me and blurted out something nasty about the stupid little kid in the choir.

That incident froze inside me. I refused to sing any songs for many years after. There were multiple reasons why I had difficulty with speech. One being that my opinions never seemed welcome to my parents.

Amazingly, my aversion to singing had not been triggered by chanting Guru Puja. Singing bhajans in a group was undoubtedly pushing against my inner blocks. Divya's including me and encouraging me out of the blue made a huge difference. Never again did Divya ask me to join her in a song. The experience was a divine miracle.

That was the turning point. After that I began, in my head only, to entertain the notion of actually joining in the singing at the evening satsangs. For several nights, I sat, and instead of just listening, I would think about singing along. I would listen carefully and imagine singing the lines.

It took a few weeks for me to actually open my mouth and experiment with chanting. It took several more months for me to be able to be relaxed about it. Chanting transformed me. Real yoga miracles have made my life dependent on chanting. Real yoga is full of miracles.

Gurudev clarified that the word *kirtan* means singing

with your total focus on the singing. Such complete immersion in the chant is different from performing or half-heartedly following along. When every person in the group gives the chant their 100%, dropping all other thoughts, then it is as if only the song exists. That is part of real yoga.

All of us who were able to sit in such groups, before cell phones or computers stole attention, were incredibly lucky. The depth of peace is not as easily created these days. Especially when someone is occupied with rapid scrolling on their screen.

Praise the Light

Praise the light

that glows within us.

Praise the song

ever before us.

Praise the light

that glows within us.

Praise the song

and sing its chorus.

Chanting bhajans became one of my favorite activities. It is deeply comforting to be able to sing, completely let go, and get lost in the chant. Nothing exists but the chant, and the voices singing in unison. Simple, repetitive bhajans are enormously conducive to dissolving into an ecstatic state of being. After a few years, the intensity of the intoxication from chanting rivaled any of my other experiences. All thoughts and concerns get erased, and I am left in pure bliss. The experience promotes self-integration at all levels. Such a huge blessing!

After that 1988 TTC, Gurudev told me to memorize the Guru Padukas and Maha Lakshmi *stotras,* short, traditional chants. A person with experience in chanting was kind enough to teach me. The discomfort with singing was not there while learning to chant these verses. These two stotras became a kind of life raft for me; they have been great friends for many years.

Master Gurudev explained, "Bhajan means sharing." When people are talking, everyone is in their own world of their own thoughts. When a group sings together, everyone is thinking of the same song.

Gurudev revealed that, with bhajans, "form dissolves into name, and name dissolves into being."

Gurudev also insisted that bhajan means more than just chanting. When people are wholeheartedly laughing together, that is also bhajan.

We All Want to Be

We all

want to be

a part of

the wholeness

that is.

Everyone

is part

within themselves.

They are one

connected.

See forever

within a glance

capture this

touch that

it is nothing.

Sing

open all the way

pull the core

to the surface

take us with you.

Chanting bhajans helps to uplift life. Gurudev revealed that there is an old saying that "Shiva sits on the planets." This means that various types of sadhana can help reduce both the impact of planetary positions and the effects of karmas that may be seen in an astrological chart.

Astrological charts are based on the position of planets at the time of a person's birth. There are methods of reducing the negative effects of a particular planet or astrological configuration. For example, chanting OM Namah Shivaya brings in positive energy and reduces negativity. For relief from a specific issue, it is important to consult with an expert.

Gurudev encourages regular use of OM Namah Shivaya. "OM Namah Shivaya chant has been there for thousands of years. The five elements are represented in this mantra, and each sound corresponds to one of them. For instance, 'OM' is the life force or divinity. Chanting energizes our psyche and our inner being. It is very powerful, and we should chant it every day. It will keep away depression. You will see that whenever you are feeling low, chanting 'OM Namah Shivaya' removes the negativity."

You can chant OM Namah Shivaya in a group or alone.

When I met Gurudev, my verbal skills still had room for enormous improvement. Even after a bit more than one year with the Art of Living, my verbal expressions were usually lackluster. I was often lacking in finesse and became a target of ridicule.

One lady made a point of putting me down. She told me about one of her interactions with Gurudev. She told me that she had been with him, talking about how the Art of Living had some people who were remarkably good at public speaking. Some of the teachers were notably skillful at talking to groups of people. She told me that she had said that my skills were lacking.

Supposedly, according to her, Gurudev's response had been to say, "All Daren has to do is open his mouth, then he puts his foot right in. The whole leg goes in." Supposedly, Gurudev even went further to say something to the effect that people would not like what I said. I was astonished. Maybe he did say those things, maybe not, but I did not appreciate being teased about it. Certainly, I had limitations and issues in this area; I knew that. Okay, someone had some fun at my expense. At the time, I did not enjoy hearing about it.

I was not in the lofty space that Maharishi or Brahmananda Saraswati occupied when they were younger. There is a story about Brahmananda Saraswati involving an incident that happened when he was younger, while staying at his master's ashram. One of the other ashram residents told Brahmananda Saraswati that the master had made some derogatory remarks about Brahmananda Saraswati. Brahmananda Saraswati calmly replied that it was not his concern; it was between that other person and the master. The same thing happened to Maharishi, such that someone claimed that his Gurudev said something derogatory about Maharishi. Maharishi gave the same kind of response, saying that it was between the other person and the master.

If I had been emptier and more centered inside, I might have been able to laugh about it. It was too sensitive an issue for me at that time. I was upset and just stuffed the whole thing deep inside. It only burst into my awareness years later, when enough had been processed that I could think about it without getting upset, and it could dissolve.

At some point, I realized that I had had plenty of bad karma to be ridiculed, made fun of, and not listened to. A lot of that got burned up through various events in those early years. The master accelerated the process, and it was an enormous blessing. Whatever skill I have in talking and public speaking is from waves of divine grace and real yoga.

Guru Purnima, 1988

In July of 1988, Gurudev came back to California for Guru Purnima. He stayed at a house in West Los Angeles. The man who lived in that house was not interested in Gurudev, but he let Gurudev stay there for a couple of nights. Just a small number of people came and went. Gurudev was not offended; he remained graceful and positive.

Guru Purnima is the traditional time to honor the master, honor the lineage of masters, and honor the tradition.

Guru Purnima is also said to be the day of the devotee.

Gratitude is a blessing. A person is lucky to feel gratitude. During most of the mid-1980s, feeling gratitude seemed rare and elusive for me.

When we honor the master and the knowledge, it helps to look back and see how we have grown. Then, it is easy to feel thankful for positive changes in one's life. It is useful and it is important to cultivate gratitude. Gratitude opens doors and promotes grace and a flow of good things in life.

When a person becomes a seeker, they often read books in search of deeper meaning. Sometimes one finds a teacher or a group where growth is possible and deliberately supported. Finding a real, enlightened master is genuinely rare and more valuable than precious gems or anything else. Reading about masters of the past can be inspiring. Paramahansa Yogananda's *Autobiography of a Yogi* (Self-Realization Fellowship) was a favorite book of mine.

But pictures and books are quite safe. We are still stuck in our comfortable nest of habits and limitations. With a living master, one gets more deeply connected with the enormous potency of divine grace. Being around a living master, we come face to face with ourselves and are given the means to become unstuck. Real yoga beckons. Around a living master, one's progress can accelerate enormously.

Masters may behave in seemingly odd, illogical ways in order to help devotees mature, become more relaxed, and become more self-aware. Inner obstacles, toxins, habits, beliefs, presumptions, patterns, assumptions, and judgments are churned up, often right in our faces, as they get washed away in the healing cleansing of divine presence. It is one thing to abstractly delete stress from the mind/body system during meditation; it is quite another to come under the umbrella of a living master's personal grace. Everything a guru does helps people become stronger. Each master has their own method, and they know what a person can handle.

Some people have developed powers, *siddhis,* but demonstration of powers is not a good way to choose a master. Siddhis can and will happen before the full blossoming of consciousness has happened. Brahmananda Saraswati, Maharishi's master, emphasized that one should not choose a master just on the basis of siddhis. Brahmananda Saraswati taught that Siddhis can be the result of birth, herbs, mantras, tapas, or samadhi. This is stated in Patanjali's *Yoga Sutras*: *"janma aushadi mantra tapah samadhija sidhayaha."*

Unfortunately, people who are not enlightened sometimes proclaim themselves to be masters, gurus, or even saints. In many different arenas of life, people low in integrity sometimes take advantage of others. That is also true in the arena of spiritual development.

Maharishi put it in sweet poetic terms by saying that one should go for the highest and capture the fort (achieve full development of consciousness). Once you capture the fort, you own the whole territory. If you only capture a silver mine or a diamond mine (some power), then you just have that one mine. If you focus on developing some power, even if you gain that power, you will have much less than real enlightenment. When you own the fort, all the mines are yours. Along these lines, realized masters can perform miracles, and they are not attached to those abilities. A genuine master isn't interested in showing off.

For me, becoming connected with a master was a happening. I had felt devoted to Maharishi, yet I didn't appreciate the depths of devotion until I had spent time with Gurudev Sri Sri. Gurudev gave me solid, personal attention full of love and caring. Every time I sat with Gurudev, it felt natural, good, and right.

Gurudev gave me many assignments, some of which seemed baffling and/or enormously challenging to me at the time. Each assignment from Gurudev carried the strong value of pure consciousness. I could feel the absence of ego behind it. Each assignment came from depths of love and consciousness. I always knew, deep inside, that it would be best for me to do what the master guided me to do.

Often, while in the room with the master, I have felt a sense of timelessness. On one hand, it was as if time outside did not exist. On the other hand, it was as if we had been together for countless years, and whatever place or event we happened to be meeting in was just one more extension of a celestial moment. Soaking in real yoga.

It didn't matter what we were doing; most of the time, timelessness pervaded my experience. This is my frequent experience when I am with the real yogi, Gurudev.

They Say that the Body Will Die

They say that the body will die

not so far from now.

It has happened

many times before.

You may remember

or you may not.

Love lives on,

and you will feel it.

Even if you remember

nothing else.

In all the future times

you will feel the love.

Ultimately, it will fill you

more than you can hold.

As you taste

part of the mystery

that is this vastness

cradling us forever.

On the day of Guru Purnima in 1988, for the morning puja and chanting, there were at first just three of us sitting with Gurudev. We started chanting. Tears began to pour out of my eyes. I couldn't stop the waterfall. I was glad for the chanting with my eyes closed because I didn't understand why I was crying. It was a happening. Everything faded into insignificance as I drifted on a sea of divine mystery, fullness, and consciousness.

Only a couple of other people joined the tiny group later on. We ended up with Janael, Claire, Michele, Chandrika, and myself. Chandrika spent much of the time in the kitchen, happily preparing food for Gurudev. That morning session was three hours, but it felt like an entire day that we were sitting with Gurudev. It took most of that time before I could stop crying. Feeling embarrassed about crying, I was glad the group was small. At a loss for this unexpected behavior, when the others were out of the room, I asked Gurudev why I was crying.

"Your heart is expanding."

Since Maharishi had mentioned expansion of the heart and Gurudev was telling me, I figured that heart expansion must be a good thing. The way he expressed it was soft and compassionate, affirming that this was valuable.

I was still thinking of myself as being "too sensitive." Without mentioning this to Gurudev, I noticed that in most lectures that he gave in that period, he talked about this phenomenon.

Many people think that they are too sensitive and think it is a sign of weakness. There seems to be a social mythic norm of endlessly doing. There is an expectation of never getting tired, never needing to eat, drink, rest, or take a bathroom break. These unhealthy attitudes get reinforced in many different contexts, with various age groups.

Gurudev said, "The law for yoga is moderation in everything."

Real yoga gives you the ability to be in touch with your emotions without being overwhelmed by them. Real yoga simultaneously gives sensitivity, compassion, courage, bravery, strength, empathy and centeredness.

Gurudev emphasized ancient understandings when he said, "A yogi is one who has a balance of activity and rest."

Real yoga promotes healthy daily rhythms that support living your best life. Real yoga promotes being in touch with actual needs and honoring them in a graceful way. At the same time, real yoga increases durability so we can endure challenges with minimal damage and recover quickly. Healthy routines are basic for real yoga and ayurveda.

Tears are Cried

Tears are cried,

for no one,

for everyone.

They come.

they go.

Who can capture the poetry,

of stunning grace,

that speaks beyond all language

to the core of your being?

Scraping your nobility

from the depths of marrow,

to leave you kneeling,

raw,

in front of the galaxy!

Most people who get lost in the pursuit of acceptance, fads, fame, power, money, and/or the accumulation of stuff become dull and jaded. Many people are burned out, relying on caffeine to get going and alcohol to unwind. This type of person is often so out of touch with their own mind and body system that many times they don't know exactly when they need food, water, exercise, or rest.

Gurudev kept emphasizing this point: that sensitivity is a strength in the growth of consciousness. Longing is part of love, and one must be sensitive to feel love and longing. He maintained that longing is valuable, and we should not try to get rid of it.

Balance in life pays off. Ayurveda emphasizes the importance of maintaining a healthy daily routine. This involves simple methods of self care. Including eating meals on time, focusing on the food and nothing else while eating, drinking water starting early and throughout the day, going to bed early, and not suppressing natural urges such as sneezing, yawning, or using the bathroom.

On that Guru Purnima day, in 1988, using fresh cilantro, Chandrika made a stunning, radiant green cilantro chutney for Gurudev. Without any garlic or onion to drown out the flavor, that chutney was as smooth as the finest silk. It completely melted in the mouth. The exquisite flavor spread through my body like a peaceful tide of comfort.

Ancient Palm Leaf Books

Thousands of years ago, in some cultures, records were kept by making markings in books made of palm leaves. When handled carefully and kept in a dry and dark place, such books could last for many hundreds of years.

In 1988, a swami who was the then-current holder of some ancient palm leaf books came to California. These palm leaf books had been in his family for many generations. The books were the notes of a sage who lived hundreds of years ago. That sage predicted life events for many people who would live during some part of the hundreds of years after his own death.

This particular set of palm leaf books held information about various people who would meet the current holder of the palm leaves. For each holder of the books, many of the people who would ask for a reading were written about. Not only were some of the people who were destined to meet the keeper of the palm leaves predicted, but details about the lives of those people were also written about.

Such predictions require great clarity and potency of consciousness. Each father would train his child in the reading of the leaves.

The swami, who was the keeper of the palm leaf books during 1988, was in California at the same time as Gurudev. I was in the room when someone mentioned the Palm Leaf Swami to Gurudev. Gurudev related that they had known each other since childhood. They had spent some time together when they were younger.

Gurudev abruptly made plans to meet the Palm Leaf Swami. Gurudev went to meet the swami on a beautiful day with blue skies. A couple of devotees followed Gurudev into the room, and he and the swami greeted each other. They chatted briefly, and then Gurudev told us that the swami would look at the palm leaves. Gurudev then asked us to leave. Reluctant to leave, I appreciated that he was entitled to have his privacy with the Palm Leaf Swami. I was curious what the leaves would have to say. It was interesting that the timing of the reading of the leaves for a particular person might also be indicated in the leaves themselves.

Upset Tummy

In the summer of 1988, Gurudev was sitting on a sofa in Jeff Houk's apartment near the beach, south of Santa Barbara. When I walked into the room, Gurudev had a strange look on his face. "Oh, tummy is not happy." With a bewildered look, he expressed discomfort and held his hand on his abdomen.

It became obvious over the next couple of years that some people liked offering random snacks to Gurudev. Bags of cookies, candies, and chips would show up. There is a general rule that it is considered auspicious to offer something to eat to a master or saint. Over the years, women have been known to have serious arguments over who would be allowed to cook for the master.

Some people didn't take the quality of the food they offered seriously. There were a lot of junk food treats coming to Gurudev. It looked at times like people thought Gurudev was a pet or a doll and not a real person, let alone a living embodiment of the divine.

Giving unhealthy snacks to any person, especially a master, seemed offensive and disrespectful to me.

Endlessly compassionate, Gurudev wanted to do the right thing. For a saint, that seems to be eating some of the offering. Which supposedly can bless the one who offers it.

Gurudev ended up eating lots of chips and cheap, mass-produced snacks and cookies made with grease, chemicals, and sugar. These eventually made his skin break out. On that day in 1988, he had eaten mango, ice cream, chips, guacamole, and salsa, which was a bad combination.

I felt sorry for Gurudev and wanted him to feel better. I realized that I could work on some points for digestion on his feet and lower leg, and it would make a difference. I offered to do that. Gurudev had a question mark on his face. Someone chimed in that reflexology and acupressure could help. Accepting the encouragement, Gurudev held a foot out.

Cradling his foot in my lap, I began to hold and press points. He noticed and commented that some of the points were tender, though he had no bruises. Tender points on the foot are a sign that that point needs attention, assuming it is not a bruise. The points relate to different organs. When an organ is not performing at its best, the corresponding point on the foot will be tender.

When working on points in the feet, the points that are the most tender should be held the longest. Often, people will then feel the tenderness fade away. Someone with sensitivity and experience working on points will feel a difference in the tissues. The instinctive response to the feeling of congestion, emptiness, or irregularity in the flow of energy at a certain point will attract fingers to work there.

This instinctive surrender to the feeling is much more powerful than merely working off a chart that assigns organ relationships to exact physical locations. In order to do the best, most effective work, one must feel the force and not be a numb automaton using a cookie-cutter approach.

In Ayurveda, vital points are known as marma points. It is understood in Ayurveda that point locations on the body can move slightly. The body is a dynamic matrix of huge complexity. Ayurveda understands that there can be many physical and emotional differences between people with identical symptoms. As Ayurvedic expert Dr. Lad said in class, "Where the tenderness is, that is the marma."

Gurudev was sitting on a sofa, and I sat on the floor in front of him. Chit chat among the others resumed about various topics while I sat silently for a few minutes working on the points. After about fifteen minutes, it felt like it was becoming complete. As I noticed the improved flow of energy in Gurudev's foot, I looked up.

With a grin of surprise, Gurudev exclaimed, "Oh, tummy is feeling better now!" It was gratifying to me to be able to do something helpful.

Janael and I were sent ahead to Los Angeles to help notify people about the Basic Course that was scheduled. We rode a greyhound bus together. Janael took the opportunity to get organized and was sorting many sizes, shapes, and colors of papers in her lap during the drive.

Gurudev gave public lectures at different locations before the upcoming July 1988 Basic Course. One evening, during one of the talks, he seemed to be speaking directly to me when he got into a discussion about pain.

Pain

Gurudev clarified that pain is an intense physical sensation, and suffering is an attitude about the pain. Pain is part of life. Pain is only felt when we are awake. It grabbed my attention when he revealed that an enlightened person feels the pain of the people around them.

In Western society, sometimes when one person feels the pain of another, that experience is judged as negative and/or frowned upon. Gurudev let us know that it is actually part of advanced human development to feel the pain of those around you.

Gurudev maintained that enlightened masters are profoundly sensitive. Average people feel their own pain, and the enlightened feel the pain of other people. He talked about the intense sensitivity of Buddha. All Buddha had to do was look at a person, and he would deeply and completely sense their situation.

Buddha's family tried to prevent the young Buddha from seeing anything bad, filthy, or disgusting. Gurudev said that the first time Buddha saw a dead body, he felt he didn't need to see anything else, something like, "That's it; I am already dead. We are all going to die. Let's go back home."

Regular people want to get rid of their own pain. Enlightened people go a step further and want to get rid of the pain of the people around them. Enlightened people feel other people's pain as their own pain, but the enlightened person does not suffer. Real yoga frees us from suffering.

Suffering is due to having an attitude about the pain. Suffering is due to how we think and feel about pain. It is possible to feel the pain and not resist. Without holding an attitude, the pain will dissolve much more rapidly. This perspective inspired me to be more of an impartial witness to the daily discomfort in my body.

Barely Keeping Things Together

In 1986, a doctor told me that there was mercury in my brain. The doctor also said that the mercury in my brain made decision-making difficult for me. Definitely part of why sometimes I felt as useless as an old string tied in knots.

During the second half of 1988, I was still troubled and limited by my physical condition. My emotional state was sometimes even worse. I would have brief moments of clarity and/or happiness and then lapse back into a fog of tiredness, confusion, and overwhelm. I had been feeling trapped in a downward spiral for many years. Before meeting Gurudev there was no perceivable way to gain consistent improvement. I could not find a way to make any significant recovery.

Personal commitments were challenging for me. My digestion was weak and extremely problematic.

Gurudev said that pain can help us be more in touch with ourselves. Perhaps I was more present in the moment due to the pain. At the time, it was often too overwhelming to think about. Appreciating the wonder of the present moment was challenging for me.

Gurudev was my life raft. I felt some wonder about the situation.

Due to my previous experiences, it was difficult to trust. Yet a part of me felt, deep inside, that I would gradually continue to be extricated from misery.

In 1988, words would often fail me, but later I was able to put my need for guidance into words.

You Be My Guidance

You be my guidance,

my best guidance,

my best guidance True.

Please be my guidance,

my real guidance,

the only guidance True.

You are the Guidance,

the clear Guidance,

the great Guidance True.

We are with the Guidance,

the eternal Guidance,

feel the Guidance True.

Love the Guidance,

embrace the Guidance,

melt in the Guidance True.

In those days of 1988, I often felt inadequate for the task of managing my life. My life seemed apt to spiral out of control. Emerging at times from a fog of perpetual exhaustion, I would alternate between certainty and uncertainty.

On the Saturday of the July 1988 Basic Course, I was tired. I didn't want to help teach the practices for the course. *If I sit behind a plant, maybe Gurudev will not call on me.* That was my pathetic state of mind at that moment.

At that point, I was too frazzled to tell whether helping to teach the course might have made me feel better. Gurudev must have approved, since I was able to do all the breathing sitting off to the side, undisturbed.

I remember thinking that Janael was counting noticeably slowly and deliciously for the pranayama. My lungs were full to bursting several times. I felt my lung capacity increase. It was wonderful to sit with Gurudev and do all the breathing exercises.

As usual, Gurudev called out the rhythms for Sudarshan Kriya from his seat. The Sudarshan Kriya breathing went on for about 45 minutes, and then the lying-down segment was about the same length. We were getting the maximum.

I felt better after that day of the course, yet I still felt exhausted. I didn't want to be with people. I had a need to be reclusive.

Chapter Six: Potency of the Sangha

When in a spiritual group, also known as a *sangha*, many people have the expectation that the members of the sangha will be good, kind, special, easy to be with, etc. Often, people expect that members of a spiritual organization will behave in a more evolved way. Especially regarding the long-term members, people expect enlightened behavior. Inevitably, this expectation leads to upset, since members of a spiritual group are there because they are learning and growing. Many members are far from enlightenment.

Many types of groups are available. Maturity levels and abilities tend to be all over the map. The expectation of enlightened behavior happens at times in other groups as well, such as families and schools. For a person on a spiritual path, any group of people they are with on a regular basis functions as a sangha.

Gurudev puts this into perspective: "From a distance, the group is very charming, but the closer you get to it, the more it pushes your buttons and brings out all the unwanted things from within you."

Everyone starts a spiritual path at whatever point they happen to be on the evolutionary scale. People who are many lifetimes short of achieving Buddha stature or Christ consciousness become teachers of a discipline. This happens in groups in many places.

As Gurudev says, "From a distance, any group is very good, if your acquaintance with them is very little. If you think a group is very good, it means that you are not yet with that group in totality."

Eventually, there will be a complaint from someone that some person did some objectionable thing. Then the complaining person may exaggerate and say that either there is something wrong with the organization or the whole teaching must be suspect due to a person doing wrong actions. Obviously, if someone does something illegal or deliberately hurtful, intelligence must swiftly be used to handle things in an appropriate way.

Here is where one of the master's key teachings comes into play. We are told to accept people, things, and situations as they are. Acceptance means we stay centered when we stand against wrong. Acceptance is part of real yoga.

Unlike most other kinds of groups, around a truly enlightened being, many different types of people will gather in the sangha. The guru told us that many points on the circle would be represented. Meditation and breathing practices do not turn us into robots or clones. Transformation happens. It is important to attend satsang, even if someone bugs you.

Even though he warned us, many forget this. People may be surprised by some of the types of personalities in the group. I noticed that, with every lecture and course taught by Gurudev, a broader array of types of people would gather around. Many types of people were there in the early 1990's: meditators, doctors, musicians, actors, people proud of their work, shy people, artists, writers, people who respected wealthy people, healers, sick people, salespeople, people eager to rub shoulders with famous people, hippies, athletes, couch potatoes, greedy people, generous people, healthy people, singers, dancers, poets, therapists, painters, truck drivers, people of different religions, some confident, some insecure, etc.

Gurudev clarified, "You find other groups better than your own group. This is not really true because **you** (his emphasis) make the group. If you are better, your group will be better! If you are good, your group will be good."

"Once you are used to a sangha, the sangha loses its charm for you. This is essential."

Gurudev repeatedly emphasized that if we blow up

over minor upsets, then it is like we are a machine with buttons. Push the right button, and a person freaks out. Pursuing a spiritual path is a way of disconnecting inner hot buttons. The path puts opportunities to grow right in front of you.

It takes some bravery to accept people who bug you. Especially if they repeatedly push your buttons. Especially if you see those people every week at gatherings.

Revealing deep secrets that I had never heard of, Gurudev said, "If a sangha is only repulsive, all the time, then nobody will be in the sangha because our nature is not to be in repulsion. The sangha has its own bonding, but at the same time, it can bring out negativity from within you, and that is what it is *meant* to do. This is a good thing, for in this way, a sangha pushes you inside, to your nature. Otherwise, you will be distracted from your nature."

This leads back to some of the basic foundations of yoga, namely forbearance and self-study. It is important to be faithful with your practices, cleansing yourself so your buttons get disconnected. Then it is such a relief to be gracefully able to choose how to respond to situations.

Path of the Brave

Several times during my early years with Gurudev, I heard Gurudev say that a person must be brave to walk this path. At first, it seemed surprising to hear him say that. As time went on, the truth of this became readily apparent. There are diverse reasons for the need for bravery.

Most people have strong desires for things to be a

certain way. Certain things are seen as good, and other things are seen as bad. People have cravings for things they want and aversions to things, people, and situations they wish to avoid. Gurudev pointed out that cravings and aversions distort our emotions and thoughts. Bravery is required to face this.

Gurudev let us know that it is a fundamental law of nature that when a person has a craving for something, the more they demand that something, the less they will get of it. Vice versa, when people can't stand something or someone, they will find themselves faced with whatever they are averse to. These dynamics are apparent in a spiritual group. The more you run from something, the more it chases you. Living with knowledge is real yoga. Real yoga requires facing your own discomforts. As many have taught, "What you resist will persist."

If someone is about to perform a criminal act, while being in acceptance you can act to stop the crime. Acceptance is not being passive. It is valuable to put up with some minor, unenlightened behavior in your sangha. Meanwhile, it is also important to stand up against harmful or mean behavior. For many people, this will require bravery.

In the *Kena Upanishad*, there is mention of being brave to see the One Consciousness that composes everything. It takes bravery to be settled with the truth.

Perhaps it is also appropriate to say that bravery is needed since the road to enlightenment is long. Patience is required. Some people will meditate or chant every day for ten, fifteen, or thirty years and then get frustrated when they are not enlightened. If the path you are on is appropriate for you, you should see some signs of growth. However, the blossoming of consciousness takes a long time. It requires patience and enthusiasm, without lethargy.

Burning Every Day

Burning every day

in some new way.

It could be years,

before this is over.

Burning every day

in some new way.

You roll through your feelings

and seek new freshness.

Burning every day

in some new way.

Miracles are dawning.

Thank you!

Some people are naturally sincere. Yet sincerity is difficult for other people. Gurudev laid it out for us: "To be successful on the path, utter sincerity is needed." For some people, this can be another reason why bravery is needed.

Vishnu is the aspect of nature that maintains the universe. Vishnu is a name for the energy that provides everyone with whatever they need to survive. *Dattatreya*, thought by some to have been an incarnation of Vishnu, was a wise, highly regarded sage who was mentioned in several Upanishads. Dattatreya taught that tremendous perseverance is required to attain perfection in yoga.

Patanjali agrees with this. The requirement of a long period of dedication is also mentioned in Patanjali's *Yoga Sutras*.

Gurudev will sometimes have a serious face when he talks about this, and sometimes he will have a little smile. He gracefully makes it seem simple when he says, "The path is long, yet the goal is at every moment."

Except for Gurudev having a full beard, in 1988 he appeared to me to be no bigger than I was when I was 14 years old. He was slender in 1988. Sometimes his graceful physical lightness made him appear to be delicate.

When I thought of Gurudev as my "little brother," perhaps I was amusing myself. On the other hand, it was increasingly clear that I was very far behind him in my spiritual development. I was repeatedly amazed by his prodigious abilities every time I met with him.

Even though Gurudev is chronologically younger than I am, I could no longer let myself think of him as a younger brother. It didn't matter that I felt rugged and street-smart. I recognized that Gurudev was filled with a prodigious level of inspirational spiritual bravery of a cosmic caliber. That bravery I longed to own within myself.

On many occasions, Gurudev made it clear that silence

is superior to words. He asserted that we can only worry thanks to words.

Gurudev used the analogy of baking bread to illustrate the ideal proportion of silence in our lives. He stated that just as we only use a tiny amount of salt in a bread recipe, that should be the situation with our use of words. The amount of silence in our lives should be like the flour in a bread recipe. Silence in our lives should be much greater than the words in our lives or the salt in bread.

This is another area requiring bravery for many people. Many people are addicted to noise and talking. Silence is quite scary for a lot of people. Yet Gurudev asserts that silence is our true nature.

Some people are so addicted to noise and distractions that they play music throughout the day. Some people prevent themselves from having deep meditations by playing music even during a meditation period. Even if it seems comforting or soothing, music can keep the mind on a surface level. Meditation should promote silence. After we finish meditation, we can be as dynamic as we need to be.

Many times, I have heard our master declare that words are the language of the head and silence is the language of the heart. One of the functions of knowledge is to put us in silence.

With real yoga you cultivate bravery in yourself. Real yoga gives us the ability to be comfortable in silence. Real yoga promotes being comfortable in diverse circumstances.

The understanding that this is a path requiring bravery stuck with me. Facing personal challenges needs bravery. In my head, I can hear the way that Gurudev murmured, one day, softly, "This is a path of the brave." That particular time when he said it, anyone not paying close attention would not have heard it. Later, I appreciated it and wrote a little poem.

Only the Brave Will Walk This Path

Only the brave will walk this path.

Only the brave will fully burn.

Only the brave will root in the sky.

Only the brave truly learn.

Tell us your story,

tell us truth.

Sand the edges with love,

till we are smooth.

Meditating with a Lecture

There were only two of us to take Gurudev to the airport for his departure after teaching the July 1988 Basic Course in Los Angeles. Before going to the airport, Claire wanted to buy and cook some food. She disappeared for a while.

Gurudev and I were by ourselves, hanging out together. With a smile, he said, "Let's sit and meditate." I was eager and ready to enjoy the moment with him.

At the time, I did not realize how truly lucky I was.

Gurudev's schedule became busier with every passing month. What a profound gift to have had that time.

Gurudev saw a cassette tape recording of a lecture that had been given by Maharishi. He asked me to play the tape. I was surprised. I was hesitant to accept this tricky idea. *Is he playing with my mind? Whatever, it will be an interesting experiment.* Gurudev was promoting wonder.

Gurudev and I sat side by side on a plain futon mattress against the wall. Sitting next to an enlightened being undoubtedly made meditation easier. We both went into deep serenity. Surprisingly, we had a great meditation while the recording of Maharishi was playing. We did some alternate nostril pranayama to end the meditation.

"Nice to hear his voice" murmured Gurudev, with a sweet, grateful feeling and a touch of wistfulness as he gazed at the cassette. It was gratifying and inspiring to be allowed to witness a private expression of Gurudev's devotion toward Maharishi. More and more, I admired our saintly Gurudev's noble qualities, including peacefulness and the complete absence of arrogance.

Stop All Exercise

At the airport, I was sitting on my heels while on tiptoe in the aisle next to the end of the row of seats. Then I could be beside the seat that Gurudev sat in. I had my arms crossed in front of me, resting on the armrest of Gurudev's chair. The dim lighting barely revealed rows of empty seats all around us. Gurudev had his head turned to his left, facing away from me. I relaxed in his presence and enjoyed the last few minutes before he boarded his plane. I was not paying attention to the conversation that was happening on Gurudev's left side.

Abruptly, he turned to me, riveting me with his eyes.

"Two months, no exercise. No exercise for you for two months. No asanas, no yoga, nothing. No exercise for two months."

His head rotated smoothly and effortlessly as he turned back to his left and resumed chatting about something. Feeling stunned, my mouth opened, and no sound came out.

As an exercise addict, I was flabbergasted. My mind verged into frozen shock. For the next few minutes, not a single word that was spoken registered in my mind.

Years of forcefully pursuing different kinds of exercise had actually interfered with the healing of injuries from car and bike accidents. I had many different, partially healed injuries in my body. I had always forced myself to do my yoga asanas and more. Even when tired, the pain was usually less when I was in motion. The truth was that I was an exercise addict. If I could get out of bed, even if I were ill, I would do my own intense session of warm-ups, asanas, and exercises. It was perfect timing to let go of this compulsion.

At the airport in 1988, one could walk all the way to the boarding gate as a non-passenger accompanying a passenger. Gurudev and I walked slowly, side by side, in silence. I drank in the moment as deeply as I could. Magically, no other passengers were nearby.

I stopped as he entered the ramp for the plane. Turning to me and stopping, he looked quite serious. He coached, "Two months. No exercise. Nothing. No yoga. Two months. Jai Guru Dev." I watched as he turned to enter the plane. With a twinkle and a grin, he was on his way.

This simple, surprising instruction was instrumental to my healing and progress. I had never given myself the space to rest long enough to heal my injuries. And now that I was doing pranayama and other powerful yogic breathing exercises every day, here was a perfect opportunity to heal more deeply than ever before.

The first three weeks were quite challenging. Frequently, I was observing the compulsion to move my body: swim, bike, dance, lift weights, climb a tree, etc. *Do something! Work the muscles!!*

After one month of no exercise, I felt a difference. My injuries were healing more than they ever had. At the end of two months of zero exercise, I realized that I was actually much more likely to be able to be entirely free of the aches and pains that had plagued me for years.

Gradually, through 1989 and 1990, I felt less and less pain in my body. The daily reality of pain, sometimes intense, was slowly getting reduced. Gratitude for relief came and went like tides of lovely ocean waters.

This experience gave me the ability to pace myself. If I have a lot of work to do, I will not grind myself into a pulp just to get some exercise in.

My abilities were actually improving after having the rest. Some things that I could not do before became possible after that two-month period.

Every instruction from the master is a blessing, even if it seems difficult, trivial, or nonsensical. Instinctively, I always did my best to follow Gurudev's requests and instructions fully. I hold myself to do things exactly the way he wants them done. Even if that meant going against my own inclinations. Even if it meant going against group opinions, ridicule, or peer pressure. The supreme consciousness knows our strengths, karmas, and prejudices. Opportunities for growth are given when you can handle them. Even if your mind disagrees. For the best and fastest results, you gracefully follow the guidance of the master.

Time is that Subtle Thread

Time is that subtle thread,

weaving a tapestry of life.

Yours is a mosaic heart,

singing across centuries.

Now is a fullness,

extending forever.

One tiny moment,

engraved on a bubble,

to float through eternity,

in condensed intensity.

When the pop comes,

it's not an end,

any more than another

beginning.

SECTION THREE: FIND CENTER

Chapter Seven: First Los Angeles Art of Living Center

In the fall of 1988, I began to look for a two-bedroom residence to rent in West Los Angeles. Some essential criteria were key to determining the suitability of a rental.

The rental had to be good for hosting meditation gatherings, bhajan chanting groups, and satsangs. I wanted plenty of space for a group of people to sit comfortably. I wanted it to be situated in a peaceful, quiet neighborhood with minimal traffic. It had to be good for teaching Art of Living courses, so it had to have plenty of windows and doors providing a good flow of fresh air for breathing techniques. Ample floor space was needed for course participants to do asanas. Convenient parking was a must. It had to be nice for the master, Gurudev Sri Sri, to come and visit. I wanted a peaceful bedroom for Gurudev to stay in and a clean, medium-sized kitchen.

I only looked at apartments since I was limited by my income. None of them met all the above criteria. At first, it was a more casual search. As place after place was objectionable, usually for multiple reasons, it seemed like a more serious effort was needed. I put all my free time into the search. Over the course of several months, 107 possible rentals were considered and rejected.

Familiar feelings of frustration over a lack of success were bubbling up. My income was not sufficient for leasing representative houses in the area.

In March 1989, a house was found by a friend riding a bicycle. This house met the criteria and was in my budget. There were lots of windows and doors. The house was light and cozy. This rental was the 108th choice.

A wonderful ocean breeze would gently move right through the house when the front and back doors were both open. Sometimes one could even smell the ocean. The energy was sweet and positive. There was a lot of unrestricted street parking close by.

On April 1st, 1989, I signed the lease for the house on Ashwood Ave. I made a phone call to Gurudev to let him know that the space was ready. Three weeks later, Gurudev came to stay for a week at the house on Ashwood Ave. in Mar Vista, a residential community in West Los Angeles.

That is how the first Art of Living Center in Los Angeles was born.

The number of people that would come was unknown, so the living room was kept open, free of clutter. In order to seat as many people as possible on the floor, there were no tables, sofas, shelves, cabinets, or chairs. Pillows were stacked against the walls for the comfort of visitors who might need them. The fluffy, clean, white carpet made it seem even more perfect.

Before Gurudev arrived, I bought a compact futon chair with a wooden frame. That chair was reserved exclusively for Gurudev. It was easy to take apart the frame to transport it. That chair ended up being taken to all but a couple of the talks and courses that Gurudev gave in Los Angeles for the next 11 years. When Gurudev was not in town, it was kept as an altar. It was the intention that nobody else sit on the chair, as a sign of respect and honor.

The chair for the master was kept opposite the entrance at a central focal point. That chair was the only piece of furniture in the living room and dining room. The stereo and small, portable video player in the dining room fit neatly into the small corners that had no view of Gurudev's chair.

Future needs were being anticipated. Certainly, all the floor space was not needed during that first visit that Gurudev made in April of 1989.

One of the first nights that Gurudev was there, he said to expect a special guest at satsang. Gurudev wanted us to set up a chair for this man so he would not sit on the floor. Our guest was Dosthora Warnasuriya, a Sri Lankan doctor. Dosthora was an exponent of the Sri Lanka Deha Dhamma system, which his family had maintained for thousands of years. The Deha Dhamma system originated from and honors the herbal medicines and expertise of King Ravana, the ancient ruler of Sri Lanka, who was trained by Rishi Agasthi. Meaning that Dosthora's family traced its lineage back to the time of Rama, Sita, and Ravana! Thanks to the scoffing of British invaders and the censorship of carefully dated indigenous histories, the exact dates of the existence of Rama, Sita, and Ravana have been debated. Some have said that Rama lived about 17 million years ago! In *Historical Rama*, authors Hari and Hari give extensive evidence for January 10, 5114 BCE, as the birthdate of Rama.

That night, when he visited in April 1989, Dosthora brought with him some ancient palm leaf books that had been in his family for hundreds of years. I don't know how Dosthora found out about Gurudev being there. Gurudev didn't talk much when Dosthora was there. Dosthora had a lot to say, and Gurudev encouraged Dosthora.

The next morning, we went for a drive. Gurudev wanted to make a stop on our way, and he didn't know the address. I asked him, "How are we supposed to get there if we don't have an address?"

He told me, "You drive, and I will tell you how to get there." I turned left or right as he guided me. His guidance was perfect. In a short time, we pulled into the driveway of a house in Brentwood. It was Dosthora's home.

Gurudev said to wait in the car, then he went in by himself. When he came out, he had a few bags of herbs in his hands. After getting back in the car, Gurudev started eating some of the herb powders. As he held up one clear plastic bag of powder, he got a twinkle in his eye. He joked, "If you are not already sick, this one will make you sick." Wholeheartedly laughing, he seemed to think that was a funny joke.

An Art of Living checking account was established at a local bank. It was used to deposit money from course fees. It would cover expenses such as the rental of commercial course and lecture venues for Gurudev's visits to Los Angeles. I never touched any of that money for my personal rent, phone, food, or utilities.

When the master stays at a place, it is typical that many types of people, some of whom you have never met, show up at odd times. Each time that Gurudev came to stay in Los Angeles, I was impressed with the ever-increasing size of the group. Friends told friends, and there was a magical feeling. Many dedicated meditators came in those early days.

One gentleman had his own special style of congenial greeting. Along with a twinkle in his eye and a big grin, he would come up to me and ask, "Have you seen my latest tattoo?" He acted and felt like a close friend from ages ago. The first time it happened, I was at a loss for words. I was trying to figure out where I had seen him before. I knew that I knew him from somewhere. But I was fairly certain that I had never met him. At least, not in this lifetime.

A Very Detached Master

New towels and sheets had been purchased for Gurudev's visit. There was also a portable foam exercise pad for Gurudev to use as a bed. He prefers to sleep on minimalistic mattresses on the floor. In some cases, I witnessed that if there were no new sheets available for Gurudev, he would just spread a shawl on the floor and use that as his bed. He would then cover himself with another shawl.

When caring for a saint, it is traditional and honorable to offer items for their personal use that have never been used by anyone else. A real saint is more sensitive than the average person. They will feel, in the objects themselves, the vibrations of anyone who has used those objects. In later trips, a set of dishes would travel with Gurudev in his suitcase. If some hosts did not have new dishes that had never been used, those crucial items were on hand.

One morning, after Gurudev welcomed me into his room, I noticed that his towel was flat on the carpet on the floor. My instinct was to hang it up somewhere in order for the towel to dry out.

As I reached for the towel to hang it up, Gurudev instructed, "That can be there." I was taken off guard by his relaxed attitude. With a giggle, I straightened out the towel.

Perhaps part of that whole scenario was to get me to break through a personal barrier and learn a lesson in detachment. After that, he seemed to keep most of his towels hanging on a hook, towel rod, or coat hanger.

Gurudev Laughs at an Old TV Show

Gurudev was not very busy during his first stay on Ashwood Ave. The pace of the day was much more relaxed than during subsequent visits. Within that context, there was space for a distraction or two.

One morning, the cart with the video tape player and small TV was wheeled into the living room. Gurudev sat in his chair. We watched an old black-and-white episode of the *I Love Lucy* TV show. Gurudev laughed vigorously and covered his face. It was fun to see him laugh a lot.

Assignments from the Master

I felt like a bouncy kid having Gurudev in the house on Ashwood on that first visit in April 1989. The first day, as he emerged from his room, it was like we were floating as I fell into step beside him, walking to the front of the house.

Tucked into corners of the dining area that did not have a view of Gurudev's chair were the stereo equipment and portable video cart. The rest of the floor space could be entirely clear. This set-up was deliberate, so all possible sitting areas that had a view of Gurudev's chair were left open for visitors to be able to sit and see Gurudev.

We could accommodate a greater number of people than many large, expensive homes that had shelves, big sofas, and tables. Each time Gurudev came to the house on Ashwood, more people showed up. Since we did not stuff the room with furniture, we were able to easily accommodate the increasingly larger groups each year. The growth of these groups was impressive. They swelled from five to sixty people.

As we were walking together past my stereo equipment, Gurudev took me by surprise by saying, "Ah, you can make the Kriya tapes."

This was completely out of the blue. Not only had I not made any request, I had not had any desire to make tapes in any official capacity. He unexpectedly gave me the assignment. Immediately, I felt a wave of bliss inside. Given that he could have asked anyone, I realized that this was truly a great honor.

At first, it was that simple. Just one sentence. Later on, he gave me more detailed instructions. One distinctive requirement was that the Sudarshan Kriya tapes should only be recorded on Mondays or Thursdays.

Later, another surprise assignment felt natural for me. Gurudev said, "Ha, you can record all of my talks."

From that point onward, wherever we were, when I was with Gurudev, I would record all of his talks and sessions on audio cassettes.

Later, Gurudev asked me to choose some of his better lectures to edit and then reproduce to sell. He specified that all the cassette tapes should be sold for $10. He made it simple. "Charge everyone $10 for a tape."

After Gurudev had left town, I would listen to the master tapes and decide which talks to edit. Once I had finished editing a talk, I would then make copies and sell them.

Some of the lectures that Gurudev gave in Canada in 1988 had been recorded by one of the Canadians. Some talks were duplicated on cassette tapes and made for sale. The sale of tapes was casual. Meaning that if you happened to be there in the room when the person who had duplicated them still had one in her bag, you could buy a copy.

Canadian talks included:
Confusion.
Can You Laugh Like Me?
Learn to Be a Fool.
Meet the Alien Called Guru.
What Attracts Us to Spirituality?

The sound quality of the tapes from Canada, though not the best, was good for a casual audio cassette recording.

There was no internet, and there were no recordings of Gurudev on radio or TV back then. YouTube did not exist in 1989. To be able to hear the master's voice delivering the knowledge is always a blessing. In 1989, it was a tremendous blessing.

Without my having any desire for it, or making any requests at all, many jobs were assigned to me by Gurudev. These included making Sudarshan Kriya Tapes (SKT), handling SKT administration, recording Gurudev's lectures, editing lectures, duplicating talks onto cassettes, managing sales of talks, and shipping orders of talks. These were all voluntary services, known as seva.

Gurudev gave my life purpose and value. He helped me grow closer to becoming a good human being. That is a lot for someone like myself, who was rough around the edges in those early days.

It takes time for real yoga to grow. Especially after years of abuse, trauma, illnesses, injuries and heartaches.

Sometimes I felt right at home, on the way to becoming more content and more complete. Yet, in the first few years, confusion, questions, and turbulence would frequently pop up and churn inside.

This was a broken record theme, from many previous years. In spite of yearning and rigorous persistence, I had not been able to bring my life into a lasting, harmonious balance.

When Will I Be Able to Live?

When will I be able to live?

Only you can help me.

When will I be able to trust?

Only you know the answer.

When will I be able to give?

You teach me by example.

When will I be able to offer?

Only you can tell me.

When will I be able to love?

Only you can help me.

You are the answer.

You are the secret.

You are the doorway and the shining light.

You are the sky.

Each breath is yours.

Editing the Sudarshan Kriya Tape

Prior to mid-1989, we were using an older version of a recording of the Sudarshan Kriya. Gurudev told me that he wanted me to edit a different recording of the Sudarshan Kriya.

Sudarshan Kriya (SKY breathing) is powerful. To prepare for editing the cassette recording, I kept silent the day before.

Two whole days of doing nothing besides editing the SKY recording were barely enough to get it right. Doing the edits to make a new master for the SKY recording felt like an Advanced Course. I felt distinctly altered in a long-term way just from performing that job of editing.

After editing the SKY recording, for the next couple of years, I made SKY tape cassettes for the entire world. In the early years, I knew every Art of Living teacher in most countries outside India.

After some time, Gurudev had Kishore make tapes for teachers in India. Later, Regina Boensel, in Germany, was asked to make tapes for Europe. Art of Living grew exponentially through the 1990s and 2000s. Gurudev made hundreds of new teachers. Old tapes needed to be replaced. Even with a reduced distribution area, in 2000 and later years, staying on top of tape administration took a huge amount of my time. It was more than a full-time job.

Back in 1989, many professionals were still recording demo tapes and interviews on cassette tapes. At that time, many musicians and journalists used the Marantz PMD430 as their professional, portable, two-channel stereo deck. Buck had spoken in glowing terms about the sturdy Marantz PMD430. When Gurudev told me to record all of his talks, I figured that I had better buy a Marantz PMD430.

Silence, an Essential Component of Lectures

When Gurudev gives a talk, he is outstandingly good at gauging and capturing the attention of the audience. The pacing of each talk is exceptional. Throughout lectures, Gurudev makes skillful use of silence. Silence can emphasize a point, grab attention, and let understanding grow.

At the beginning of a talk, most everyone has their eyes open. Gurudev might sit for a minute or two, or ten minutes, without saying a word. Imagine experiencing that with zero digital devices in the room. This helps to get people's attention, settle the room, and promote a state of wonder in the minds of listeners. That silence is a deep, rich place, full of energy and innuendo.

The silent pauses were more silent during those early years when we did not have laptops or cell phones. Picture an audience without phones or any digital devices. The lack of distractions helped to create a lively, magical atmosphere. Longer silences often put people into varying degrees of self-awareness or confusion, happy alertness or expanded consciousness.

The 12 Second Rule

As time went on, Gurudev gave more specific details in his instructions for editing the talks. Coughing and other loud noises were to be edited out. Silences under 12 seconds in duration were to be left in. Silences longer than 12 seconds he wanted reduced to 12 seconds. This is an important guideline, as most of his talks before editing have multiple periods of silence longer than 12 seconds.

When you attend a lecture in person, these longer periods of silence help to make the knowledge easier to digest. Silence can bring up unexpected feelings. While listening to an audio recording, long gaps of silence can be quite annoying. Especially since people have shorter spans of attention than they did in the 1980s and 1990s.

Gurudev's 12-second rule is perfect to give recordings the best of the feeling of Gurudev's relaxed, real-life pacing without losing people. Often, a pause of, for example, five to nine seconds helps the mind to grasp a point in the lecture and then be fully ready to receive the next knowledge point.

Some of the talks that were originally recorded and copied on cassette tapes were later reproduced on CDs. Unfortunately, since the year 1998, other people have edited many silences in those audio recordings down to a maximum of one or two seconds. This gives the lectures a rushed, artificial, mechanical feeling. The natural pacing of Gurudev's words is lost. Without the silent pauses, knowledge is often reduced to rapidly pumped-out information bullets. It sounds unnatural and becomes difficult to digest.

When talks on wisdom are edited, it would be skillful for people to remember the 12-second rule. Many people know that knowledge should lead us to silence. It is easier for that to happen when recordings of lectures keep the original silent pauses that are up to 12 seconds long.

At first, editing and duplicating talks was a simple industry. Duplicating tapes, one at a time, at normal real-time speed to preserve sound quality, took plenty of time. After setting up the duplicating equipment, I would do other things as the recording was being made. Before the end of 1989, copies were not being made fast enough. I bought a double cassette deck, which enabled me to simultaneously make two copies. After a few months, this was still not efficient enough to keep up. I bought another double deck. Then I could make four copies simultaneously. This worked well for a while.

An East Coast resident made some low-quality copies of talks that Gurudev had given on the East Coast. The sound quality on many of these talks was unbearably poor. It was so bad that even with the volume turned all the way up, it would be difficult and sometimes impossible to make out what Gurudev had said. Some of the cleanest talks were copied and distributed as a lending library for centers to have available for course graduates. Lending library titles were:

>*Introduction to the Art of Living.*
>*Intensity, Satsang, Devotion, Gopis.*
>*The True Nature of Love and Service.*
>*Truth Can be Felt.*
>*Fulfillment of the Shruti.*

Janael recorded a talk of good quality that went into the lending library collection. This was *Sanskrit, Language of Innocence.*

Demand for tapes kept growing. By early 1990, I ended up shipping tapes all over the United States as well as to Canada. By the fall of 1990, I started paying for professional duplication in order to make 50 to 100 copies of lectures that would then be sold. Tape copies were always duplicated in real-time, not at high speed, in order to have the best sound quality. A list of talks that were available was typed up, and people could order from that list. After 1991, tapes were also being shipped to Europe, the United Kingdom and other countries. At first, for a short while, it was manageable.

Resistance to Change

Ayurvedic five-element theory uses earth, water, fire, air, and space as the basic elements. Vedic culture and saints throughout the ages have been articulating wisdom about *panchabhuta*, the five elements, for many thousands of years.

Ayurveda describes *doshas* as functional principles that help us understand all aspects of life. Doshas are composed of the five elements. The three doshas are *vata* (air and space), *pitta* (fire and water), and *kapha* (water and earth). Their dynamic interplay can either maintain healthy bodily processes or cause disease.

Ayurveda says that water and earth elements, and the dynamic energy that organizes these elements to work together in the human body, are known as kapha dosha. Some of the qualities of kapha are heavy, cold, wet, slow, thick, and resistant to change. Kapha promotes holding on to the past and being sluggish. Bodily waste products are often kapha in nature, like mucous.

Toxins in the body will also produce resistance to change. Ayurveda tells us that toxins in the body will influence our thoughts and feelings in an effort to prevent us from doing things that would eliminate the toxins. Toxins have a nice, cozy place to live in our body, and they don't want to leave. This is another reason why it is important to follow our wisdom and not our feelings.

Some stresses have been with the system for an immeasurably long time. On an unconscious level, we are used to them. Whatever is familiar becomes comfortable to us just because it is familiar. For many people, change is unsettling and sometimes scary. Rapid change, even if undertaken for good, noble, and healthy reasons, can sometimes be extremely unsettling and upsetting.

It is also possible that people can get imbalanced to another extreme, such that they are addicted to change. They usually will not remove old stress and toxins through any of those compulsive changes. Some changes, such as frequent changes of residence, channel surfing, random bedtimes, irregular schedules, frequent travel, or random mealtimes, increase stress and make the mind and body weaker.

Addiction to change is often another way of avoiding feelings and avoiding the digestion of emotions. Ayurveda tells us that the digestion of emotions is an important component of health and healing.

Along with meditation, the breathing techniques; pranayama and Sudarshan Kriya (SKY), have a lot of potency for cleaning toxins and emotional garbage out of the human mind/body system. This cleansing can sometimes provoke a person to feel some resistance to the positive, healthy changes of real healing. Inner stress and toxins try to stop the cleansing.

Resistance to change is common. I have noticed some people experience resistance to doing spiritual practices, especially daily sadhana. Maharishi talked about it in poetic terms, with an analogy about shadows moving in the room when we are cleaning house. It is good to clean, but we may sometimes feel uncomfortable about the process of cleaning.

Sometimes people will feel resistance to doing some pranayama, meditation, or other practice. Some people may just start avoiding doing their sadhana. Or in the middle of breathing practices or meditation, they may feel a strong urge to stop prematurely and do something else.

It is important to follow your wisdom. Keep your commitment to yourself, and finish each round of sadhana. Don't give in to the toxins in your body. Keep doing your practices every day, all year. Go for freedom with real yoga.

It is important and valuable to keep going, stick with the practice, and get the benefits! I had a brief stage of saying to myself, "Oh, I'm tired; I'm not going to do the breathing. I'll just meditate." Then I would start meditation and zone out in a dull state. Fortunately, I kicked myself out of the rut.

The Sudarshan Kriya, SKY, is a potent technique. It is a powerful tool for cleaning out old emotions. Some people become uncomfortable with their changes and reduce the frequency or duration of their practices. It is important to keep going and get past the sludge of the old garbage.

The human body gives us a venue for the digestion of all of our experiences. In Ayurvedic understanding, one is stuck with whatever emotions have accumulated and not been digested. Ayurveda says that if you don't digest the emotions in this life, you will have to digest them in a future life. It's better to get it over with, don't you think?

One technique that Gurudev has emphasized for personal use is known as the Hmm! technique. Hmm! is actually a sacred mantra. Over and over, I heard Gurudev say, "This is a million-dollar technique! Use it!"

Gurudev taught this to the European Parliament in 2015. Prior to that, we would only teach it in the context of a course. If SKY is the jet, Hmm! is the warp drive. Hmm! quickly and dynamically flushes out stress, emotional gunk, and negativity. It creates a space around us of positive energy and vibrant sattva.

This rapid shift is intimidating for some people. Some people avoid using it because they are uncomfortable with change, even if a change brings sattva, health, and harmony. Tamasic energies will resist the use of the Hmm! Toxins and tamas can also make people more comfortable with using drugs, eating junk food, avoiding fresh air, drinking alcohol, not drinking water, avoiding healthy food, sleeping past sunrise, not bathing, smoking, and/or other bad habits.

During a certain time period, when a friend and I were doing sadhana together, that friend refused to make the Hmm! sound. They even asked me not to make the sound on my own when we were in the same room!

Publicity

Before he finished that April 1989 visit, Gurudev told our group that we could invite our friends to take the course. He stated that if everyone brought ten people, then we would grow rapidly. We asked if we should place some ads. Gurudev insisted, "We don't need advertising. It will grow very naturally. We should not spend money for advertising."

One thing that he said stuck with me: "A picture of a candle doesn't shed any light. We are the light, and people will be attracted to the light." Gurudev wanted us to use word-of-mouth.

In groups, one sometimes has a person who insists on doing things their own way or being contrary. Especially around enlightened masters, with all points of the circle represented, there will be widely divergent opinions.

In 1989, someone thought that advertising was necessary to get people's attention. My reminder that Gurudev requested that we not pay for any advertising was ignored. Private donors, who did not know about Gurudev's instruction not to buy advertising, paid for ads.

It surprised me that someone would argue against the master's instructions. As far as I was concerned, the master was the final authority. I was disappointed that someone wanted to go against Gurudev's instructions.

At the time, I did not realize that it was an opportunity for me to observe myself and my limitations. I was still learning how to drop expectations. The master had set up a good play of opposites. Briefly, I felt discouraged and unsettled. Since I wasn't able to accept and drop it immediately, I was bound to run into more of these scenarios. Eventually, in later years, Gurudev stopped voicing disapproval of advertising.

Amazingly, Gurudev came back to California less than two months after his April 1989 visit.

Surrender

Appreciation of the ultimate, which has created everything, can be called surrender. Many people have a misunderstanding of what surrender is. It is not about defeat in battle. Gurudev has offered an enlightened understanding of surrender.

"Surrender is not losing something. Surrender is recognizing the beauty. Surrender is recognizing the love. Surrender is recognizing that which is great."

"Dropping that which is bothering you. Dropping that which you cannot do for yourself. Letting go of your cravings, your desires, and your efforts and recognizing that which is, is surrender."

"All that negativity in you that you cannot handle, drop it, that is called surrender."

"Surrender means having trust."

"Surrender is the only way for security. There is nothing to surrender; it already belongs to the infinite. It already belongs to the divine. Everything already belongs to the divine."

Gurudev's most eloquent words on surrender have undoubtedly been a soothing life raft for many people.

We can understand surrender as being centered in the moment and alert in a relaxed way. Surrender is both a way of finding yourself, and a manifestation of living according to higher principles. Gurudev said that surrender requires courage. Surrender is a fundamental part of real yoga.

When we surrender our negative qualities, they get reduced. This rescues us from feeling bad about negative qualities.

When we surrender our positive qualities, they increase. This helps prevent the tendency to become caught in the ego trip of being arrogant about our positive qualities.

Surrender is helpful when dealing with resistance to change. It is as simple as bowing down and offering.

"Your thought of possessing is false. You don't possess anything. What do you possess?"

"You can't even hold on to your own body. It can stay with you only for a few years."

"All that you think of as yours will drop away from you anyway."

Dealing with Feelings

On the first day of June 1989, about 17 of us gathered with Gurudev at Jeff Houk's house in Montecito, the southern part of Santa Barbara, California. We sat on the sofa and the floor in the living room. Often, as he was about to give a lecture on knowledge, Gurudev would chant all or part of the following:

> *OM namah pranavaarthaaya shudignani kamoortaye*
> *Nirmalaaya prashaantaya Dakshinamurtaye namaha*
> *Gurave sarva lokaanaam bishaje bhava roginaam*
> *Nidhaye sarva vidyaanaam Dakshinamurtaye namaha*
> *Ishvaro gururaatmeti murtibheda vibhaagini*
> *Vyomavad vyaapta dehaaya Dakshinamurtaye namaha*

Since it was a small group, casually assembled in a private living room, I was impressed when Gurudev chanted all of that. It made the satsang more special and magical.

Gurudev pointed out that our issues start when we feel bad. We don't consider it trouble when we feel good.

He stated that feelings are like water; they flow. When he stated that it is important to allow ourselves to experience feelings without reacting to them, I felt both puzzled and intrigued. I don't know how the others felt hearing Gurudev say that it is important not to try to turn off our own feelings.

Many people have a habit of turning off their own feelings in order to avoid pain. He suggested that when you feel low, if you go deep into it, you can come out of it sooner. Getting free of painful feelings faster sounded like good incentive to try this bold, refreshing approach.

Gurudev pointed out that the ocean is full, and it is also the lowest. Infinity is the greatest, and it is the lowest.

He explained that we should not go to a doctor when we feel depressed. To feel better, instead of fighting with our bad feelings or pretending they are not there, he encouraged us to love our bad feelings and get into them.

He gave a technique for feeling good: to digest being upset by accepting feeling bad. One must simply be with whatever comes up and watch it. Observe our own inner upset without doing anything to make it worse.

If I hadn't made use of this technique, I might have forgotten about it. After hearing these ideas, I trained myself to go into the burn of upset. I could feel it get intense, but I could tell that it would fade a lot faster than if I had avoided the pain. If we dive into the bad feelings with a sense of being an observer, we will rise up much faster than if we try to sweep the upset under the proverbial rug.

As you observe, some sensations will come. If you fight with your feelings, it will take longer to get over them. It is important to let feelings come, observe them without judgment, and then they will go on their own. This technique of dropping resistance to feelings, surrendering, and letting go is very valuable. This is a key in real yoga. Gurudev even proposed that it could put psychiatrists out of business.

This is interesting in the light of Ayurveda. Ayurveda says that most illnesses derive from emotions. We must digest our food completely, or there will be toxins left. Ayurveda says that we must completely digest our experiences. Many people have not caught up with their own lives and have a gigantic backlog of undigested experiences.

Any undigested experience will sit in the system until it is processed. If you have a big upset and try not to feel the sad, angry, mad, frustrated, jealous, anxious, or whatever feelings, they will stick in your system. At first, it may be more on a subtle level. The longer feelings remain in the system, the denser they become. Eventually, some physical problem will show up somewhere in the body.

From my personal experience, I know that this method of watching the feelings and allowing the uncomfortable emotions to be there is an efficient way to get out of feeling bad. This helps people feel better. More rapidly than not.

Love Is Anguish

Gurudev brought up Rishi Narada, a wise saint from long ago. It would be a full year later, in 1990, when Gurudev gave weeks and weeks of commentary on Narada's *Bhakti Sutras*. That June day in 1989, in Santa Barbara, Gurudev revealed, "Rishi Narada said that 'The nature of love is extreme anguish. If you have not had extreme anguish, then you have not had supreme love.'"

This may have sounded a little harsh or weird to some people. Yet I was probably not the only person in the room who felt that they could relate to what Gurudev was saying. By that point in my life, I figured I had already gone through enough anguish for more than this lifetime.

Gurudev pointed out that, to get to long-term, peaceful bliss, we have to transcend anguish. Undoubtedly, most of us shared the feeling of wanting to pass beyond anguish and stay in long-term bliss.

As Gurudev emphasized, you'll get better results if you follow your commitment and don't follow your feelings. Allowing the emotion to be there does not mean running with some impulsive idea that degrades your clarity. Follow truth, wisdom, love, kindness, generosity.

"Make decisions based on wisdom. When you are in your big mind, you will feel calm, collected, and serene."

Since that day, Gurudev has talked many times about the importance of going through our feelings to get to bliss.

We all want bliss. Everyone is searching for the juice in life. The bliss is on the other side of our feelings.

Bliss, a fundamental part of real yoga, is a result of rest. To reach the love and happiness we all want, we have to relax. We have to digest our experiences. And relax.

Religion Versus Saints: Banana Peel or Banana?

Just a couple of days after the talk in Jeff's living room, Gurudev was scheduled to give an evening talk at a church. This small church was in the Santa Barbara Mountains, near Ojai. The remote location had almost zero lighting for the outside of the building and parking area. I enjoyed standing with Gurudev under the night sky, looking up at millions of glittering stars.

At first, it was just six devotees there with Gurudev, then maybe five to ten more people showed up, bit by bit.

A person working for the church had an office door open. Their large, old, loud, dot matrix printer was spewing out printing nonstop. I asked them politely to close the door since we were having a lecture. That person refused. Surprised that they would disturb an event that had rented space at their own facility, I was at a loss.

Gurudev began by asking for topics to discuss. It was sweet to hear Gurudev speak. There is always a lot of silence around his words. That night, the loud printer was antagonistic to silence. After a few minutes, Gurudev asked that the door be closed, and only then did we get cooperation. Once the door was closed, it was much quieter and easier to hear Gurudev's words.

Gurudev explained that the self within us is untouched, and because it is untouched it is virgin. This virgin space within us, when we go deep within ourselves, gives birth to the Christ consciousness. This made sense to me, yet it seemed experientially a bit out of reach at the time.

"The peak of any emotion can lead us to that virgin area of self."

It was clear that Gurudev was talking about our true

self, not the small self, which is identified with ego. He clarified that knowing the imperishable self can happen with meditation. "If you go deep into that virgin area of yourself, you become Christ."

I thought I sensed, within the audience, a wide range of responses to this idea, ranging from shock to discomfort to blankness to excitement. It was clear though, that Gurudev was just innocently speaking the truth.

Gurudev explained that we are still intact after death; the soul lives on. He spoke against suicide. Suicide is like feeling intensely cold and then removing all your clothes. Whatever a person is feeling before they commit suicide, that is stuck with them after they die.

Gurudev spoke about various religions, giving an understanding of the cultural context of each religion. Different aspects of God are emphasized in different religions.

At the time of Muhammad, there was a lot of cruelty in that area of the world. It made sense for the merciful, compassionate side of God to be emphasized in Islam.

Creating fear in people is a common method to bring law and order. The Jewish religion would emphasize fear because, in the Middle East, there was a lot of disorderliness in society in the early days of Judaism. Fear of God was used to reduce chaos and get people to obey laws.

When people are unhappy, it is hard to recognize beauty. People were happy when Hinduism developed thousands of years ago. Earlier, in the Vedic period, God was known as *Satchidananda*, meaning truth, consciousness, and bliss. Later, *satya*, truth; *Shiva*, consciousness as innocence; and *sundara*, beauty, were emphasized as *Satyam Shivam Sundaram*. God was identified with innocence. Shiva is innocence, auspiciousness, and consciousness. There was emphasis on beauty, or *sundaram*, as part of God.

Usually, when people see some beauty, they want to possess it. Ego wants to possess things, and knowledge can bring ego. Pride can destroy the divinity in you. When you see the divinity in beauty and surrender to the divinity, then you can overcome wanting to possess it. Real yoga promotes such surrender to divinity. Gurudev told us that, when a person surrenders to their partner, "that is Radha Krishna."

"It is important to see innocence as an aspect of God, spirit, divinity. And surrender to beauty." Gurudev told us that we will not be able to hold all the beauty since our senses are too small to contain everything. By surrendering to beauty, we can dissolve the desire to possess it. With surrender, negative emotions will fade. Surrender will help us to have detachment, so we don't get lost in desire.

Gurudev told us that Jesus proclaimed that everyone of us is a child of God. Due to problems caused by translations of misinterpretations of translations, it became falsely understood that Christ was the only son of God.

People were bound by rules at the time of Jesus. Jesus emphasized the fatherly, loving aspect of divinity. The intimacy of one's own, personal connection with God was emphasized by Jesus.

When Buddha came, there was prosperity in his region. People had time to study. Many people had a lot of concepts. They had read a lot of teachings, and felt like they knew wisdom. Dealing with that, Buddha did not talk about God. Whether people believed in God or not, Buddha smiled and agreed. Buddha taught meditation.

Mahaveer was a contemporary of Buddha. Mahaveer founded Jainism, which emphasizes nonviolence.

Guru Nanak founded Sikhism, which emphasizes the brave aspect of divinity. The idea that a saint should be a soldier does not get much emphasis in other religions. Some people object to this idea. When you look more deeply, it makes sense. If an unholy person has a sword, it can be disastrous.

Yet a saint would never harm innocent people. Many kings, who were not saints, hurt people in many countries. Good people are needed to protect others from evil people. If only evildoers have weapons, who will protect the good people? Saints will never harm good people.

Gurudev declared that organized religion has been responsible for promoting disagreements and conflict. Obviously, when people believe that their religion is the only acceptable way, people of other religions will be judged as wrong, bad, or foolish.

I think he shocked some members of the audience, when Gurudev declared that there is no need for organized religion. Gurudev said that humanity would be better off without organized religion. He insisted that freedom is necessary in order to experience love.

One point that Master Gurudev has made many times is that there is a difference between spirituality and religion. Spirituality promotes the development of humans through consciousness. The spiritual practices of real yoga clean out stress and enable people to be their best. Spirituality is upheld by authentic, living masters.

A favorite topic of Gurudev is the importance of upholding the positive values that all religions teach and applying these values to all people. We can overcome conflicts around the world when we identify ourselves as one humanity and drop any negative feelings about other cultures or other religions. Since all religions arose out of the same consciousness, we can say that the big mind is the source of all religions.

Many masters have come and gone. Often, the followers of a master will do their best to preserve the wisdom and teachings of that master. Organizations, full of unenlightened followers, develop and continue this preservation effort.

When the original master is gone, without authentic saints, the organizations eventually lose the real juice behind all the teachings. Such organizations become religions.

Religion focuses more on symbols and procedures. It is like comparing a banana to the peel. Spirituality will nourish you like a real banana.

Love and God are already there. Real yoga helps us to get in touch with love and God. We use these practices to perceive the divine. Our meditation and practices are to keep the cup upright so that it can hold the soup, the nectar, the grace. Repeatedly, real yoga coaxes us onward in this journey of moving from the head to the heart.

Some religions honor God as female, and some honor God as male. Language falls short. God is beyond gender. Gurudev explained that by saying "he, she, or it," one does not convey the totality of God. Real yoga functions regardless of the gender of the experiencer. Real yoga allows perceptions of supreme consciousness beyond the concepts of gender. Much later, I was relating to some of this with the following poem.

We Can Do Nothing

We can do nothing

other than worship the Divine.

For It is our very life,

our true blood.

Flowing joyfully through our veins.

Singing the Divine Song

that bubbles up

and tumbles out of our lips.

The flower, so soft and beautiful!

Others' eyes, so deep and bright!

Sing! That He may hear you.

Offer! That you may know Her.

Gaze! That One may share love.

Enjoy! That All will be happier.

Secret Questions Finally Answered

Some people have questions tucked away inside themselves that they have carried for a long time. Coming into the presence of a master sometimes yields opportunities to get an answer to that old, buried question. Often, Gurudev will answer more than one person's secret and unexpressed questions in a single group lecture. For some, the relief of having an answer is huge. They treasure and hold the wisdom in their hearts.

A friend of mine revealed that when he first went to a lecture by Gurudev, there were two questions he had wondered about for years. In the course of the talk, without my friend saying anything to anyone, Gurudev answered those questions. Those answers gave my friend certainty. He gladly took the Basic Course after that. That same man became a teacher, eventually working full time for the Art of Living.

Mistakes and Acceptance

Many times, I have heard Gurudev assert that we should make new mistakes. He helps people avoid making the same mistakes over and over. He says, "I don't tell people not to make mistakes; I tell people to make new mistakes." It is easy to appreciate this more positive way of looking at making mistakes.

Gurudev explained that lack of awareness is what causes people to make mistakes. People tend to repeat patterns. We get into the same moods with different people. It is important to observe and be aware. Gurudev claimed that not being aware of our own mind is a big mistake.

It is important not to get stuck with obstacles. Gurudev confirmed that being intelligent means moving through obstacles. Real yoga gives greater ability to face obstacles.

People who have never gone through hardship tend to be shallow. Gurudev emphasized that difficulties help us to grow. With the positive perspective of the master, he pointed out that "only rains bring a rainbow."

We can pass through challenges, either crying or smiling. Real yoga increases our ability to smile.

Acceptance means not carrying events from one moment into another. Gurudev grabbed our minds by saying, "One day you had an argument with somebody. Okay fine, that is finished. Tomorrow, you can go in for fresh argument. The next day, you can go in for a fresh argument. That is acceptance."

As he was saying this, I remembered that I had been in an argument with someone less than 24 hours before Gurudev brought up the subject of arguments. It was impressive that Gurudev was giving this fresh perspective on arguments when I had not revealed anything to anyone about any disagreement I had been involved in. During talks, people in the audience may notice that Gurudev weaves in wisdom about things that those people had experienced prior to the talk.

Gurudev said that we can accept and still argue. He mentioned that sooner or later, intelligent people will disagree with each other. He must have caught the attention of many when he asserted that the only ones who can completely avoid arguing are "stupid people and sheep."

He said that we can agree with whatever comes up and keep going forward. It doesn't mean that we never get angry. If we have to argue, it is best to do it and then drop it. It is important to relax and drop the past. Be fully present and enjoy whatever we are doing. That is real yoga.

With a grin, Gurudev insisted that we can be happy, smiling, and enjoying ourselves. He encouraged us to go so far as to say, "Today I had a good argument." Once again, I felt my awareness perk up with Gurudev's lively, inspiring, and unexpected perspective.

Be Hopeless

Gurudev talked about how people base their lives on hopes. Some people think having a lot of hope is a positive thing. According to Gurudev, having a lot of hopes is actually disempowering because hope takes you out of the present moment. Hope is a focus on the future, having some desire, and an energy drain.

He pointed out that hopes are gone when you are either in bliss or feeling upset and hopeless. Living life in the moment is blissful. Revealing true mastery, Gurudev helped us understand the nuances of now.

"The now is very deep. The now is a mystery. It cannot be understood."

"Knowledge of now has only pushed the mystery further away. It has not resolved the mystery."

"Now is infinite, vast… One thing you can never know is the now. So, keep wondering about the now. You can't have any concepts about now. But you can totally live now. The present moment is inexhaustible."

Doubts are an opportunity to observe something

passing through your mind. Gurudev compared hope to starlight. Stars appear to be bright lights, but they do not give enough light to get things done. He asserted that when the last hope is gone, then you can get enlightened. With joy and love, increased by real yoga, hopes will drop by themselves.

At dawn, we start to see some light from the sun, though the sunrise has not yet happened. Light is increasing with the dawn, and the stars have disappeared. Gurudev compared this to losing the last hope. He emphasized that this type of dawn, losing the last hope, is precious.

A number of times, I have heard Gurudev say that Buddha kept silent after he got enlightened. At the time of Buddha's silence, this caused some concern. Buddha was questioned and prodded. Buddha responded that there was no point in his talking. Gurudev told us that Buddha argued, "Those who know, already know. Those who do not know, words will not help." The response to Buddha was that there are people who know a little and need some help to achieve full realization. Buddha finally agreed to talk.

Not everyone can sense the presence of divine energy. Most people are stuck on words. Most are not sensitive enough to feel the divine presence. Many people were stuck in their intellects in the time of Buddha. Buddha spoke day and night for 40 years. Gurudev noted that Buddha said only people who were in the dawn would come to him.

Gurudev emphasized that if we feel upset, it is a great opportunity to examine ourselves. He told us that we can stand up and challenge our typical patterns.

Our own patterns have obscured the clear skies of our own life. We can watch and observe whatever pops up inside us. It is possible for us to be free of inner clouds and enjoy sunny skies. Turning within can bring real joy. When we can experience this, it means that we are lucky, insisted Gurudev. Our inner, true nature is unconditional love.

'Positive Thinking' Causes Depression

Gurudev insisted that, if we have a negative thought, it is important not to suppress it or try to get rid of it by thinking a positive thought instead. He explained that forcing a positive thought makes the negativity stronger. If we observe and simply watch the negative thought, then it can begin to dissolve. People need to learn how to stay free of negativity.

Over time, when we do daily sadhana, the negative thoughts will arise less often. Gurudev explained that we should not encourage or suppress negative thoughts. This way, our freedom will come. That is real yoga.

Gurudev asserted that the root of criticism is discontent. Discontent is rooted in desire. When you don't know that you are the source of joy, that will cause desire. Frustration comes when desires are not fulfilled. People tend to forget that fulfilled desires can also end up giving us frustration. Gurudev was skillfully motivating us to rise above our desires.

Many times, I have heard master Gurudev talk about the difference between an intention and a desire. With intention, you decide to do something, and then you make any necessary preparations at appropriate times in a calm, skilled way. With intention, you stay relaxed and trust it will work out. Feverishness happens when you repeat your desire over and over and get worked up about it. Not all desires are good for you. Repeatedly reminding yourself of the desire is actually counterproductive and disempowering.

Using intention to get what you want is like planting a seed and watering it. It has to be buried a little bit, not right on the surface or too deep. If you keep digging up a sprouting seed to see how much it has grown, you will kill it.

Intentions similarly need to be given space to grow.

We started out as "lumps of joy" when we were children. Our joy shrank as we got older. Gurudev made it seem simple when he noted that it is possible for our joy to increase and expand. Joy can be infectious.

He declared that we could become so soaked in joy that anyone thinking of us would feel some joy. "Consciousness can retain the flavor of name and form."

To get to that space of joy, we have to "remove the emotions stuck in every cell of the body." This a fundamental part of real yoga. We have to remove blockages that interfere with our natural rhythms.

This is where ayurveda and sadhana perform well. Herbs, oil application, yoga exercises, breathing practices, meditation, and chanting all help to remove blockages in our bodies.

Many people have reached out to me to get help with identifying or taking their next step. Each person is unique. If you would like some help, please let me know: PracticalAyurveda.com

Chapter Eight: Second Teacher Training with Gurudev Sri Sri

In the early summer of 1989, a few of us met in a peaceful, private home in the Santa Barbara foothills for a Teacher Training Course, TTC, with Gurudev. The core group was about ten people. It became clear that Janael had been focusing a lot of time and energy on Gurudev's knowledge, and bringing more people to learn. I was impressed by her commitment. For most of the group, including Jeff, John, and Michael, it was their first TTC with Gurudev. These were peaceful, innocent times, without laptops, email, or cell phones to distract us.

Many points covered on this, the second TTC, were the same as on the first TTC. However, the structure and content of the second TTC were not the same as the first.

There were techniques that Gurudev taught on the first 1988 TTC that were not even mentioned during the 1989 TTC.

Both courses felt like a different reality. We were in a special, timeless place, far out of the flow of regular society, steeped in the grace of the master.

Another common factor for me in both TTC courses was intense cooking in the custom-made soup pot of the master. This was *tapaha swaadhyaaya ishvara pranidhaan* brought to the forefront with tremendous potency.

The master knows exactly how much heat from divine cooking any given person can handle. Some people are quite delicate. I have observed him softly, gently encouraging, and only giving the most minimal, lightweight assignments to some people, as if they were extremely fragile. A select few, sturdier people, will get higher temperatures of heavy-duty cooking with the guru.

People have different buttons. A true guru can have

situations occur that push various buttons of multiple people in several different ways, all at the same time. It is a big mind miracle supportive of growth, the development of knowledge, and personal strength.

Another time, on one silent Advanced Course, while the majority of people were meditating, Gurudev sent a few guys on a secret mission. They opened suitcases to scramble and rearrange luggage and clothing within and between rooms. It was crazy, colorful, button-pushing chaos that was intensely unpopular.

One man stopped Gurudev on the first day of that 1989 TTC and asked if Gurudev himself could fly. As in levitate with the flying sutra. Gurudev responded, "No."

The man immediately started to walk away with an annoyed look. Gurudev confessed that nobody was able to fly these days due to the denseness of the atmosphere, from the low level of consciousness on the planet. But the other person was obviously put off, not interested in any explanation, and just continued walking away, looking irritated.

During the first two TTC courses with Gurudev, I was in an almost constant state of something approaching shock due to having the maximum 'heat' of the Guru's grace cooking me profoundly.

I was grateful and lucky to be there. At times, I was floating in a vapor of bliss. When miserable feelings came up, sometimes I felt quite bleak and inadequate. I did my best to observe the feelings and allow them to dissolve. I was determined to persevere.

Another common point that Gurudev spoke about for those first two TTC courses was the development of our perception, observation, and expression. Gurudev would put it forth as a question to ask ourselves, "Has my perception, observation, and expression changed for the better?"

A couple of times, during my first year with Gurudev, he did this without further explanation. He was in a serious mood both times. It was clear to me that it wasn't great timing for me to interrupt his flow.

Perception, observation, and expression are things that can vary depending on one's state of mind; this is obvious. Yet, I felt it would be nice to have Gurudev discuss whatever nuances he wanted us to master.

Later on, when he gave some explanation, he revealed that this can be a type of gauge of growth on the path. I pounced on it and attempted to digest it with honesty.

Is our perception becoming more accurate? Can we perceive without judgment or bias? Are we able to observe ourselves so that we do not react blindly to situations? It is important to deactivate internal buttons, so we can decide how to respond. Then our expressions will likely become more congenial and life-supportive.

Real yoga promotes being centered enough to perceive complete truth without being overwhelmed.

"Willingness to be corrected is a great characteristic." Classic wisdom from our saintly master, Gurudev.

During TTC, we did a number of processes that could be challenging and/or button-pushing.

When it was my turn to say something, I did my best to tune in to the truth. I hoped that what I had shared could be used as a tool for growth by others. I wanted to extract what could truly be helpful for me.

Some processes were much more challenging than others. We managed to go through without any major blowups. Though a couple of people seemed truly annoyed or irritated after one session. When that session was officially over, I felt inward and kept silent, as instructed. One man seemed quite smug as he delivered a putdown about me, which he gave while we were about to serve ourselves some food. Not appreciating his enjoyment of his show of superiority complex, I felt violated and raw. I kept silent in response.

Purpose of Knowledge

Many times, Gurudev has made the statement that "the purpose of knowledge is ignorance." When hearing it for the first time, that statement can be confusing. Gurudev definitely likes to open people's minds.

As Gurudev revealed, "The purpose of knowledge is to know that I don't know. An ignorant knower thinks he knows. When you move beyond knowledge, ego disappears."

Many times, he has spoken about "the beautiful 'I don't know!'." During the 1990 Bhakti Sutra Tour, we would have a more in-depth discussion of "the beautiful 'I don't know!'."

Generally, people identify themselves with some particular place, time, and/or outer phenomena. It is important to grow beyond such attachments. Knowledge is essential in this process. Daily sadhana makes it possible to grow beyond limited identifications.

"When you move beyond love, the other disappears. What remains is bliss, is you, is power, is strength, is enlightenment. Take your identity beyond time, beyond space."

In the evenings of the 1989 TTC course, we would sit in the living room for satsang. Other people from the area would join us for knowledge and bhajans. Many nights, we ended up having three, beautiful guitars in the group. John had a guitar that he held, eagerly waiting for an opportunity to lead a bhajan. One evening, Gurudev deliberately played with that situation and continued to draw out the discussion. Gurudev kept the talking going long after the guitar had been picked up. Gurudev remained super relaxed. At least one person was ready to burst.

Free of microphones and electronic equipment, the sweet, simple purity of those times with the master was profoundly full of grace. Keep in mind that, at that time, people's attention spans were longer than they are now. There were no cell phones. Nobody had email. There were no digital devices to interrupt us.

The satsangs were small and intimate. Floating in the presence was easy. This was often the healing balm that would wash away the upset from the buttons that would get pushed during the day. Though, for some of the singers and musicians, the satsang itself could be the biggest button pusher. Even so, we could harmonize with the group and come to a place of sweet oneness.

At least one new bhajan would be introduced by Gurudev to our growing satsangs with each trip that Gurudev made to California. Sometimes we were learning new bhajans every night. We were still mostly Westerners who had limited experience with group chanting. Our blissful bhajans were mainly two to four short verses in Sanskrit, repeated for three to six minutes.

Basic Course at Casa de Maria

Before teaching the Basic Course in June of 1989, Gurudev gave an introductory talk. He told people they would lose stress and tension and see how big they are by doing the course. Gurudev encouraged people. He said that, by taking the course, we can get a glimpse of how full of love we are.

Gurudev pointed out that usually people say that we should not be foolish. He advised that it is okay to be foolish if we are aware. The important thing is to be aware of what we are doing in the moment, while we are doing it.

We have to take care of the body every day. We have to brush the teeth, bathe, and eat. Gurudev pointed out that most people do things without awareness of what they are doing. For example, most people think about other things while eating, shoveling food in and barely tasting it.

Revealing a deeper truth, Gurudev emphasized that if we hate someone, that energy goes out around us. If we get depressed, it pollutes the environment wherever we are.

In June 1989, Gurudev taught a Basic Course at the Casa de Maria facility in Santa Barbara, California. Most of the new teachers were helping to facilitate. People came from many cities for this course.

During breaks between meetings, Gurudev would sometimes discuss surprising topics within intimate clusters of people. During a break on that Casa de Maria course, Gurudev said something, in a small gathering, about Moses. Moses was rigidly strict and bound by rules, which can create a need for a soul to promote balance by breaking many boundaries during a subsequent reincarnation.

During that course, Gurudev advised the new teachers to stay away from the 'old-timers' and not give instructions to us. Along with a couple of other people, I was one of the old-timers.

He asserted that old-timers could go very deep during the Sudarshan Kriya and that giving us instructions could be quite disturbing. After doing Sudarshan Kriya regularly over a long period of time, breathing with circles during Sudarshan Kriya becomes second nature. At times, the breathing can appear to be extremely subtle.

On the other hand, in subsequent years, Gurudev noticed that some people with more kapha (water and earth elements) and/or more toxins in their system would sometimes tend to fall asleep during breathing practices.

Gurudev told some heavier people to stay alert when doing Sudarshan Kriya and make a strong effort to breathe fully with each breath.

Some tired, dull, or overweight people may have to apply a little more focus in order not to fall asleep during breathing practices. It is worth doing if you are in that category. Those who fall asleep should not give up. It is not correct to think that you should never fall asleep during breathing or meditation practices. If you are exhausted your body will want to collapse during breathing or meditation. That is natural. You do not need caffeine. Let the body rest.

Be kind to yourself. If judgement comes, observe it like a cloud drifting by. It is important to keep going and continue doing meditation and breathing practices regularly. Eventually, you will get past that phase. Each person has their own, unique journey. Inner, lasting changes take time. Be patient. With persistence, you will make it!

Gurudev taught that most people are tangled and hung up in words. He maintained that words are not a good foundation for life. Gurudev specified that love, beauty, and gratitude do not require words. Real yoga helps us to be better able to live with and express love and gratitude.

Heavy Duty Blessing

We drove north from Santa Barbara to Carmel, in California. A small caravan of cars included Gurudev and some of his teachers. We stopped near Pismo Beach for a break. There was a nice view of the ocean. Someone brought out a camera (cell phones were nonexistent) to take some photos.

Gurudev and M sat on a bench that faced away from the view of the ocean. I stood right in front of Gurudev, facing him and the ocean. Gurudev effortlessly changed his persona and flipped his head to toss his hair to one side of his shoulder. Then, while grinning and batting his eyelashes, in a seductive voice, he said to M, "So, do you come here often?" M and I burst into laughter.

Since Gurudev had kept his voice low, the rest of the group did not hear what he had said. M was choking on speechless surprise and grinning. Some of the others wondered why we had cracked up.

One of the photographers lamented having missed the moment when Gurudev looked extra charming. A request was made for Gurudev to smile like that again.

Gurudev had been giggling, but it stopped because he did not like being asked to repeat an action for the sake of a photo. Gurudev took on a sour look. He abruptly got up, making commentary under his breath on the pursuit of people, taking pictures of him, and not living in the present moment. This happened sometimes with Gurudev when nobody had a cell phone. He ended the photo session by walking back to the car.

I was bubbling with happiness and contentment to be with Gurudev. Even while being serious, Gurudev felt like a beacon of positive energy. It didn't seem to matter where we were or what we were doing. I loved every possible moment of being near Gurudev and his calm, soothing energy.

Masters can give blessings in any number of ways. Just a simple look or a slight, brief touch can be enough to give a blast of energy. Some masters will hold a flower or a peacock feather and tap it on a person's head to transfer energy, which is known as *shaktipat*.

I have seen people ask that Gurudev bless a strand of beads. Gurudev only held the beads for a second or two, then gave them back. Any food touched by the master is considered as *prasad,* sacred, blessed, and energized. Even a light, quick flicker of a touch can transfer strong energy into food.

In the middle of the drive, the two cars were side by side as Gurudev held up a packet of cookies to get everyone's attention. He passed out cookies in the car that he sat in, then he rolled down his window and held a cookie out. The first cookie toss got blown back down the road between the cars due to the cars traveling at over fifty miles an hour.

Both cars kept slowing down to make it easy to toss a cookie from one car to the other. Finally, at roughly fifteen miles an hour, we had a successful toss. A cookie flew from his hand through the window into our car. With lots of laughter and smiles, the cars sped up to resume the drive.

We stopped at a gas station before driving the last leg of the trip to Pacific Grove. Gurudev was asking if they had Limca, a soft drink from India. I was standing beside him while he sat in the car with the door open. I was simply enjoying being near Gurudev. He kept looking at the soda pop vending machine. Michele was checking the choices. Gurudev seemed uncertain. Choices of soda were repeated, and Gurudev finally said that 7Up would be good.

I was wondering if he was going to drink the soda. The

entire time he was holding a vanilla cream sandwich cookie in his hand. A can of soda was handed to Gurudev. When he got the soda, he also held that in the other hand.

Wondering what Gurudev was up to, I was chuckling inwardly about the whole thing. Gurudev and I didn't say anything, just enjoying the moment. He sat, sometimes looking at his hands with the cookie and the drink, and sometimes just staring off. *What is he going to do with the soda and the cookie?* After a while, all the restroom trips were finished, and the cars were full of gas.

Gurudev turned to me. Holding out the cookie and the 7Up, one in each hand, he insisted, "Eat this and drink this." I just looked at him in disbelief and stood still, keeping my arms at my sides. I had not had a soda drink in many, many years. I had not had cookies in many months, and would not have considered a white flour, white sugar cookie as something to put in my mouth.

To break through my disdain, he repeated the instruction, "Eat this and drink this. Now. Finish it. All of it." His imperative broke through my reluctance.

Having been in his hands for more than five minutes, they were supercharged items. That fact made his instructions seem both more reasonable and beneficial. I would never have consumed those items on anyone else's suggestion. In a bit of a state of shock and wonder, I accepted the cookie and the drink.

As I sat in the car, I ate the entire cookie and drank the whole can of soda. A tide of giddiness crept over me.

About 20 minutes later, I started feeling strange. My stomach was cramping, and I felt a fever coming on. It hit me hard before we reached Pacific Grove. By the time we were at the house of a person who had donated rooms for followers to sleep in that night, I was too weak to even lift my luggage. It was embarrassing for me to have to ask for help carrying my bags. Usually, I was strong enough to carry my own bags, in spite of injuries.

Since Gurudev had asked me to record all of his talks, I brought recording equipment wherever I went with him. There was a talk scheduled for that evening. When I realized that I was too far gone, I felt sad that I would not be able to record. Let alone be present at the talk. Interacting with people felt impossible in my lousy condition. I was desperate to close my eyes and lie down.

In a large house that was in an area of town central to the community, the room where I stayed was on the basement level. Only one window would open in that room. The window was close to the ground outside. The air inside and out was quiet and still, which made it difficult to ventilate the stale, stuffy, and dusty room. I felt truly strange being there by myself. Knowing that Gurudev was somewhere with a crowd of people, not far away, it bothered me that I was not with him.

Opening the window all the way, I curled up on the bed. In hopes of getting fresh air, my head almost touched the screen. Outside the window, I saw lots of mossy growth in the enclosed garden. It seemed like an eternity before anyone came back from the public lecture. When I finally heard some voices, I did not recognize all of them.

F was to be my roommate. When he returned from the event, he immediately walked over, reached across me, and slammed the window shut. I was too weak to argue or explain my urgent need to breathe. I slowly opened the window again. In a flash, F was slamming it shut.

Maybe I can try leaving it closed for a while. After just a moment, the stale, stuffy air was making me feel dizzy. I started to choke. I had to have some air.

Gently, quietly, I opened the window only halfway. "Bam!" The window was closed again. I waited for a little and opened it just an inch. "Bam!" The closing was immediate. *Why would someone be mean to a sick person?*

The whole night was quite surreal. It occurred to me later that I must have mistreated some people, and therefore I was reaping the bad karma. It felt terrible to talk, but my need for air was strong. Weakly, I pleaded with F, "Please, let us have some air." He burst out, "No!"

I realized that I did not have the energy to fight or to continue that drama any more. I had to get some fresh air and sleep so I could recover. As a last resort, aching all over, I staggered out into the hallway and tried to find another place to sleep.

All I needed was a quiet spot with some air. I felt delirious and extremely weak. I had no idea of the layout of the house or who was there. In the dark, I slowly crept along in vaguely shadowed hallways. I wasn't sure where I went. I had no idea what the layout of the house was.

I didn't know who I would run into. Or if anyone else was awake. Then I heard a faint sound of voices, which guided me to some people who were surprised to see me. Since I was out of sorts, I was not communicating clearly at all. It felt like I had gone to some unknown place, like Alice in Wonderland. Barely able to talk, I unskillfully conveyed some portion of my dilemma. I was not sure of what I was saying or if my words were understood.

Feeling wobbly and dizzy, I was also unclear about how I ended up standing in the bedroom of the owner of the house. I waited while Michele informed the hostess of my request.

Our hostess didn't say much that I could understand at that moment. Later, I heard that she thought I was blaming her or complaining about her house. It was nothing like that at all. I was just desperate for undisturbed rest. I didn't feel able to attempt to explain to the owner of the house the bizarre, comedic drama of the window opening and F aggressively closing it, nor did I have the energy or clarity to do so. Another space was made available, and I passed out.

While I was helping to clean the kitchen the next morning, I attempted to express my gratitude for having a peaceful place to rest. When she ignored me, it became clear that the hostess wanted nothing further to do with me. I was puzzled and sad. I did not understand her cold shoulder. Wearing a big smile, his chest pushed up, F literally strutted through the kitchen. He babbled glib banter and was greeted with charm and grace.

As everyone left, the empty house seemed like an uncharted land from an ancient book. Silently, feeling rejected, sad, confused, and alone, I watched dirty water drain from one side of the sink. I finished washing the dishes.

When a group of us sat with Gurudev, Polly got upset with Michele for supposedly complaining about the house we had stayed in. Polly was making a big deal out of it, implying that possibly the hostess might make a big deal out of it. Polly was concerned about her own reputation and the reputation of Art of Living in the community. Michele had no fault, but blame was being thrown at her.

I was drained, spaced out, and unable to talk. I was flabbergasted. The true facts of the situation were ignored. Michele was upset. No mention was made of the basis of the situation being an attempt to help take care of a person who had not been feeling well. Michele had not complained she had simply asked if another space was available. In my fog of fatigue and recovery, I had no clarity or energy to say anything. In shock and dismay, I was mute.

Gurudev was a silent witness. Sitting at his feet, I felt like a useless, empty container. I was incapable of expressing truth, unable to speak. Gurudev sat, watching the happening, not speaking up to the women in front of us. He was letting the pile of karmas get rearranged.

What a strange scenario. An absurd nightmare. Briefly, I wished that I had a movie of the events to show people. To reveal what actually occurred. It struck me that I might not see the owner of that house for a long time, probably never. I would not have a chance to make amends for a misunderstanding. Wistfully, I felt defeated, caught in the grip of events far beyond my control.

When I was alone with Gurudev, I asked him about the illness. It seemed to me that the illness had happened in order to purge an old illness from which I had not completely recovered. I also sensed that two old, serious illnesses were coming out together. I was surprised and grateful.

I felt amazed and deeply blessed. The whole thing happened to help reduce karmic baggage. Only years later did I realize that it was also my karma to get mistreated, misunderstood, blamed, falsely accused, and have people turn against me. This had all been a perfect set-up to relieve some of those bad karmas. Years later I discovered that by putting awareness on a situation I could sense the karmic cause of that situation. Sometimes, in my mind, I see actual events that were the underlying cause of some issue.

During the days that we stayed in Pacific Grove, we would travel to nearby communities where Gurudev gave public lectures. This was when I recorded the following lectures given by Gurudev:

> *What is the Meaning of Life?*
> *You are the Blue Pearl.*
> *Somebody, Nobody, Everybody.* (Years later, this talk was put on CD and titled; *Two Steps to Enlightenment.*)

Casa de Maria Advanced Course

Starting the first week of July 1989, we had an Advanced Course at Casa de Maria in Santa Barbara. We had a week of silence at Casa de Maria, which had close to sixty people attending. There were people from different cities and states.

Most of the men slept in a poorly ventilated dormitory. The beds were upstairs, and the windows were locked shut. Fresh air only came up the stairway. Since there were at least twenty-five of us in that upper room, the use of a fan to move the air was critical. Several times I woke up hot and sweaty, feeling like I was choking, because someone had turned the fan off. Someone would sneak over and turn the fan off after most of us were asleep. That made it miserable for the rest of us.

The first morning, we met in our meeting room, preparing to do a long session of Sudarshan Kriya. Gurudev came in and was quiet for a while, looking around the room. He announced that we would not do the Long Sudarshan Kriya since there weren't enough windows.

People began begging and pleading. Someone suggested keeping the door open. Gurudev still did not agree. Another idea was to use fans to help move the air. Reluctantly, Gurudev agreed to do the long session of breathing, based on having multiple fans on and the door and all three windows open. Electric fans were bringing fresh air into one window and blowing stale air out another.

On that course, we did many sessions of meditating and observing the breath. Gurudev said that it was important that we sit still and not move during the meditations.

During one session, as I sat with my eyes closed, I suddenly felt a sharp pain in my lower back on the right side. It was like being stabbed with a hot piece of metal. My instinct was to shift my position to try to get rid of the pain.

Before I could actually move, Gurudev snapped out, "Don't move!"

My eyes popped open to see him looking right at me. I was surprised by how he had followed my thought process more rapidly than I could on my own. It was amazing that he could get that instruction out in time to prevent my moving.

During discussion time, Gurudev stated that there will be some people who do things that bother us. He contended that it is much more important to observe what is happening inside our own system than to try to correct the other person.

Gurudev told us to see everyone as his agent. Whatever the other people do, it is big mind working through them. The way he said it made it an instruction both for the course and also for life in general.

This sounded cute at the time and got some chuckles from the group. In my mind, I can still hear a small, distinctive piece of laughter that came from a person sitting behind me.

It is a healthy challenge to stop yourself from reacting. And to stay in the mindset that a much bigger reality is the cause of other people's actions. To accept this, one has to accept that the master is an embodiment of the supreme consciousness. The supreme consciousness effortlessly delivers karmas to every creature.

This goes along with Gurudev's idea of seeing people as rag dolls. Several times in 1989, he talked about understanding events as happenings. Such that people around us are just rag dolls being moved around by divine energy.

Gurudev asserted that complaints and criticism happen when we are unaware. A remark can just come out of a fact, but our inner, negative habits give rise to complaints.

He stated that we can thank people who are courageous

enough to criticize us. Revealing noble goals, he emphasized that if we can laugh easily after receiving complaints, then we have achieved something worthwhile.

Often, a master is able to perceive and address the inner tendencies of the students. This can be inspiring for some and intimidating for others.

He told the story of Shiva swallowing the poison that got stuck in his throat and turned his throat blue. Gurudev revealed that this is a beautiful story to illustrate that when we complain or show negative emotions, we should not let them go into our heart. If we take negativity into our heart, it can destroy us.

Gurudev pointed out that we want people to only say nice things about us, even if they don't feel that way.

With his distinctively fresh perspective, Gurudev expressed, "If someone appears to be against you, they are against themselves."

To appreciate this, one must look at it from a broad perspective. Looking at the law of cause and effect helps.

If someone is mean to you, that person is reducing your karma and creating karma for themselves. They then have to receive similar, cruel treatment at some point in the future.

Gurudev sweetly insisted that the purpose of words is to create silence. He encouraged us to be aware and see if our words are creating silence or agitation in ourselves or other people.

When we want to say something, we should see if the person can actually listen to us. Some people are too tense to listen to anything we wish to discuss. Some people only want to talk about themselves, and they won't be receptive to what we want to say.

Sounding reminiscent of advanced mathematics (Gödel's Incompleteness Theorem), Gurudev revealed, "No word can ever express the truth totally as it is." It seems to be rare for many people to actually see beyond the words.

Gurudev asserted that the more agitated a person is, the harder and louder the music they will listen to. The less stress we store inside, the more developed our consciousness is. Then, the more sensitive we will be to sound.

Gurudev encouraged us to go beyond words. He confirmed that it was possible to get into an ecstatic state by being silent.

"This silence is most precious."

"Silence is not just keeping the mouth shut and chattering in the mind. Silence is unification of the mind."

I did my utmost to keep strict silence. No matter how many frustrating circumstances popped up, I kept my mouth shut.

Exercising focused willpower, with the help of the master's grace, I uttered not a single word. This was a true, crucial breakthrough with important benefits. It's not a big thing to just speak a little less. It is much more challenging not to speak any words at all. Especially to not say anything at all for days at a time.

Anyone can try periods of silence on their own. You can do this responsibly when you have periods of alone time. Try it. Keep the phone, radio, TV and computer turned off and see how long you can go without listening or talking.

Obviously, a structured retreat setting helps enormously to make early attempts at silence successful.

Be patient with yourself. Most adults have learned that we are rewarded for speaking well. Not for keeping silent non-stop for several days in a row.

It is worth facing the challenge of keeping silent. Do it skillfully so you are not harming relationships by evading communication. No reading, writing, talking or listening. Do pranayama, yoga, and meditation. Walk in nature. Every hour of silence adds to your own, personal vitality.

Blast Away

Blast away

that outer covering,

the dry, restraining husk...

with the flood

of standing silent

in your blazing light.

This was a potent silence course.

It was on this course that I first heard Gurudev use the term "hollow and empty." The first few times he said it, it came out sounding like, "hollow and yempty." We did many meditations. We would breathe and observe that we were hollow and empty. The Casa de Maria silence course was also the first place that I heard Gurudev chant "*Asango Ham Punah Punaha*," which he often chants when leading Hollow and Empty meditations.

At the end of the course, Gurudev sat alone under a tree and met people one by one. Boldly, while looking into my eyes, he told me, "You kept good silence. I have seen!"

Pausing, he shifted his attention to gaze into a diffused distance. As if talking to a group of friends that I could not see. Gurudev then spoke more softly: "Daren kept very good silence." It was a significant achievement to be able to receive that praise from the master. I was deeply grateful for Gurudev's orchestration of that course.

Recording Bhajans

During that June 1989 visit, Gurudev asked me to make a collection of bhajans sung live in his presence. This ended up being one of the more externally challenging of his instructions. Getting a good live recording of bhajan singing during a satsang with the Guru present can be anything from a major feat to a magical miracle.

In nearly every satsang, someone would start a private conversation with another person when they were close to a microphone. While the chanting was happening. People will need to have a word with a friend, cough, bump into microphones, unplug cables, play tambourines right next to a microphone, change the volume of various inputs, (making some instruments and voices much louder than others) practice a different song in the middle of another, play out of rhythm, etc. All kinds of things happen to interfere with making a decent recording. Trying to have the giddy crowd be mindful for the sake of recording chanting was often hopeless.

I did notice that the bhajans sung while Gurudev was sitting with the group had a stronger effect than the bhajans sung when Gurudev was not there. I felt a subtle but definite difference in the energy. I made a point of editing only those chants sung with the master physically present in the room. Then I noticed how I felt more uplifted and refreshed by listening to the recordings of chanting with Gurudev present.

By that point in time, I had been experimenting with leading bhajans for several months. I had even composed a simple bhajan, which I sang during our final satsang at Casa de Maria. When I edited the recording of myself singing, I did not like the way my voice sounded. Discouraged, I judged myself and stopped leading that song.

The Guru Had Me Keep a Secret

Gurudev sometimes had me massage his feet. It was a secret. When the two of us had privacy, he sometimes would slip his feet out toward me and say, "You can work on the feet." Sometimes he would be focused on reading a letter written to him, and the feet would silently come out of hiding. Then he would just glance at his feet, indicating his request without words.

One day, the feet slipped out, and, after only a few minutes of massage, someone knocked on the bedroom door. His feet tucked back under his cloth so fast that I was left holding my hands in the air where his feet had been, like a cartoon. Gurudev had the person come in, and a long conversation began. I felt laughter bubble up; there was some humor in what the feet had secretly been up to.

One afternoon, Gurudev asked me to massage his back. I was eager and grateful to be given such a special opportunity. As I started working on Gurudev, my mind went into a state of expanded awareness. I was aware that I was having random thoughts. I noticed odd factors about the present moment. It struck me that Gurudev would feel all the details of any thought or feeling that I experienced. I felt shy. *What if I think of something embarrassing?* That settled a little after a while, yet I felt exposed in a hyper-aware state.

I focused more intently on the movement of my hands and what I was doing. I was still concerned that my mind seemed on the verge of randomizing. In an effort to achieve stillness inside, I made my breathing deeper and slower.

It felt like I was floating in a sea of Gurudev's energy. I wasn't sure how much I could handle. As soon as I had those thoughts, he stopped me and told me to go and meditate. Right away, I went into another room and sat with my eyes closed. I was not confident about my ability to meditate at that moment. I felt caught in the grip of a powerful process. The process worked like magic and I felt a sense of returning comfort and self-assurance. Meditation brought me back. I was relieved to feel like myself again.

The Karma of Received Instructions

It happens sometimes that someone thinks they know better than the master what to do and how to do it. This is generally a sign of arrogance, ego, and being out of touch. In 1991, during the Ashtavakra talks, Gurudev spoke about the phenomenon of a person wanting to be guru to the guru. Some people will not just offer advice but also insist that their ideas are better. They try to correct the guru. In the Bhakti Sutras, it is said that ignorance may be overlooked, but not arrogance. A serious trap for someone on a path is to be overly proud of what one thinks or has accomplished.

The enlightened master is connected to everything and is a living repository of pure consciousness. Any instruction from a true master is drawn from many possibilities including the most sattvic choices. The most advanced computer on the planet does not have anywhere near the expansive vision of the master. I'm talking about a fully enlightened master, not a partially developed wannabe. Anyone who goes around saying, "I'm a guru, I'm a master!" is not a real master.

Gurudev does not like to say "no" to anyone. When people ask questions, Gurudev will only tell them not to do something if it is seriously bad for them. Rather than say "no," Gurudev will suggest alternatives, or keep brushing aside the issue by saying something indefinite. For example, "We'll see." or "Ask me later." or "What else?" or "Don't you have some other commitments?" If you ask a question and Gurudev won't say "yes," it means you are definitely better off with a negative response to your question. If the master suggests something else, go with it.

Gurudev became concerned when some followers would ask for advice and not listen. Some would then turn around and do the opposite of what they were told.

Gurudev clarified that, if you ask for guidance and the master says to do something, it is very good karma to do what the master says to do. It is very bad karma not to do what the master said to do. After you ask for advice, it is extremely bad karma to do something that the master says not to do. Deep within, that was my sense before Gurudev articulated it.

Even after articulating the workings of karma with regard to seeking guidance, it was sad to see that some people would disregard the wisdom of the guru. Some would do whatever came to their mind.

There is an old saying that the person who does not have faith in the words of their guru cannot hope to have success or happiness in life, not even in a dream.

Often, Gurudev seems very relaxed and casual. Some people think they can do whatever random thing strikes their fancy and not take the guru seriously. It is worth paying utmost attention to the guru's guidance and following wisdom emanating from the living master.

People who do what Gurudev says not to do end up regretting it, or much worse. In 1991, at the Bangalore, India, ashram, several different groups from various countries came and went. We had four, ten-day-long silence courses back-to-back during the first two months that I was there. For each course, new groups from various countries showed up at the ashram, and others left.

Hardly any people from India were involved back then. It seemed like most of the people came from Europe. There was a young girl from some other country who was obviously anxious for attention. She was making eyes at many of the men. She charmed a certain European gentleman.

He went to Gurudev and said that they wanted to travel to Goa for a vacation. Gurudev instructed that they should stay at the ashram. But the couple was eager, and they left anyway. Quite some time later, word came back that the man had been robbed. His passport, airline tickets, and all his money were stolen. He tried to return to the ashram but was detained somewhere. Someone eventually brought him back to the ashram. Totally dejected and feeling ruined, he was in a serious mess. A tragic lesson. That man expressed that he deeply wished he had followed what Gurudev had guided.

Several years later, there was an incident in India in which someone died by not following Gurudev's instructions. Gurudev was making a tour of some cities, and there was a group of devotees traveling with him. One day Gurudev was scheduled to speak somewhere, and he told everyone to stay back and not accompany him. Several people were pushy and foolishly kept pleading to come with him to the talk.

After some long deliberation, Gurudev finally assented, reluctantly, with an instruction that everyone must sit in the cars in exactly the seating arrangement that he set up. They all agreed.

On the day of departure, Gurudev organized everyone exactly in each of several cars. Left side front, left side back, middle, right rear; the seating was exact and specific. The caravan set out. It was a long drive. Stops had to be made.

During one stop, some people got giggly and were joking around. Conversations started up. Some people sat in different seats, so the seating arrangement was mixed up.

They had an accident, and one of those people was killed. The other riders were shocked and upset. Some promised they would take this as a powerful lesson.

Gurudev gave me clear, specific instructions on how to administer the Sudarshan Kriya cassette tape recordings. He specified that there were to be "no exceptions" to his rules. Gurudev repeated the Sudarshan Kriya tape rules multiple times in front of multiple people. Gurudev dictated the Sudarshan Kriya tape contracts, with a small group of teachers witnessing.

The Sudarshan Kriya tapes were only to be given out to teachers that Gurudev had approved.

If some other teacher decided or heard that a person was eligible and relayed that information to me, I had to check with Gurudev before issuing the tape. If the master was sitting in a satsang and someone requested a tape, the master might say "keep hosting satsangs" or give another ambiguous answer. Some eager people, after hearing a response like, "Keep bringing people to courses" or "keep attending satsangs," would interpret that to mean that they should get a tape. I was supposed to check with Gurudev regarding all possible tape eligibilities.

Several times, people insisted that they were supposed to get a tape, even though it was not certain. Upon checking, the guru sometimes would say "no." Maybe they needed to do more silence courses. Sometimes a suggestion was given. Sometimes there was no suggestion, just a negative response.

Then it would be my job to convey the unwanted answer. Some people became angry with me. They blamed me and insisted that I had made a mistake. In a couple of noteworthy instances, people were angry with me for many years. Their anger lasted long after they finally got a tape that had real, complete approval from the master.

Never once did I give out a tape based on my own personal feelings about someone, friend or not. Regardless of whether a person loved me or hated me, I treated everyone equally with respect to Sudarshan Kriya tapes.

Gurudev insisted that if a Sudarshan Kriya tape broke, the person that tape had been checked out to would have to return the tape to me. I had to receive the old tape before I could send out a new tape.

One lady called me and told me that her tape had broken and she would like a new one. I consented, "Okay." Then I reiterated the instruction that I had to receive the old tape, before I could send a new tape. The lady insisted that her old tape was super special. Gurudev himself had personally handed the tape to her. I maintained that I understood, yet the master had given me strict instructions that I had to follow.

That lady blew up and yelled at me. Foul language burst out of the phone. Slowly, I lowered the receiver from my ear as the obscenities poured out. I hung up the phone. I was feeling surprised and disappointed at her nastiness.

Fortunately, I was detached at the same time.

A couple of days later, I received a call from a gentleman who was pleading her case. He asked me to reconsider. I explained that I couldn't do that as Gurudev had stated clearly that there were to be "no exceptions."

That man asked me to ask Gurudev about this case because it was unusual. I replied that that didn't seem respectful. It seemed to me to be insulting to the master to ask if it would be okay to do the opposite of what he had instructed. I did not want to insult Gurudev by asking if it would be okay to go against direct guidance. It was a repugnant idea. That man kept asking, over and over. Again and again, he maintained that it was a special situation. Finally, reluctantly, I agreed to check on it.

When I called Gurudev on the telephone and outlined the situation, without hesitation, he emphatically declared, "Why should she be the exception! Get the old tape back before you give her a new tape."

Unfortunately, this type of scenario, in which people expected to be the exception to the guru's rules, was repeated as time went on. When people made demands, diplomacy occasionally failed to give satisfaction, and people would sometimes be upset with me.

Some people got enthusiastic about throwing trash at my name and saying nasty things about me behind my back. I got to see a huge range of responses to my activities. After receiving a new tape, the few people who took the time to express gratitude clearly operated from a higher place.

A few years later, when I was alone with Gurudev, I mentioned that people would sometimes get confrontational with me. They would get nasty and insulting with me when I was clearly following his instructions. I said to Gurudev, "Sometimes it's very challenging to have the strictest job, to be the administrator of Sudarshan Kriya tapes."

Gently and sympathetically, he soothed in warm, rich tones, "I know." That kind moment was comforting and reassuring. It helped to know that I was understood. At the same time, it was obvious that it was appropriate and necessary for me to continue. I had to stay in that sattvic role of selfless service, known as *seva*. I needed the opportunity to lose more karma of being disliked and falsely accused.

Private Puja

A friend of mine received a meditation mantra from Gurudev. When I found out, I took my next private opportunity to ask Gurudev if he would give me a mantra. He agreed, and we arranged to perform a puja in his bedroom.

When Gurudev sat on my left to give me the mantra, I recognized the wisdom of the teacher sitting on the left side of the student.

A wise healer once told me that there is a subtle bio-circuit of energy coming into the body on the left side and going out on the right side of the body. Sensitives, who feel the moods and energies of other people, may sometimes be less affected by keeping other people on their right-hand side. The natural outward moving energy on the teacher's right side helps the student receive it via the natural incoming energy on the left side of the student.

Real yoga increases our awareness. Real yoga includes the awareness of both subtle energies and gross happenings. Real yoga expands our abilities to deal gracefully with a wide range of situations.

Chapter Nine: Guru Purnima 1989

A week-long silent retreat was planned for Guru Purnima in 1989. The rented facility, roughly two hours' drive outside Montreal, Canada, was in a place called Lennoxville. Gurudev's Basic Course and Advanced Course were happening concurrently. Both courses joined together for joyful evening satsangs.

I was lucky to have a dorm room in the same building that Gurudev was staying in. Not only that, I was close to the stairs that lead right down to Gurudev's room.

A musician from New York City, P, showed up because his friends had rushed to be there with Gurudev. P took his first Basic Course there.

One afternoon, I knocked on Gurudev's door. These were dark wooden doors with panels of glass. The glass was translucent. You could not clearly see through it. There would only be a shadow on the other side if someone stood close to the glass. When Gurudev answered "yes." I entered and found P sitting motionless with Gurudev.

After stealing a rapid, surreptitious glance at me, P studiously ignored me. Gurudev looked calm, confident, and serene as he stared into my eyes. Gurudev continued soothing P. The three of us were a frozen tableau. There were a few moments of deep peacefulness. None of us spoke a single word.

After standing there for a few seconds in the silence, I decided I ought to allow P to have his special moment in peace, so I left. My small mind was wondering. My big mind thought it was a good scene.

Each day was precious and magical. One day, during one of the sessions, Gurudev chanted Sanskrit verses from the Ashtavakra Gita. He didn't give any translation. In the middle of the chanting, one lady began sobbing.

Someone wrote a note saying that they felt some negativity, and they wondered whether it was from inside them or from somewhere outside. Gurudev answered that it doesn't matter; just let it go. He pointed out that we don't examine or take apart the garbage; we just throw it out.

On Advanced Courses, people noticed that Gurudev would have profound awareness of the people in the room. In the early years, if someone were missing from a meeting, Gurudev would send another person to bring the missing person back to the meeting. This happened at the Lennoxville Guru Purnima course in 1989.

There were questions about whether certain behaviors, such as sitting on silk or only wearing white clothes, are necessary to get enlightened. Gurudev expressed that imitation is present in many cultures, but that imitating outer actions is childish. How much centeredness and unconditional love are in a person is what is important.

It is not possible to judge an enlightened person based on their outer behavior. Perfection is in consciousness, in the big mind, in the being.

Understanding God

Many people have limited concepts of God and small ways of thinking about God. Surprising some people, Gurudev said that we can have God as our friend.

Gurudev revealed that the junction of presence and the present moment is God. "God is the totality. Everything is in God. Nothing can be outside of God."

All types of life are manifestations of one divinity.

He maintained that everything, whether seen as good or evil, exists inside God. "God is omnipresent, so God is in both the wicked and the wonderful."

It is important to look deeply and see beyond emotions and people's garbage thoughts.

"Ego is harshness. Ego is hard."

When you try to dissolve it, your ego is still there. *Doership* is thinking that your actions are the cause of events. Doership is a sign of ego. The master cautioned that "doership is evil." By getting soaked in presence and the present moment, ego dissolves. Gurudev stated that "I" is a big bother. Following the path, we can lose the "me, me, me, give me, I want, I, I, I" orientation and get a taste of eternity. Wise people must be careful to avoid falling into the trap of the ego trip of thinking that they are great.

Most people are caught up in duality. Gurudev taught that silence gives us a taste of a lack of duality.

Silence can happen when your mind is not stuck thinking about the past or future. Silence promotes presence and the expansion of awareness.

Pushing our minds into awareness, Gurudev declared, "You can never meet God. When you meet God, you disappear. In your true, real nature, you are God. That is the ultimate goal of all life."

If you trust yourself, then it is easier to trust the master. Gurudev maintained that if we have difficulty trusting ourselves, then it helps just to focus on the master.

Everything is in the big mind, including all of our future possibilities.

"The big mind is in the tree. The big mind is everywhere. The big mind is total."

"Things that you don't know will come to you. Knowledge comes spontaneously. Getting into your big mind, all knowledge is spontaneous."

Gurudev noted that with this silence course, we were just taking a small step. However, he said it is worth congratulating ourselves for taking this important step.

One of the key points of the Lennoxville course was the understanding of "That is it!". When something happens, that is it; it is whatever it is. Some glass thing fell and broke; that is it. Nothing you say or do will go back and save the object of glass from being broken. Okay, finished. Move forward. Whatever mess is there, clean it up, drop it out of your mind, and move forward. Things can be as they are without a label of good or bad.

He told us that innocence is seeing the present as it is without coloring it with an impression or opinion of the past. When you forgive, it means that you think that something is wrong. By repeating "That is it!" there is no valuation of right or wrong.

Something happened in the past. If your mind keeps going back and chewing on it over and over, you are wasting your life energy. Embracing "That is it!" frees the mind and brings you to a place of innocence.

The past is gone and cannot be changed. When we look, we can see that the past is just a dream. "Past is past; throw it out. Life is a game. Don't take it so seriously."

"That is it!" means experiencing without having an emotional reaction or judgment. People's minds often spit out judgments when they see certain things.

Gurudev claimed that our efforts to laugh and smile have been making us miserable. He told us that we just needed to relax. "Life itself is an expression of joy. Everything is being done by the big mind."

Gurudev encouraged us to accept and relax. He told us that we can live knowing that everything already belongs to the divine. Real yoga helps us break free of judgements.

The future has not yet happened. The past and future

are not now. Awareness gets pulled away from the present moment by both the future and the past. For most people, the mind oscillates between the past and the future.

Right now, it is possible to be centered and happy. We can allow ourselves to be simple and alert. "That is it!" is being with what is happening now with relaxed awareness.

With different groups in various settings, Gurudev has asked, "What is happening now?" When the group was not in silence, people would throw out random answers. Gurudev would keep asking the same question until there were longer and longer moments of silence. This is a provocative technique in public, and especially so on a silence course.

In Lennoxville, Gurudev would ask, over and over, "What's happening now?" When some people started answering, Gurudev reminded us that we were supposed to be keeping silent. Some people made little noises as comments. Again, Gurudev told us to keep silent.

"What's happening now?" The question activated awareness. You could feel the focus in the room becoming more vibrant. Alertness would increase. Most everyone would be sitting quietly in their seat, in a state of wonder. After the course, I noticed that my mind was quieter and more present in the moment.

He told us that our silence could not be a failure. It doesn't matter whether we thought we had a good experience or a bad experience. Regardless of experiences going up and down, something deep and substantial happened in silence.

Gurudev taught us to say "So what!" if something happened that we didn't like or if we kept thinking about it.

On that course and others, he revealed that the highest does not come to us from our effort. Gurudev taught that the greatest comes through prayerfulness. Gratitude turns into prayer. Prayer is being in the moment, being total.

Some of the food prep and most of the cooking for our meals had to happen in a parking lot, as there were problems with the kitchen. One time I watched as a large pot was cooking on a portable gas burner in the parking lot. A young girl approached the pot with a clear glass measuring cup full of a white substance. She had to stand on her tiptoes to dump the cup into the pot. I was not sure whether it was sugar or salt; neither alternative seemed appealing. Perhaps it was a type of flour.

With us on the course was Dr. Varma, an elderly Indian doctor. Dr. Varma did an "Anthropometric Analysis," whereby he would take many precise measurements of distances between body parts, such as the distance from the top of the ear to the tip of the nose and the distance from the ear lobe to the outside edge of the eyeball. After compiling a chart of these measurements, he would then give a reading with some suggestions for the person. After he had taken Gurudev's measurements, he got down on the floor and bowed down at Gurudev's feet for several minutes.

Dr. Varma claimed that he had some good "spinal cord exercises." Gurudev instructed me to learn them from Dr. Varma. These "spinal cord exercises" were a type of massage whereby the person receiving the treatment would lie on their back. The person giving the treatment would reach around the recipient's torso and hold both index fingers right next to the spine to elevate the torso slightly off the ground. This would stretch the muscles and give some decompression to the space between the vertebra.

Moving slowly, Dr. Varma briefly gave a minimalistic demonstration of the technique. It felt good. Suddenly, his habitually sedate pace vanished as his movement accelerated. He quickly whipped off his shirt, eagerly laid on his back, and asked me to practice on him. After a few minutes, he had a big smile on his face. He asked me to repeat the sequence. As simple as the technique was, it was quite time-consuming. It took some strength and ended up being a strain on my back. I was glad that Gurudev preferred a different style of massage.

One afternoon, when just the two of us were in his room, Gurudev played a cassette recording of some chanting. I heard the word *"upanayanam"* in the recording and mentioned it to Gurudev. His reply, concerning that particular text of chanting, was, "Everything is in there."

The Guru Blasted Them with Anger

The morning of the last day of the course, I had the thought that I would like to see Gurudev in his room. I wanted to visit before the flurry of departures consumed everyone. My room was on the upper floor of the dormitory building. Gurudev's room was a corner room, directly downstairs, at the convergence of two hallways.

After rapidly packing my things, I rushed downstairs. *Nobody else in sight. How lucky!* I knocked on the door.

Opening the door with a look that implied he was expecting me, Gurudev invited me in and said, "Come." Gracefully conducting me in, he walked over to a big chair in the corner and sat down. He motioned for me to sit a couple of feet to his left, beside him. I was surprised that he had gestured for me to sit next to his chair, along the wall. Usually, people visiting him would sit on the floor.

It was blissfully peaceful for a short while. Often, being in the presence of the master has a timeless quality.

You could be anywhere; it wouldn't matter. All that matters is that you are sitting with the master. We were just grinning, leaning back, and hanging out with each other. Enjoying the peaceful silence together.

A knock came on the door. Smiling, Gurudev casually, with a welcoming tone, called out, "Yes." Two ladies came in: Tanya with a woman on her right. Tanya spoke, "She can't find her bag."

Becoming serious, Gurudev seemed less relaxed than he had been before they came. He advised, "If you look, I'm sure you will find it. Okay." He was already adopting the tone of voice he uses to conclude a meeting.

"But. She can't find her bag," urged Tanya, full of concern. Gurudev was annoyed. To Tanya, he snapped, "She may fool you, but she can't fool me!" To the other lady, he exploded, "What do you take me for?! Why are you wasting my time? Why do you do these stupid things just to get attention??! Get out!"

Softly, quietly, Tanya began to object. "But."

Like a thunderbolt, he stood and roared a powerful command, "Go Now!!" Stunned, I was impressed by Gurudev's potent anger.

Sometimes people will remain sitting, even after being asked to leave, in order to milk out a last precious moment. When the master stands, it is important to stand with him in order to catch the upward movement of prana. Unless he instructs that you remain seated.

That morning, the potency of the anger of the guru blasted those women. The shocked ladies popped up from their seats, eyes stretched wide. They were not enjoying having the anger of the divine directed their way. The energy bounced me quickly into standing as well.

As the ladies scurried to the exit, Gurudev glanced at me. With a motion of his head, he indicated the front door.

Frowning, he muttered, "Lock the door." As he walked into his bedroom, I locked the front door.

There were some other people gathered in the hallway. Knocking at the door started up instantly. Mindful of the mood of the master, I quietly walked to his bedroom door and peeked in. Pausing, I wasn't sure if I should go in.

He had calmed down. He gave a soft, closing comment on the pair of ladies, "What people do to get attention," while shaking his head. Emotions pass rapidly with real yoga.

It seemed easy to be in the "That is it!" frame of mind while I was in the good graces of the master.

Often, the master will be smooth, patient, and calm with people. I have noticed that he limits the amount of time that people spend in his presence. Sometimes he will get fed up and put his foot down. Maybe he was giving me a little extra time in his presence to give me a boost and help me be more prepared for unexpected events later that day.

Gesturing around the room at things spread over the floor, he observed, "The suitcase has to be packed." I felt lucky that I had run downstairs when inspiration came to me. I was lucky that I managed to get in before the drama with the ladies about a missing bag that was not truly missing.

As we packed the bags, knocking on the front door happened repeatedly. As knocking continued, Gurudev surreptitiously tried to peek out into the hall through a crack in a window covering.

"Should I answer it?" I asked him several times. For a while, Gurudev was just silent. Eventually he shook his head, indicating "no," and we continued packing.

There were a lot of things to fit in the small bag and suitcase. A few odds and ends had to be left behind. They looked mostly like things people had given after Gurudev's arrival in Canada, like packages of snack items, candles, etc.

Gurudev asked me to carry the suitcase for him. We

opened the door to the hallway to find a large group of people.

One lady was upset and planted herself right in front of Gurudev. She confronted Gurudev with anger: "You locked us out. We wanted to see you."

Smiling, Gurudev replied softly, "Ah, later." The upset lady blocked Gurudev's way and persisted in disbelief, "Couldn't you hear we were knocking on the door?" She drilled Gurudev with an angry glare.

Gurudev gave everyone a big smile and glided slightly to the side of the angry woman. He started walking, and the crowd parted as he walked down the hallway.

That same lady turned to me with rage and gave me a dirty look. As if addressing a filthy criminal, she blasted me, "Why did you get to be in there with him??! I have important things to discuss with him! Didn't you hear us knocking?!"

Her anger made her face red. She was squinting so hard that her eyes were nothing but tiny slits. She was so angry that her whole body was trembling like a rapid earthquake.

Focusing her stress on me, she planted herself in front of me to block my way. Everyone else followed Gurudev. Suddenly we were alone.

Surprised by this vehement outburst, I calmly explained, "It wasn't my choice. He asked me to lock the door." My mind wanted to make a comment, but I wouldn't let it. I wanted to stay in my "That is it!" zone.

It wasn't the first time that I had seen someone think that their needs were more important than the needs of the guru.

Holding my breath, I slipped past as her complaints continued behind my back. I started down the hallway, trying to catch up to the group that had vanished. As I walked down the hallway with Gurudev's suitcase, someone briskly came walking toward me. "Is that Gurudev's suitcase?"

"It needs to be put into the car. Can I have the suitcase, please?"

After handing over the suitcase, I quickly ran upstairs to get my own luggage. "That is it!" still prevailed in my mentality. Feeling a bubble of excitement and wonder, I joined the group in the parking lot.

A caravan of five cars and a motorcycle was leaving the course. The plan was to take Gurudev and others to the airport. Gurudev was in the lead car. Once we got onto the main road, someone pointed out that a lady was on the back of the motorcycle. With the wind whipping her hair, tilting forward, and as if holding on for dear life, she did not look comfortable on the motorcycle.

Surprise Adventure in a Foreign Country

We stopped somewhere in Montreal. A vacant office space was being considered as a potential center for teaching and holding satsangs. It was a perfect opportunity to get Gurudev's opinion on the space.

Misty thought she remembered that there was a store close by that had fresh juice. She asked if anyone was interested in getting a juice. Most of the people wanted to stay close to Gurudev. At that point, my tummy was typically empty. I was happy to go along to get something. Misty asked Gurudev if he would like some juice. He smiled and declined. All the luggage was left in the cars while the group went across the street to view the office. Simultaneously, the search for juice began.

It was supposed to be a five-minute walk. After ten

minutes of nonstop, brisk walking, we still had not found any sign of fresh juice. We realized we ought to get back to the car to meet the others. Even though we walked with rapid briskness to get back, we found that all the vehicles in the caravan had left. No word, no note. Certainly, none of us had cell phones or email!

We were stranded. I was dumbfounded. It seemed unbelievable and crazy. Several people knew about the search for juice. How could they just leave with people missing from cars?? It did not occur to me to say, "So what!"

My vacant stomach was now feeling like it was falling towards my legs. My mind was reeling. Being empty-handed and abandoned in a foreign country was a new experience for me. *What to do now?*

I wish I had not gone for juice. Realizing that with that thought I was not centered in the moment, no longer in "That is it!" mode, I felt even more deflated.

Misty suggested calling other devotees to see if one could be found who had not yet left home to go to the airport. At a payphone, she called the number of some person living in Montreal. It rang with no answer.

We ended up moping mournfully in silence under a tree in a small park. I was not able to get into a "That is it!" mental state. I felt numb and in shock. Time stretched on slowly. I didn't know what to think. Uncertainty prevailed.

Magically, the gentleman who had been on the motorcycle as part of the caravan turned a corner. He was by himself, slowly driving past the park. Jumping up, waving arms, and yelling, we got his attention. He stopped, and we ran over to him. He offered, "You can come to my apartment."

I still hoped to get to the airport to say goodbye to Gurudev. The thought of not saying goodbye was bugging me. After being abandoned in what was, for me, a strange city, I was feeling dejected and droopy.

At the apartment, Misty got on the phone and managed to catch hold of some other local person, but that person was not going to the airport.

Upon sitting, I felt like I was shrinking down to a lumpy blob. In a bubble of inspiration, I had the idea to call the airport and have them page Gurudev to have him answer the phone. Making the call, I asked the airlines to page passenger Ravi Shankar to have him take my phone call. After a few minutes, they said that nobody had responded.

After waiting a little longer, I called again. With the second call, they successfully found the mischievous master.

"Did you enjoy your ice cream???!" Gurudev asked me as he got on the phone. He was laughing. I was speechless. I had not eaten any ice cream in many years. It was confusing. *Why is he talking about ice cream?*

"I don't eat ice cream. We went to get juice."

In a loud voice, he asked again, "Did you enjoy your ice cream?!" By now, Gurudev was laughing hysterically. In that moment, I was baffled. My mind was blown. There was still some wistfulness about not getting to be at the airport with Gurudev. I felt my alertness increasing.

"You had some ice cream! Jai Guru Dev!!" Gurudev happily insisted with enthusiastic finality as he abruptly hung up the phone. Startled, still holding the phone, I felt some calming of the feelings of rejection happening within.

My mind had truly been blown into a real state of wonder by the unusual phone conversation. It was an odd juxtaposition. I felt the residue of rejection and dejection, which was being flushed away with intense alertness and a tingling sense of wonder. I had no convenient descriptive label to put on that experience. In an unusual way, I felt cared for by the master.

Looking back makes it easy to see the grace operating

through the experience. The abandonment experience had not lasted a long time. A safe space was provided where I had been able to use the telephone. The call to the airport had actually gone through, and I had spoken with Gurudev himself. Some odd karma of being forgotten and abandoned had been worked off in a relatively easy way.

A missing link in that adventure was how I ended up getting reconnected with my luggage. The luggage was in a random car. By that point, I had no idea what type of car it was or who the driver was. Miraculously, the luggage and I ended up together at the airport. I had my luggage when I took the flight home. Probably both residual shock and the expanded state of wonder helped to keep it all blurry.

Have you noticed how your mind wants to label things? Have you seen how people usually feel more comfortable putting things into categories? Real yoga is beyond labels. With real yoga, there is great value in digesting all of our experiences. Then we are better able to be present in the moment without judgments, expectations, or hang-ups distorting reality. It takes practice. It is worth it.

Real yoga is experience and more. Words are used in an attempt to describe. It feels like home. It looks like a rainbow. It smells like roses. It tastes like cardamom. Real yoga is ultimately beyond words. Look for deep knowingness inside yourself, beyond influence from senses, habits, social norms, preferences, attitudes, or beliefs.

A master is quite adept at being able to gauge exactly how intense an experience a person can handle. I guess he thought I was strong enough. To deal with an experience that I would rather have avoided. The experience definitely helped me to be stronger and more centered. Real yoga enables not freaking out, digesting the input, and then completely washing away any residual upset or feelings. In spite of the chaos, I still felt that I was on a noble path.

Choose One Noble Path

One noble path

leads us

to the truth.

And the truth is

all encompassing.

One noble path,

if you are brave enough.

One noble path,

if you have the strength

to accept the fullness.

Miraculous Rescue

One of the dramatic ways in which Gurudev saved my life happened in the summer of 1989. I decided to go camping on an island off the coast of California. I chose the more remote dock as the landing for the boat trip. I wanted to get far away from well-traveled pathways.

The goal was to avoid people and be isolated in nature as much as possible. Instead of following a path, I forged across rough fields. It looked like going straight up the steep hill to reach the top of the bluffs would be a lot faster than following the meandering fire road.

About halfway up the hill, I realized that I would fall off the hill if I leaned back at all. If I even stood up straight, the weight of my backpack would pull me backward off the hill. That hill was probably the steepest I had ever climbed with a heavy pack. The whole time, I had to hunch forward, so I was essentially climbing up on my hands and feet. At the top, there was a lovely view. With an old barbed wire fence to protect the endless rows of spiny cacti.

Finding a flat, clear space to set up the tent required walking around a large section of rusty barbed wire and cactus. After dodging a lot of cactus thorns, it was looking quite hopeless. The area that was not eroded into deep, narrow, tiny canyons was covered with cactus. After walking onward and searching, a flat space large enough to allow a tent finally became visible. There was some space between the cacti to allow a narrow passage to reach the flat space.

By the time the tent was set up, I sadly realized that daylight would not last much longer. I was sweaty, and the dust and grit felt itchy. The ocean below the bluffs looked much cleaner than any of the beaches along the Southern California coast. The inviting water was incredibly clear. Details of rocks and fish underwater could easily be seen.

It was irresistible. I climbed down and rinsed off in the tide pools, quickly getting cold as the light just started to fade with the sunset. It was deeply refreshing. The need to get back to the tent before dark was growing.

I turned around and was astonished by how sheer the

cliff was. I couldn't see how I had scrambled down in the first place. There was no discernible trail. It was a vertical chalk cliff. I wondered how to get back up.

A family of goats perched motionless at the top, staring down. The baby goat looked puzzled, apparently asking its parents something about the unusual human predicament unfolding below. Goats understand vertical cliffs.

Having no equipment or other recourse, I began to climb the chalk face. I had to use my feet and hands to make my way. Every other foot or hand hold would give way and break off. I was moving carefully and changing grips rapidly, but only making slow, upward progress.

At different times, the master has noted that when a person feels helpless, they can turn that into worry, tension, etc. Or they can turn that helplessness into prayer.

When I was about half way to the rocks above the chalk, both hands and both feet suddenly lost grip. I began to fall.

Gurudev, help me!!! The thought was immediate.

My fall abruptly stopped without anything visible supporting me! My mind was suspended in wonder as my body was suspended in space. In less time than a blink, I decided not to look down or question my experience in any way.

Resolute in embracing the miracle of safety, I had no iota of doubt that might cause me to fall. I was being held up by invisible hands. I scrambled as fast as I could to reach solid dirt. It was a huge relief to reach the top.

Wind Takes Me

Wind takes me.

Wind carries me…

yet…

I am the wind.

You are the wind.

We are swooping across the terrain!

Magnificent!

Powerful!

Sweet and delicate,

Wind moves through all.

Wind moves through everything.

It is only a current of the Consciousness.

Each river is the One!

Blessings

When you have a remote control, you can pause the movie you are watching and go get some water. Do whatever you need to do. As long as you are within a certain short distance and aim the remote at your device, you can control the device.

With the development of consciousness, a connectedness with nature develops. To such an extent that it is as if one has some type of remote control which can enlist the assistance of natural forces to help. This is noticeable with enlightened masters. Many times, people have witnessed miracles around Gurudev.

The master does not need a physical remote control to aim at the sky, yet the sky will respond. Sometimes when Gurudev visits hot, dry areas, clouds have gathered in the sky. Rain might fall to relieve the heat and dryness. Some would say it was due to the grace of the master. Whether the master even thought about it, wanted it, or the rain just happened due to darshan or an abundance of prana is sometimes a mystery.

Nature aligns itself with the intentions of the enlightened, whether intentions are expressed outwardly or not. The physical presence of an enlightened being brings harmony to the surrounding environment. Many people feel more relaxed and happier, for example, after attending an event with Gurudev.

Seekers, followers, and devotees have experienced some development of their own personal 'remote control devices,' you could say. Especially when they intend for some positive event or circumstance and they see some results of their intention happen. The phenomenon of giving or sending blessings is one example.

Gurudev can think about someone and tune in to that person easily. He can know what is going on with them, regardless of where that person is physically located on the planet. Blessings can be sent from a person in one country to a person in another country. Nothing will pose a barrier to the blessings. Space, distance, buildings, or location will not block blessings. How is this possible?

Ayurveda talks about the five elements of nature: earth, water, fire, air, and space. These are user-friendly reference points, sort of a condensed version of the science of matter.

Air and space are subtle. If you hold some air in your hands, can you guess how many molecules of oxygen, nitrogen, carbon dioxide, etc. are contained therein? If you have some experience with chemistry and physics, you could make an educated guess based on the average composition of air in a certain location and the relative amounts of various components per 100 ml. The experience of internal knowingness that there are, for example, 20 ml of O_2, 10 ml of CO_2, 60 ml of nitrogen, 8 ml of H_2O vapor, so much sulfur dioxide, methane, etc., contained in a sample is not possible for even an expert person. Accurate quantitative perception requires special equipment.

We understand that air is there. Air is important to us because we breathe it, and from that air, we get the oxygen our bodies need.

Known as *akasha,* space is even more subtle than air. There are different kinds of akasha: the physical space that we inhabit, the psychological space of our mind and thoughts, and the infinite space of consciousness. As people progress, it is easier for them to understand these distinctions. For thousands of years, advanced seers, sometimes called *rishis,* understood the nuances of space.

Consciousness is more subtle than physical space.

Many wise masters have stated that everything,

including the entire universe, is contained within pure consciousness. This is a very advanced understanding.

You can see in many books on yoga or Ayurveda that the word 'ether' is used instead of space. Ether was a theoretical construct invented as the proposed substance filling the universe to explain the perception of the transmission of light at different speeds. Before it was proven that the speed of light is constant, it was thought that light travels at variable speeds. In order to explain the possibility of the perception that light could travel at variable speeds, ether was postulated as a slightly elastic substance filling our universe.

We know, of course, that the speed of light is constant. Thus, the theory of the imaginary substance known as ether can be relegated to the trash heap of time.

Unfortunately, some believers in ether were quite adamant that we should no longer use the word 'space.' They thought there was no space; the universe must be filled with a subtle substance called ether, quite like helium in a giant balloon. Some people from Britain in the 1800's and even sometimes during the early 1900's, did their best to eradicate the use of the word 'space' in schools and publications.

This partially correlates with the general effort of foreigners to stamp out the ancient culture and history of India. Unfortunately, some were persistently successful in turning Indians against their own true heritage. Many Indians came to look down on yoga and ayurveda during British rule, as well as during the years of India's independence from British rule.

We can restore truth, talk about space, and eliminate the use of the word 'ether'. Let's break free of fake-scientific, antiquated, colonial, and anti-indigenous sentiments, wherever we can. Space is a reality; the falsehood of 'ether' stems from flawed thinking. The concept of ether lacks both truth and depth of consciousness.

Many people in multiple countries recognize the importance of keeping alive the wisdom of yoga and ayurveda. Gurudev has sponsored a multitude of projects in many countries to promote yoga and ayurveda.

There are a few versions of the ancient text *Yoga Vasishtha* that Gurudev will sometimes have groups of people read out loud. *Yoga Vasishtha* says the same thing that many masters have said. Everything is made up of consciousness and exists within pure consciousness.

Consciousness is more subtle than any element, including space. Real yoga helps us to perceive this.

Whether this is your personal experience or not, it may make sense that communication through consciousness can be instantaneous. This is why a blessing can be sent by Gurudev from one part of the world to a person in another country. That person in the other country may feel the effect of the blessing right away.

When people from another country need help, it is possible to bless them, even if you have never met them. Sending a blessing or effecting a change via the use of mantras can happen because consciousness connects everything. The entire universe is inside consciousness, the formless divine. Some people spend their entire lives dedicated to pursuing the ability to have direct experience of this reality. Real yoga promotes this advanced experience.

If someone asks permission to give a blessing, they are making themselves the doer. This is not correct. Blessing is a happening via surrender, not doership. Divine grace is the doer, not the person offering blessings.

Gurudev has contributed an abundance of knowledge and techniques to help people of all ages to connect with pure consciousness, the big mind, aka the one true self. Regular use of such techniques promotes blessing abilities.

Sankalpa

The greater the infusion of pure consciousness, the more you will be in contact with the big mind. As explained by Gurudev, when a seeker progresses on a path and is carrying more of the value of pure consciousness within them, their thoughts become more powerful.

Intentions are *sankalpa*, and the fruit of sankalpa ripens in response to the presence of sattva (purity or harmony), satya (truth), and divine shakti (energy). Thus, it is important to say what you want in positive terms and avoid describing things in negative terms. This is basic to real yoga.

The more a person embodies pure consciousness, the more divine energy will be carried in their actions, words, and whole system. In a positive way, the forces of nature will respond more to such a person. The words of a master have the potency and power to create what they describe.

For many people, not all desires are good. When you have a desire and it does not get fulfilled, that often feels bad. Assuming that the desire is of a positive nature, lack of fulfillment may be a sign of bad karma, lower consciousness, or poor timing. When it takes a while, but the desire is fulfilled after waiting for some time, that is fortunate. When a desire is fulfilled right after it is expressed, that is very fortunate. But most fortunate are those whose desires are fulfilled before they are even aware of having the desire. That is a sign of real yoga. It requires high consciousness and good karma upholding life-supportive desires.

Samadhi makes a person more sensitive and aware. Clearly stated by Gurudev, "When you become sensitive, the world and nature become sensitive to you."

When *vrittis*, the activities of the mind, are well managed, this will happen more. This is real yoga. This underscores Rishi Patanjali's first definition of real yoga in the *Yoga Sutras*. The five vrittis are proof, wrong knowledge, fantasy or imagination, memory, and sleep. When the vrittis are transcended, then you can see things as they actually are. Not through a filter of comparison (memory), likes or dislikes, or any other distortion.

Gurudev bluntly explained that most people are not able to be truthful or objective in their thoughts due to aversions (dislikes) and cravings (likes). Patanjali listed likes and dislikes as types of misery. Removal of misery is an important purpose of real yoga.

Ancient wisdom says that it is important to speak the positive truth, the sweet truth. By speaking positive words, not only do you uplift people around you, but you also create positive energy. Positive outcomes become more likely. Sensitive people will notice this.

For example, suppose you try to tell someone something and they are not paying attention. Especially within families or intimate groups, you may have heard someone say, out of frustration, "You never listen to me!" This actually promotes the person not listening to you, especially if you have some power of speech.

We are better off saying things in a positive way, such as, "I like it when you listen to me." You can even go as far as saying, "You are such a good listener!" Which then might bless the person to be a better listener.

Our Gurudev does this every day. He will say to people, "You are looking so bright!" or "You look very fresh." or "You are getting so strong." or "You are doing so well!" and "You are much better now."

There was a person who had told me multiple times, "You are so weird." After that, I actually did feel more weirdness in my life. There was a period of time when I found out that that same person was watching TV and movies on a frequent, regular, daily basis.

Gurudev gave a talk, during which somebody asked about cursing and blessing. Gurudev explained that cursing and blessing are two sides of the same coin. As you go further on the path, your power of speech develops. This is why many scriptures say to speak the truth, and speak only the sweet truth.

Still addressing the entire audience, Gurudev then looked right at the frequent TV viewer and declared, "When you watch TV and movies every day, you burn your prana down. When you watch TV and movies a lot, you lose your power of speech."

I felt some relief knowing that their words would have less and less ability to affect me.

The power of speech or potency of sankalpa, as well as intuition, can be developed. First, by doing spiritual practices on a regular, consistent basis. Also, by promoting *satya,* truth, and sattva, purity and harmony in daily life.

Masters have said that the means to success gather around sattva. It is important to make positive choices based on wisdom, not whimsical desires. Repeatedly, Gurudev has asserted, "When you follow fun, misery follows you. When you follow knowledge, fun follows you."

Chapter Ten: Airport Tricks

A living master is skilled at helping people get past their stuck emotions, limited thinking, and unconscious habits. Often, people insist that things be done in a certain way. Limited, narrow thinking is bound to get shaken, challenged, stretched, and stirred when a living master comes into your life. Without this dynamic, devotion to a master from history is less challenging. It feels cozy and safe to many people.

Gurudev moves gracefully, with barely perceptible effort. His being is dominated by fullness and sincerity, brimming over with kindness, caring, contentment, and peacefulness. Yet many people, in a group around a master, will find themselves challenged in different ways, about different issues, during the same span of time.

Once, when Gurudev came back to California, he gave further proof of being a master of unpredictability. I went to meet him at LAX airport in Los Angeles. I had parked my car in short-term parking at the airport. It was a treat to be in the baggage claim area as Gurudev entered. Various people there to meet him were milling about, greeting, and chatting. John and Jeff huddled together, having a private meeting as they were moving toward the conveyor belt, to be ready to look for luggage once the conveyor turned on.

Gurudev was standing next to me, and I followed beside him as he veered away from the conveyor and took a few steps towards the door. He had a far-away look in his eyes as he gazed out the windows. Wondering what he saw, I started to look out the windows. Abruptly, my focus came back to Gurudev when his head tilted towards me. Then, in a minimalistic voice, whispering so nobody else could hear, he asked, "You have your car? Your car is here?"

I replied, "Yes."

Softly, "Can you get it?"

In disbelief, I asked, "You mean go and get it right now?" He replied, "Yes." Then he urged me, "Don't tell anybody."

I thought that was strange, since the luggage had not even started to come out. As I walked in a state of wonder, I then figured that he probably wanted me to help out by putting suitcases in the car. Then I felt a little silly, like maybe the right thing would have been to have the car ready and waiting to load bags into it. However, the police will tow unattended vehicles. Airport police unhesitatingly ask you to leave if you are not actively loading or unloading.

Gurudev's request not to tell anybody didn't make sense to me. Regardless, it is always best to do what the master says. I went and brought my car around to the curb outside the baggage claim. I figured that if the bags were not yet coming out, I could just get out of the car and look busy by randomly moving around the car, opening and closing doors, to possibly delay any police disapproval.

As I drove up to the curb, Gurudev was standing further up the sidewalk with Michele. The two of them looked like they were engaged in a deep, serious conversation. They were intently focused on each other. I felt that I should not do anything to disturb them. Everybody else was inside the baggage claim area.

As I stopped the car, they both casually strolled along the sidewalk, vaguely in the direction of the car, while gesturing to accent points and keeping their conversation going. I turned off the engine. Before I could get out of the car, abruptly, they both put on a burst of speed and quickly jumped, through separate doors, into the car.

I laughed at this new sport, and then I sat there for a second, looking at Gurudev. I figured he would ask me to go grab a suitcase, so I had already unbuckled my seatbelt. I was enjoying looking into his bright eyes, which were opened wide above a big smile. The smile abruptly shifted to serious concern as he saw me remaining relaxed just looking at him. I hadn't caught on to his game.

Impatiently, he raised his voice as he looked at me with urgency. "Go! Go!"

My brain was processing for a fraction of a second. But Gurudev did not think I was responding fast enough.

"Drive!! Quickly now!" He commanded as he sat next to me, looking me in the eyes.

My mouth was hanging open. I was shocked by the unexpected rushing out of the airport. Quickly, I buckled up and drove off. My mind was in a state of wonder. Gurudev had me drive all the way to Santa Barbara.

First Camp Whittier Advanced Course

Camp Whittier was a run-down summer camp facility. It was located just north of Santa Barbara, on the east side of the mountains. We rented it for the silent, residential Advanced Course, in November of 1989.

There was a large building that we used as our group meeting hall. On one side, in the rear of that building, was a hallway with a few bedrooms spaced along the hallway. Gurudev stayed in the end room furthest from the meeting hall. A number of people had rooms off of this hallway.

Poison oak grows easily along the coastal zones of California. Poison oak was all over the hillsides of the area around the course. A momentary, faint touch of this plant is all that is necessary to create a severely itchy skin rash. This was brought up in the meeting by several people in the hopes that everyone would steer clear of the poison oak.

Gurudev claimed that this was actually a good sign. He claimed that nectar would flow in the midst of poison.

Then Gurudev told the story of gods and demons churning the ocean of milk. He explained that this is symbolic of how our lives get churned by the opposites. It is said that when poison comes first, nectar will follow.

If you are attached to orderliness, you will be put with people who are disorderly. If you are used to being disorderly, you will be subjected to orderliness. This dynamic is often a fundamental component of every silence course when Gurudev is there in person. Even if nobody verbalizes it. I have heard Gurudev discuss this a number of times, with a big smile on his face.

Chaos vs. orderliness is easier to observe when you can relax and approach it with awareness.

On the day we were planning to do a long session of SKY breathing, I was walking down the hallway in hopes of catching a moment with Gurudev in his room. In front of me was a lady who was carrying her portable cassette player.

At that moment, I did not know that inside her player was a recording of the long Sudarshan Kriya. I did not know that I was about to witness the beginning of some chaos.

She stopped walking right in front of me. She muttered to herself, "Have to be sure." As I walked past her, I watched her hold the player up in the air in front of herself. Then I saw her firmly and deliberately push the buttons on her tape deck. She didn't realize that she was pushing the record button. I kept walking. From behind me, I heard her blurt out, "Oops!" because she became aware that she had pressed record. Then I heard her stop the recording.

Later that day, we ended up using that same cassette to lead the long session. It became a surreal moment for me. In the midst of Gurudev's voice calling out the rhythm from the recording, there was a sudden click and silence, then, "Oops!" The same "Oops!" which I had heard a short while earlier.

My eyes popped open for a second, wondering why "Oops!" was being broadcast over the sound system. Nobody else seemed to notice. Realizing the cause of the unique phenomenon, I quickly closed my eyes.

Besides the lady who had said, "Oops!" I was probably the only person in the room who knew what had happened. Probably most people in the room did not even notice. Most of us in the room had taken courses in which Gurudev would lead the long SKY breath meditation on his own, without using a tape.

Over the years, we tried on several occasions to record a better-quality version of the Long Kriya. Every time, it would end up getting ruined by some person or other who just had to make loud noises for that particular session.

On that Camp Whittier course, I felt droopy and inadequate. I felt bogged down by my own shortcomings.

My yearning to become more like Gurudev felt like an ache for something incredibly far out of reach. At those moments, I imagined that I was like a wild bear in a forest. Gurudev's graceful qualities were present every moment, and they seemed like a dream of perfection.

I wrote a note about this and put it in the question basket beside Gurudev's chair. He surprised me by reading it out loud to the group. Without looking at me, he gave his response, "No, no, no, don't think that. You already have these qualities." His kindness was soothing and inspiring.

Real yoga enables us to develop positive qualities in a natural process of accelerated evolution. This is my experience, and it can be yours also.

Answering Questions

Often, people are amazed by huge quantities of wisdom that comes forth easily from Gurudev. Without any strain, he can answer questions on many different subjects. On the other hand, he will not answer every single question that is asked. Once in a while, he will smile or frown as the only acknowledgement of a question.

It is a phenomenon worth witnessing to see Gurudev ignore a question. Usually, when Gurudev ignores a question, there is not a flinch, quiver, or a speck of an indication of avoidance. It is as if the question simply does not exist. Many times, I have seen him calmly ignore a question without any perceptible change in his bearing.

Many people have found Gurudev's voice to be soothing. On the one hand, Gurudev can be bold, dynamic, and seriously emphatic about making a point. On the other hand, sometimes Gurudev's voice is so soft and soothing that his voice alone brings relaxation and starts to alter one's state of awareness.

It has also happened that he will admonish people for asking stupid questions. One lady, in 1988-1990, used to ask whatever random, irrelevant, or trivial question popped into her mind. Things like, "Does it matter what time of day I comb my hair?" or "Why does that person wear clothes like that?" or "How do I know I really did something?" or "Am I really tired?"

I was in a car with the two of them when Gurudev got fed up with it. He got stern and told her that any question she wanted to ask, she should first repeat it to herself ten times, silently. And only then, if it was a worthy question, should she ask it out loud. Gurudev made it clear that answering all of a person's questions is not the purpose of a master.

Many times, people have asked about dreams. Often, the response is that dreams are not worth holding on to. Dreams are like soap bubbles. Interpreting dreams can reinforce an impression of the stress that was released by the dream.

One time, a lady asked about dreams, and Gurudev revealed something that stood out. Gurudev taught that if we see all the past as a dream, it helps to reduce karmas. By seeing life as a dream, we become more alert and aware of the present moment.

Disneyland

After the November 1989 Silent Advanced Course at Camp Whittier, we went back to Los Angeles. Right around the time that Gurudev was arriving in Los Angeles, someone brought up the idea of taking him to Disneyland. Some people were excited about this idea. The idea of taking a saint to Disneyland seemed disrespectful to me. Inside myself, I did not want to go, but I did not want to miss out on spending time with him if he actually ended up going. The prospect of Gurudev being taken to Disneyland seemed oddly paradoxical to me.

Without me saying anything, Gurudev resolved my dilemma nicely by agreeing to go with everyone else to Disneyland while instructing me to stay back at the house on Ashwood with his sister, Bhanu. He told me to make a recording of Bhanu chanting that we could sell copies of.

Bhanu's First Vocal Album

Bhanu and I happily stayed back at the house. Many of the people I knew would have made some comment about how sad they were to be missing Disneyland. Bhanu did not make a single remark or indicate any feeling of missing out on Disneyland in any way, which raised my respect for her.

At first, she was a little cool toward me, since we had not spoken much to each other before that. But when she saw that I was focused on preparing for recording without wasting time, she relaxed. She could tell I was being respectful. We were both happy to be following an instruction from the master.

While I set up my minimal equipment, Bhanu thought about the songs that she wanted to include. We sat down and got right into it. An energy of serene repose seemed to fill both of us and the house. Many of the songs that Bhanu sang were new to me at that moment.

It was quiet for recording purposes. Nobody else was in the house. We recorded Bhanu's first album with no accompaniment. Almost every song was good on the first take. Bhanu and I did not say much to each other. It was pleasantly easy for us to get into a smooth, working rhythm.

Bhanu explained the meanings of some of the things she sang, which made the experience all the richer. There was a poem, which she shared and sang, that I ended up thinking about many times since then. The repeating verse sounded to me like *Guru Deva dayakaraa deena janeh*. Written by Vivekananda to his master, it is a plea from the devotee asking the guru to be merciful.

Devotion is an inner treasure. Devotion is something that, like the underground root system of a tree, grows quietly deep within a person. Real devotion is not seen in showing off. Gurudev would talk about how some people put on a big smile in front of him, put hands together in prayer position, and say a big "Jai Guru Dev!" Then those same people turn around, get mad at the person behind them, and give a tough, nasty look. Real masters are not fooled by salesmanship. Hypocrisy catches their attention.

As I sat with Bhanu, recording her singing, her devotion was revealed to me. Like a beautiful rainbow that is seen unexpectedly. I could feel the devotion behind Bhanu's actions. I was humbled, inspired, and encouraged all at once. I was humbled by the depth. Inspired because she was authentic, simple, and natural. I was encouraged, because instinctively I knew that Gurudev could rely on Bhanu and that she would do a lot of good service.

Choosing a Cook

As time went on, more people would offer to cook for Gurudev. Usually, Gurudev was quite selective about who would cook for him. Whatever energies prevailed in the cook while the food was being prepared would easily be felt by Gurudev when he ate the food.

One time, he mentioned that he had gotten a headache from eating something that a certain lady had cooked when she was angry. Sometime after the fact, when the issue was brought up with that lady, she denied that she had been upset. Gurudev chuckled and rejected her denial.

Gurudev revealed that several other women had asked to cook for him. He seemed amused by it. When one lady in question was not around, Gurudev thought out loud that she would only be fit to cook for him after spending a year at the Bangalore, India, ashram.

Make Rasayana with Gurudev at 2 AM

More people showed up for Gurudev's late 1989 visit. The evening satsangs at the house on Ashwood Ave. would attract a well-packed room of people. Days were busier with meetings than during previous visits. More people wanted private meetings. It was not likely we would close up the house at an early hour.

One of Gurudev's two suitcases had bags of powdered herbs. Several times after he arrived at the house, he enthused, "We will make some *rasayana*!" In Ayurveda, rasayana is a single substance or compound of multiple antioxidant and protective herbs that rejuvenates the body and mind. Rasayana has anti-aging and immune benefits.

Some plants, such as *amalaki*, Emblica officinalis, are considered rasayana on their own. I was fascinated. Each time he said "Rasayana," I would get more eager. The idea of mixing herbal recipes with a guru seemed superlatively fun to me. Between meetings, lectures, and satsangs, after a couple of days, it appeared that the plan had evaporated.

One night I was dragging with fatigue, and Gurudev perked me up at around 10:20 p.m. by saying that we could make the rasayana that night. Time seemed to crawl by as one person after another just had to ask a question. Around midnight, I noticed that the chitchat gave no indication of ending. I didn't want to interrupt. It seemed that Gurudev wanted privacy for making rasayana. I figured that he would know the ideal timing and the ideal procedure.

Around 1:00 in the morning, I figured that we would just have to wait for another night. I was discouraged. Gurudev was scheduled to leave soon. *What if the herb event didn't happen?* I set up my sleeping bag and turned off some lights. I was waiting for the last cluster of conversations to end. Sleep seemed very appealing.

The last person finally walked to the front door after 1:30 a.m. I locked it behind them. I made a last stop in the bathroom. I was fading out. Ready for sleep. I went to say goodnight to Gurudev and make sure any final requests were met.

Gurudev seemed as bright and alert as ever. Effortlessly, he instantly stood up with a burst of enthusiasm. He said, "Let's make the rasayana now!"

This was an activity that was inherently fascinating to me. I urgently wanted to do it. My fatigue made it seem like a dream. My mind thought that important events like this should be done during the day. I felt like a vague semblance of a person.

Gurudev was bubbling with enthusiasm. "Let's bring everything to the kitchen!" He led the way, and I followed.

We gently heated some ingredients and carefully mixed them together while chanting OM namah shivaya.

OM namah shivaya
OM namah shivaya
OM namah shivaya
OM namah shivaya
Shivaya namah OM
Shivaya namah OM
Shivaya namah OM
OM namah shivaya.

After additional stirring with the flame turned off, Gurudev instructed me to take a spoon and taste it. I got a spoon and put a small, 1/4 teaspoon-sized blob on it. Gurudev encouraged, "Come on, take a bigger bite! Have enough so you can feel the effect on the consciousness!"

Sure enough, a larger bite gave me a feeling of inner warmth. A glow traveled into my head. I felt calm, clear, and settled. There was a wave of freshness and clarity.

Shortly after that, we exited the kitchen. Going to bed, I fell into a deep, peaceful sleep.

Gurudev had brought a large quantity of amalaki powder in plastic bottles in his suitcase. Amalaki is well known in Ayurveda as an adaptogenic, dosha-balancing, and anti-aging herb. Amalaki is one of the world's best sources of vitamin C. Amalaki is often called amla. We used a large amount to make the rasayana blend.

During the time that he was staying at the house on Ashwood, I would now and then see Gurudev helping himself to a spoonful of the amla.

Perhaps the day after the rasayana was made, I was alone with Gurudev at some point. He was again taking some amla.

Gurudev was staring at me the entire time while he chewed and swallowed the amla and while washing it down with a swig of water. I wondered why he was staring at me.

After Gurudev finished, he handed me the bottle of amla. Gurudev told me I should take it every day. Then he turned around and bent down toward his suitcase. He came up holding yet another bottle of amla. Then he quietly dropped the second bottle into my hand. I was surprised and elated in response to this blessing. I felt lucky to be taken care of.

Run on the Beach with Gurudev

One night, a group of roughly twenty people were gathered in the living room of the house on Ashwood. Someone brought up the idea of going for a walk on the beach. Other people were opposed. Many in the group thought it would be nice to go for a walk in the coolness at the beach. The weather was warm. One of the closest beaches was actually one of the nicest of the beaches within many miles.

Some in the group were up for whatever Gurudev wanted. Others didn't want to go to the beach at night and wanted to stay put. Gurudev wondered how we would all get down to the beach. It was clear that we would need several cars. There was some discussion about parking. The big public lot near where we intended to go charged a high set fee no matter when you arrived. We were also concerned that the lot might be closed. We decided to take a chance with parking along the street near the beach. The general idea was to follow each other and try to park close to each other. Gurudev said, "Okay."

Once we had arrived at the street on which we were planning to park, we discovered that there were only a few parking spaces available. Unfortunately, some people had to park many blocks away.

A handful of us walked out on the sand with Gurudev. We got close to the water. More people came running up at scattered intervals. Keeping silent, Gurudev abruptly sat down on the dry sand. There was a lot of laughter. A few different conversations were quietly in ebb and flow.

It was a cloudy night. Once we had walked onto the sand, away from the condominiums, there were no lights.

Silently, without any warning, Gurudev jumped up and started running along the shore. It was astonishing how rapidly he went from sitting to full speed, leaving people in varying degrees of distraction, bewilderment, or obliviousness. Right behind him, I jumped up and ran as fast as I could on the dry sand. Gurudev's speed was phenomenal. We disappeared into the gray mist.

Everyone else was still sitting, just beginning to notice or wonder what was going on. Some people apparently thought that our little saint had abruptly become invisible. I was determined to stick with Gurudev, no matter what. After a minute, he stopped running. The two of us walked slowly and silently, side-by-side.

Various people, catching up with Gurudev over the next few minutes, asked, "Why were you running?"

"Was he running?"

"Why was he running?"

"What happened?"

"Did he go somewhere?"

"What did I miss?"

Gurudev just smiled and ignored all the questions coming from different directions.

Sadly, it looked like only a bit over half of the people who had been at the house on Ashwood actually made it to the beach. I felt lucky that I got to be a part of the adventure.

Enjoy Something You Don't Like

Whenever Gurudev came to the house on Ashwood, he stayed in the nicer, back bedroom. When Bhanu, his sister, was traveling with him, she would stay in the front bedroom. I slept in the living room on the floor.

Each evening had its own timing and flavors. It was quite variable as to which guests would show up and when Gurudev would finish.

After all the visitors were gone and Gurudev had given his final goodnight, I would double check that the front door was locked. Then I could set up my sleeping place on the floor. Some nights I would get to bed at midnight, some nights at 2 a.m. Every morning, I would be up at 6 a.m. On Tuesday and Thursday mornings, I would rush to meet a personal training yoga client at 6:30 a.m. Towards the end of the week, I would be more tired and find myself speaking less to conserve energy.

During one of his lectures, Gurudev asserted that someone could say something to you that you don't like, and it would be possible to enjoy it. This seemed like a lofty, distant goal. It seemed like situations were set up by divine timing to give people opportunities to rise toward enjoying things they didn't like.

Often, Gurudev is able to defuse explosive situations with minimal words. One instance happened during one of his visits to Mar Vista.

Once in a while, one person or another used to assume that it was legitimate to hang out anytime at the house that Gurudev was staying in. One night, Gurudev had already retired, and there were still a few people lingering in the living room.

I checked the kitchen and made sure the lights were off. Everything was ready to be completely finished for the night. Except that the people in the living room didn't seem to get the hint that it was time to go. Even after all the lights were turned off. Even the quick contrast of having all the lights in the room go dark did not stop the remaining conversations.

I then turned on the porch light to help motivate people

to leave. At 1:00 a.m., I opened the front door a little wider and stepped back to let people leave. Nobody seemed to notice. The gossip continued. Gently and politely, I spoke to them in a whisper. I asked them to please take their conversations outside since Gurudev had closed up for the night. I was keeping my voice gentle and quiet to avoid disturbing the women in the front room who had already gone to bed.

Mr. Push had a big grin on his face. He was talking to a pretty girl wearing a short, black skirt and a black leather jacket with metal studs. As soon as I had made my request, he jerked away from the woman and stepped right in front of me. He abruptly got angry and yelled at my face, "We were talking about the course!"

I was surprised, and my ears hurt from his outburst. Apparently, the girl was also shocked. She ran out as fast as possible and was never seen again. Mr. Push ignored her. I didn't say a word and stood there passively, watching.

"I'm not leaving!" shouted Push, as I stood there looking at him and not saying anything.

The other people quietly and quickly slipped out into the dark stillness of the night, eager to get away from the explosive Mr. Push.

In a state of peaceful acceptance, I was also exhausted. I didn't have much energy to respond. Feeling blank, like a bystander watching the ripples of someone else's illusion, I wondered how to respond to this crazy drama.

"I want to talk to Gurudev! I'm not leaving till I talk to him!"

It was obvious that he did not care that Gurudev had already said goodnight. The loud outburst was clearly inappropriate. Insisting on talking to the master was, at that point, selfish and disrespectful. Not wishing to fight and feeling empty in silence, I turned away. I walked to the back bedroom, and gently knocked on the door.

From within, Gurudev responded, "Aah, what is it?"

I opened the door. "He wants to talk to you."

Gurudev nodded yes. I went in, and Push followed. We all sat on the floor near the bedroom door.

We looked at Push. Gurudev seemed resigned about having to speak to him. "What is it?"

"I'm angry."

"You are angry."

"Yeah, I'm angry."

We sat for a moment in silence.

"It is late. You should go and rest." That was it. That was all that was needed to turn the situation around and bring some peace.

Push got up and avoided me as he made brisk, stomping steps to leave. Just that brief moment with Gurudev was enough to reduce the tension in the situation.

Gurudev told me to rest. I locked the front door, and unrolled my bedding right there in the living room. I fell asleep almost instantly as I zipped up my sleeping bag.

Close Call

One day I ended up riding as a passenger to the venue for one of Gurudev's talks. It was with a person that I had just met. This fellow was new to the Art of Living. He was talking nonstop. It was just the two of us in his car. I was in the passenger seat. We were heading in the direction of the small Santa Monica airport on a two-lane street. That man was animated as he spoke at length about his experiences.

I noticed that the light in front of us had turned red, yet the driver was not slowing down. We were already exceeding the speed limit by several miles per hour. I looked at him, looked at the red light, and looked back at him.

I asked, "Are you going to slow down?"

He kept talking as if I had not said anything.

I could see that, within a matter of seconds, we would pass the point at which he would be able to stop outside the intersection. Since he had not reduced his speed, I started repeating myself, "It's a red light; you should slow down and stop. It's a red light; please slow down and stop."

He kept ignoring me and was enjoying his own discourse. *He's not slowing down! He is about to drive through the red light!*

I did not want to be in a car crash. I yelled forcefully, "**Stop the car! NOW**!!!"

Luckily, he responded immediately. With squealing tires, and a murky cloud of smoke from burning rubber, we stopped with the front half of the car in the intersection. His only comment was, "Boy, you would make a good gym coach!"

I was grateful to be safe. Briefly, I wondered about the karma of the situation. I was glad that I did not feel angry about the situation after it was over. Though I did think it was best to avoid riding with that person in the future.

The driver had been telling me about how he had been at work, on a type of job that he had done many times. He was walking down the middle of an aisle when he hit his head. His hat got knocked off his head by an overhead cross beam. He was glad that his head was not badly hurt, yet he was still surprised that his hat got knocked off his head. He said repeatedly that that had never happened to him before.

Gurudev was giving a public lecture just a couple of hours later. Someone asked about karma and the effect of spiritual practices on karma. Gurudev explained that some karmas can be reduced. This is one of many benefits of real yoga. He gave the example of the karma to be shot in the head, but instead your hat just gets knocked off your head.

As Gurudev spoke of this dramatic, life-saving type of reduction of karma, he looked directly at the driver of the car that I had been in. The man who had been wondering about his hat getting knocked off of his head received an explanation in the lecture. The explanation amazed him.

I figured that I must have lost some karma because of that man. By virtue of being in his car when it nearly went through an intersection during a red light.

Snack for One Is a Meal for Another

One morning, as I was getting ready to leave early to meet one of my clients, I fixed myself a small snack before leaving. I cut a banana in half and ate it with a date and a couple of soaked almonds. I thought that it would be nice if I were to leave a little something for Gurudev to enjoy.

For Gurudev, I put a date and three soaked and peeled almonds on a plate, along with half a banana. Later I was told that Gurudev had looked at the plate and said, "Oh, such heavy food!" I was surprised because it seemed minimal to me. Impressively, Gurudev ate it all.

Never Hate Anybody

Gurudev Sri Sri said many times that when you hate someone, you become like them. Unknowingly, people absorb the qualities of whomever they hate. It is important, for your own sake, not to hate anybody or anything. You can avoid someone without hating them. It is possible to be free of hatred while working to promote good and reduce bad.

You Are Not Your Emotions

The public talks given by Gurudev in Santa Monica in the fall of 1989 were rich with a ripe harvest of wisdom. For some, it felt like a continuation of the Advanced Course. The concerns of newcomers were also skillfully addressed.

Gurudev compared emotions to types of music. He said, "Life is based on rhythm. Creation is based on rhythm." He said that rhythm is the basis for our mind and emotions.

Gurudev told us that we are the experiencers, not the emotions. He asserted that we are actually making the music that is our life. In music and in life, it is best not to get stuck on one note.

People are often taught not to feel certain things or not to allow certain emotions. Gurudev pointed out that the more we try not to feel a certain thing, the more it will come.

One way to master this is to direct all emotions toward one thing. For example, be angry at the divine. We can direct all emotions toward divinity, or the master himself.

Lots of people have experienced that their rhythms get

off track due to stress. Many times, I have heard Gurudev say that the Sudarshan Kriya, SKY breath meditation, resets our natural rhythms. When we eliminate the blocks and stresses in our system, we feel contentment more easily.

Contentment is foundational in yoga. Contentment is both a practice and a result of real yoga. Gurudev made some eye-opening observations about contentment.

"A few moments of contentment can destroy the sorrow of a million years."

"A few moments of contentment can dry up the ocean of sorrow."

"That mind which is contented ... becomes wise."

Someone asked about forgiveness. Gurudev's response was, "Forgiveness comes from ignorance."

You are making yourself bigger and the other person smaller when you say that you forgive someone. An enlightened being would not limit you that way. Enlightened beings see all people as divine.

Gurudev explained that, from a divine perspective, everything that happens has a place. We can learn something from everything that happens.

When people say that something was a mistake, they mean that it should not have happened. Gurudev commented, "Love knows no mistake; it simply looks to the purpose of every event."

"Love is recognition of divinity."

At that time, it was challenging to hear Gurudev say that everything that we experience contributes to our growth.

"Forgiveness is simply a model to remove guilt." People caught up in duality will feel guilty about making mistakes.

Gurudev told us that, in general, people of our era are more sensitive than they were 1000 years ago. He asserted that we can get rid of guilt "by knowing, 'I am nobody, I am the pure consciousness, I am joy.'"

On many different occasions, Gurudev has insisted that the joy of getting something is a childish joy. It is important that people learn to give, starting as early as possible.

"Get, get, get. What will you do with it?!"

"What did you give? How many things have you given away?"

"What is my contribution? Every day, every week, every month, every year!"

Desperately in Need of a Nap

The days were quite full during the week. Through the quiet mornings, I would move efficiently. I would do my asanas, pranayama, kriya, meditation, and breakfast before the phone started ringing or people started arriving. People came and went throughout the day. We would have a public talk in the evening at another location and rush home to have a more intimate satsang. In November of 1989, more people were showing up at the house. There might be thirty-five to forty-five people gathered at night.

When Gurudev arrived before the advanced course, he brought a suitcase full of incense sticks. The incense had been made according to his own recipe. The intense, memorable fragrance was unique and, in my experience, never duplicated. It became known to some as "Punditji Gold." (Gurudev was known as Punditji at that time.)

I purchased plastic tubing and a heat sealer. We set up an incense packing assembly line in the living room. A few people from different cities had shown up for Gurudev's visit, and some of them helped with the packing of the incense. The incense sold rapidly.

After being back from the course for several days, by Thursday morning I was running low on sleep.

Gurudev and Bhanu needed to have some paperwork processed for their visas. The Los Angeles branch of the Indian Consulate office, which I drove them to that day, no longer exists. We had to park some distance away and walk.

We were extremely lucky to have the consulate office to ourselves. Amazingly, the processing did not take much time. Especially compared to the current lengthy processing times. Meanwhile, during the driving, walking to the office, processing of visas, walking back to the car, and driving home, quite a large crew of people was assembling at the house on Ashwood.

It was actually the day of Judy and Chris Reed's wedding. The wedding was scheduled to take place later that afternoon and evening. By the time we got back to the house, every available space seemed to have people engaged in various activities. People on the front lawn were sorting deliveries of flowers and food. Flower arrangements were being constructed behind the front gate outside the kitchen. The living room had clusters of people making plans in between buckets of flowers. Piles of fancy garments were stacked on the floor. Food was being cooked in the kitchen. Ladies were trying on garments in the front bedroom. Gurudev started making phone calls and meeting people privately in his room.

I was overwhelmed with fatigue and hunger. The kitchen was packed to the brim with various stages of food prep, and there was no way I could make a snack right then.

Finding a corner for a nap seemed like a great idea. I wandered around and found hallways and doorways full of movement and clusters of people all over. Near despair, I realized there was only one area with a little empty space and relative quiet without cross traffic. The back yard, behind the kitchen. I slipped outside, hoping that I would not be noticed by anyone.

Wanting to hide myself from prying eyes, I took an old, yellow blanket and covered myself entirely. Including my face. There I was, lying quietly on the lawn. Foolishly convincing myself that I would be overlooked by all. I imagined I would finally be able to drift off to sleep.

Out of the blue, there was a voice in my left ear: "The phone is ringing."

Keeping still and not responding, I hoped silence might earn silence in return. No such luck.

"The phone is ringing."

Note how bizarre it was to be assailed by a random voice while lying wrapped like a mummy. And being asked to answer the phone. This was happening when the house was full of people. Many of whom were simply hanging out with no specific task to do. *Any sane person would grab a pen and paper and do what was needed, wouldn't they?*

"Then you can answer it and take a message," I said. It seemed like elementary logic; why would I have to spell it out?

The presence was gone, and I resumed settling down.

"It's for you." They were back.

This was truly frustrating. *How did my hiding spot get compromised?* I was still resolutely wrapped head to toe. I was an incognito yellow mummy.

I pretended that my voice might not give me away. "How do you know it's for me?"

"Well, they asked for Daren."

The thought came that perhaps someone was determined to stop me from taking a nap.

Buying time and seeing what would happen, I stalled. "How do you know that I'm Daren?"

"The phone is for you."

"I'm not available. Take a message." Thank goodness the person left. Earnestly, I resumed settling down. But not for long.

The presence was back. "They don't want to leave a message. They want to talk to you."

Emphatically, I spoke strongly: "I'm not available! Have them call back, or I can call them back! Leave me alone!"

"It's difficult for them to call back because they are in Germany."

Surrendering to the inevitability of conflicting needs, I got up to answer the phone.

Wedding for Chris and Judy Reed

The wedding was to begin with a guru puja. Gurudev had told me that, since I was the man of the house hosting the wedding, I should perform the puja. I was glad to be involved in a sacred way. Sometime in the early part of mid-afternoon, I was dressed and ready in the front living room.

Sometimes, when Gurudev wants to motivate someone who is reluctant to leave his room, he will ask them to look for someone else who is far away. Or give the person an assignment that takes plenty of time. Carlton came bustling out of Gurudev's room, saying, "Gurudev asked me to get the puja started."

It was clear that it was not anywhere close to the time

to begin the wedding. Most people weren't in the room, or even near being ready to start. This was one of those times when the master had given an assignment in order to have one less person in his private space.

Michael, Chris, and I were just sitting quietly in the front living room. None of us responded to Carlton.

Carlton kept the ball rolling by turning to Chris and briskly asking, "What kind of flowers would you like for your puja, Chris? Long-stemmed roses?" It happened that a vase with a dozen red roses was sitting right there.

"Well." Chris drawled, typically letting the moment flow onward. Chris glanced around. There were a large number of different types of flowers around the room to choose from.

"Roses are nice; do you like roses?" Carlton continued urging.

"Sure, roses are alright." Chris agreed. Chris was still lounging and relaxing, acting like we were talking about something that would be happening far away in the future.

Abruptly brisk again, Carlton snapped up the agreement and grabbed the roses, while saying, "Let's use the roses then."

Carlton handed flowers to Chris and Michael. He had one rose in his right hand and several in his left hand, clearly ready to start doing the puja immediately.

The rest of us were surprised by Carlton's anxiousness to begin. Chris said, "Shouldn't we get some more people in here first?" Michael's voice chimed in, "Why don't we tell everybody before we start?"

Carlton said "okay" as he took up his position, standing, ready to start, directly in front of the puja set. It was abundantly clear that the urgency spilling off of him was from his determination to be the one performing the puja.

Ordinarily, I would have spoken up and reminded him

that I was supposed to be the person performing the puja. I would not have put up with being bulldozed out of my proper place. Without my intention, I found myself in a peaceful, floating space of silent acceptance and witnessing.

I noticed that Carlton had not even bothered to trim the stems on the roses. Long stems on the flowers get in the way of puja performance. Long stems can create awkwardness and close calls. Long stems easily knock things over. Perhaps he was afraid that if he left his spot, I would step into my rightful place and stay there.

Remaining in the starting position, Carlton did not budge. We waited for the group to drop what they were doing and gather in the living room. Feeling an odd mixture of resignation, distaste, detachment, and peacefulness, I simply stood, observing without speaking.

Perhaps twelve or thirteen minutes later, we had a roomful of people. Flowers were passed around to make sure everyone had one. Most of us were poised to start. At the last moment, someone in the group noticed that I did not have a flower, and she handed a flower to me.

Carlton and I stood side by side to sing the puja. A large, ornately framed picture of Brahmananda Saraswati was in front of us.

It took a while for me to get up after the puja was finished. In spite of the awkward, surprising circumstances, I was in a silent, deep state. Time seemed meaningless for a while. I was surrendering to the moment and centering myself. With my mind inward, I gathered myself to get up. By the time I was able to stand up, everyone else had moved on to doing other things. Most of the group had left the room.

In contrast to a strong sense of detachment, there was also a lingering pinch of feeling rejected. It was a slap in the face to have been bulldozed out of my puja responsibilities. The turning inward and taste of rejection combined with a feeling of keeping silence. After the puja, I just wanted to be in silence. Nobody seemed to notice or care.

The crowd had dispersed to finish the final touches on flower arrangements and get dressed. Most people left the house to go somewhere else. I was confused since I was not aware of what nearby house or apartment that group of people might have gone to.

A request was made that I cook chapatis that had been rolled out but not cooked. As I was walking out of the living room, I heard Michael behind me telling someone that he didn't like the way that Carlton "took over the puja."

My intellect told me that I had been treated with disrespect, and therefore I should be upset. On the other hand, I recognized that it was valuable to not have gotten upset. Quietly going with the flow felt inevitable.

By that time, I had not fully assimilated the wisdom that when someone treats a person with disrespect, that someone is taking away some bad karma from the person who is being poorly treated. If you blow up and are rude back to the other person who mistreats you, then you are harvesting back the bad karma that they took from you.

Intellectual understanding is one thing; it is quite another to get to a state of calmly responding instead of reacting. That day, it seemed like a state of real detachment had been imposed on me. It gave me a chance to learn by doing as I went through the motions. Mainly, I was in a state of wonder and confusion, feeling alone while in a group.

The kitchen was empty as I stood in front of the stove, heating and flipping chapatis. Being simple and alone with an elementary task promoted my being deep in wonder.

As I stood facing the stove, on my right side was the doorway to the living room. Carlton abruptly stuck his head in the doorway. Feeling blank and empty, I looked at him as he stood halfway into the kitchen. In rapid-fire speech that was a little hard to understand, he said, "I'm sorry, Daren. I didn't mean to mess up your morning."

I looked at him in quiet surprise. Before I could speak, Carlton disappeared like a magician's rabbit. I had to replay the moment in my head in order to be sure that I understood what Carlton had said. *It's the afternoon, not the morning.*

The empty kitchen and seemingly silent and almost empty house also promoted a surreal feeling that I was entirely alone in the house.

Could the day get any weirder? Would Gurudev find more buttons in me that needed to be pushed to see how I would react or respond? I felt like a large balloon, almost entirely drained of air.

The noise of the group sounded like it had been turned off. It felt like I was in another realm. Slowly cooking chapatis for ages, one at a time on a skillet. In complete silence. The kitchen remained empty. The house oozed stillness. *Where is everybody?* I was mystified about the way that over twenty people had quickly and quietly vanished out of the house. That day was long and surreal.

After an indeterminate amount of time, the silence began to fade as people started trickling back into the house. As the front rooms of the house filled up with people for the wedding, I remained withdrawn and relaxed. It was as if I were only an insubstantial, silent witness.

The Hindu wedding process includes a fire ceremony called *homa*. The fire pit, made of bricks on top of aluminum foil on a piece of wood, was right in the center of the living room.

As the priest lit the fire, flames and black smoke rose toward the ceiling. It was quite dramatic. The doors and windows were partially open. I was glad that Lloyd was alert. He urgently got everyone's attention by saying that all the doors and windows ought to be opened all the way.

In my quiet, inward space of silence and fatigue, I felt like my presence was totally trivial and inconsequential. In that space, I was having a glimpse of what Gurudev meant when he urged us to "live as though you don't exist!"

That day, I was just another random rag doll in the group. My identity, from my perspective, was vague.

In this indefinite space, I was undergoing accelerated, rapid change. I did not feel enlightened. I did not feel completely ignorant, and I did not feel familiar with myself.

I felt insignificant and uncertain. Definitely, that day, I was not thinking about the truth that when you keep yourself open to the possibility of changing, then you don't know who you are. It took me quite awhile to feel grateful for that long, mystifying day.

In the context of the *Yoga Sutras* of Patanjali, Gurudev clearly stated that concluding about yourself is wrong. This wisdom gave me perspective long after that surreal day was over. We are changing all the time. All cells in the body get replaced on schedule. Some tissues change faster than others. By doing daily sadhana, a person can grow in wisdom more rapidly. Real yoga offers significant growth potential.

Patanjali says that the purpose of real yoga is to reduce misery, called *klesha*, and bring harmony and samadhi. Avidya, or ignorance, is a cause and a type of misery. Ignorance makes you hold on to the past and your concept of who you are. "Ignorance is considering that which is changing to be non-changing."

"Your body is new. Your mind is new," Gurudev emphasized. "As you are awakened to this truth, you don't identify with the past."

The wedding also gave me brief freedom from the other kleshas: *asmita*, I, me, mine. Identifying yourself as your body, opinions, etc.; *raga*, strong wanting or craving; *dwesha*, aversion or hatred; and *abhinivesha*, fear.

All the Past Is Gone

All the past is gone.

There is only this moment.

Does that mean that, having any feeling,

about the past,

is a type of holding on?

Clinging to a dream

that ended long ago?

I don't have to feel any cravings or aversions.

Sometimes it feels like

a blank space,

an empty space.

Perhaps some joy is there.

But it has nothing to do

with the past.

So where does divine love fit in?

Is it there all the time?

Just floating in that space,

regardless of what is happening??

If each moment is new,

then

perhaps we do not need to have any feelings

for anyone?

Except when they are right in front of us?

Is this how to have relationships?

Gurudev's words helped me to see the deeper wisdom behind the events.

"A fixed idea about who you are destroys you totally. It stops your growth. It brings a limit to your possibilities."

"If you have an idea of who you are, you are gone, finished. Because you are stuck."

When the week was over, I was going to drive Gurudev to the airport. When he got in the car, he abruptly turned to me and commanded, "What did you learn? Quick, say what you learned!"

Feeling on the spot, I tuned in, and the first thing that came out was, "I can sleep anywhere."

He had a surprised and clearly disappointed look on his face. "That's what you learned!?"

"Yes." He could see I was speaking the truth, which was significant for me due to my history of fatigue and problems with sleep. He accepted it and moved on.

Swiftly, he turned to face the stragglers who had pushed into the back seat and sternly snapped his fingers at them. "Quickly! What did you learn? No thinking, speak the knowledge out!"

At that moment, I briefly felt some self-judgment. I was disappointed that I hadn't come up with some profound, deep knowledge as my first thought of what I had learned.

What Use Is Poetry?

*What use is poetry,
if it doesn't take me
to the pinnacle
where you live?!*

*What use are words,
if they don't speak
from that Empty Space?*

*Let us enjoy playful laughter,
that bubbles up
from divine presence!*

Chapter Eleven: Assistant Teaching with the Master

It is always magical to watch Gurudev Sri Sri orchestrate the energies of groups of people. I was tremendously fortunate to have been able to facilitate several Basic Courses per year that Gurudev himself taught in those early years, from 1988 to 1992.

When the master is leading, there is plenty of silence. Gurudev will effortlessly give out knowledge points, using a minimum of words to get us to understand the meaning. He would lead from one experience to another, as smooth as silk. With knowledge artfully interspersed. Many people have felt that the master always had the right thing to say with just enough words.

Usually, Gurudev would lead groups with gentle, melodious, changing tones in his voice. It seemed like he calibrated his voice for the group in order to help keep everyone focused on what they were doing.

In those early years, Gurudev led the Sudarshan Kriya Yoga breathing, SKY, in person. It was awe-inspiring to assist him in the process of guiding new students through SKY itself. In larger groups, Gurudev would sometimes get the attention of the assistants by snapping his fingers. Then he would point at the person who needed correction. Somehow my attention would always be grabbed when the snap of the fingers was for me. Usually, I would not be diverted by a snap meant for another person.

Gurudev asserted that we should avoid walking through the group during breathing or other practices. The rule of thumb is to walk only when necessary to deliver instructions to a specific person.

He wanted us to respect the space. He clarified that if

we walk aimlessly through the group during breathing sessions, it will disturb the space and disturb the people. People will not be able to go as deep. If we were not actively giving instructions to someone, we were to remain still, quiet, and keep breathing the circles. If we didn't get called on, after being in one spot for a moment, we were to sit down right where we were, close our eyes, keep breathing, and thereby help keep the group settled.

While helping, we were also to keep breathing the circles in rhythm with everyone else the entire time. Even when we had our eyes open. The first time I did this, it turned out to feel like an intense, advanced technique.

On one course, Gurudev snapped and pointed at some man who was a little behind me. As I turned and looked at him, I was carefully watching to see how the man was not following instructions. I became puzzled because I could not see a need for any instructions to be given to that man.

But then he did something incorrectly. The need for instruction appeared several seconds after the master had indicated that some instruction was needed. Gurudev had predicted the need for instruction before it happened.

On one course, a surfer dude was in attendance. It looked like he had been in the waves earlier that morning. Gurudev snapped and pointed at him while catching my gaze.

Looking at the surfer, I saw that he had stopped breathing with the rhythm. His head sagged forward with his chin on his chest.

Softly, I began to instruct him to keep breathing. There was no response; I had to keep at it. Gradually, I got closer to the Surfer Dude as I continued repeating the instruction. Gurudev had said to keep repeating instructions until people followed the correction and made the appropriate change.

Nothing happened. By now, I was standing next to his left side. There was no perceptible change in Surfer Dude. Bending down, I kept raising my voice and received no response. Finally, I was squatting right next to that guy, repeating instructions. He was still lost in some deep, gone place. I felt foolish, speaking loudly next to his left ear, over and over.

But I didn't want to fail either the surfer or the master, so I persisted. I knew it was important to keep giving the instruction, so I kept repeating it. Surfer Dude remained like a statue.

Time was passing, and I thought I might end up spending the entire session just sitting there. I glanced at Gurudev. He got a serious look in his eye, then indicated the surfer with a tilt of his head and a minimal flick of his gaze. It was clear that I needed to keep repeating the instructions. I went at it with renewed enthusiasm.

Several repetitions later, there was still no response. Then I thought, *"Please let him start breathing again."* Surfer Dude slowly raised his head as he began to breathe with the circles.

It was always a huge inspiration to be there with Gurudev. At the same time, it felt like I was being stretched in multiple directions in order to lose my own limitations.

Showing consummate skill as a superlative teacher, Gurudev never beat anyone over the head with too much talking or long explanations.

Over time, I saw that each group of people had its own particular dynamic or quality. No two courses were exactly alike. Every course was different.

Gurudev declared that "A real teacher simply *is*." (His emphasis)

"So much wealth is in the consciousness. Such a huge gift."

In those early years, we sometimes did a type of *kapalabhati* breathing as a part of pranayama practice. Kapalabhati involves a forceful contraction of the diaphragm for each exhalation. Gurudev does not want people to do kapalabhati during Sudarshan Kriya, SKY. This was one of the things we were supposed to keep an eye out for. During SKY, the diaphragm is moving without jerks or snaps. The exhalation is usually as long as the inhalation. Gurudev explained that the breathing for SKY should be smooth.

Many people feel relief from doing the breathing practices. These practices are so refreshing that people have described them as blessed relief.

I observed that there were times when people would spontaneously have a deeper, more profound or more blissful experience. These times were usually when they were completely absorbed in the SKY breathing, relaxing and entirely letting go with the breathing. In a space of innocence, something might happen that would surprise them.

Sometimes this would coincide with an involuntary bodily movement. Or an unconscious noise, that escaped from them in complete innocence. Sometimes nothing could be seen outwardly. But the person would feel that that particular session had been extra special and more profound.

Humans often want to repeat such experiences. The mind can be wiggly and tricky. It may tell us that we are being totally innocent. When actually, if we are completely honest, we know that we are not being innocent. Some extra effort, however sneaky, is being made to make something happen.

Gurudev said that one of the best things we can do is make people aware of their own minds.

In later sessions, I noticed that some people would repeat the movement or sound that had accompanied their more profound experience. In some cases, the repetition became a habit. Every week, month after month, sometimes for years, those people would make the same sounds or movements while doing the SKY breathing.

Gurudev advised that the best experiences come to us when we relax and let go of expectations. To have good experiences, follow the instructions with innocence and awareness. Gurudev made it clear that we don't resist involuntary movements that happen spontaneously with true innocence. At the same time, he explained that it is important not to encourage movement during SKY breathing.

By allowing the breathing to clean out random thoughts and emotions and keeping our focus fully on the process, we give it our 100%. The 100% includes both full mental alertness and a minimum physical effort. Just enough effort to keep eyes closed while sitting upright and keep the breath on the rhythm. The body is relaxed, but not so relaxed that we flop over. All awareness is on the breathing. This is how to get more out of yogic breathing practices.

Gratitude and Less Talking

Gurudev told us that all that we need in life is to be grateful.

"The more grateful you are, the more will be given to you."

Challenging the habit of complaining, Gurudev maintained that we can be thankful for anything that comes to us. We can even be thankful for obstacles.

He used gardening as an illustration, saying that when

you apply manure, it stinks. But the plants will grow well after receiving manure and compost. Whatever difficulties we face, it is valuable and important to keep our focus on the path and keep moving. Persist. That is real yoga.

When we talk too much, problems come. Gurudev's advice was to be friendly but socialize less. He insisted that this would strengthen our minds.

Another key is to allow for the truth that everyone has a place in the divine mind. Each person is unique and has a specific role to play.

It is important not to depend on the outer gestures of others. Closeness to a person comes from inside one's own self.

Only by knowing your inner being can you gain real fulfillment. Overdoing or overindulging, produces tamasic fullness, which will drag you into inertia and is not true fulfillment. Real yoga brings authentic fulfillment.

Lectured About Clothing Choices

The master is supremely skilled at helping people break inner boundaries. While a group of us were in a caravan to LAX, Los Angeles International Airport, Gurudev got stern with a man who was good at keeping silence. This man, M.S., wore the same white clothes repeatedly until they had a grubby, worn-out look. While in the car, Gurudev told M.S. that he should look more presentable when traveling with the Guru. Gurudev stated that it didn't look good to wear such old, worn clothing in public. It reflected poorly on the teaching. As soon as we arrived at the airport, M.S. found a shop and bought some new shirts. He returned to the group wearing one of his new white polo shirts.

While we were all still standing near the shops, Gurudev was facing away from Lily. Standing behind Gurudev, Lily raised her voice. With a tone of disbelief and disapproval, Lily asked Gurudev, "Did you really tell him to buy new clothing!?" Not accepting her judgment, Gurudev whipped around, became stern, and told her that she was too limited in her choice of colors.

"You are always wearing these same dull, green, brown colors. You need to wear more colors!" Lily was stunned into mouth-opening, surprised silence. Some others wondered if they should wear different colors.

"Are my colors okay?"

"What color is good for me??"

Gurudev grinned and paused, effortlessly avoiding answering them.

Gurudev whirled around and quickly moved on. The group flowed around the columns and storefronts. Like a surge of water keeping up with the wave of Gurudev.

At the time, I was glad that I was wearing a clean, bright shirt. My habit, since months before that moment, was to save new garments after purchasing them and wear them for the first time when I was with the guru. It felt good to be as fresh as possible with the master.

In the years before 9/11, we would enjoy sitting with Gurudev near the boarding gate at the airport. In small groups, a bit of surprising knowledge might be mentioned. One such time, a lady mentioned a spiritual group that had experienced a split within the group. Gurudev revealed that the split happened because that group had mispronounced some mantras.

Satsang on Our Own

After Gurudev left California, the routine of hosting satsang on Sunday evenings resumed at the house on Ashwood. We would also have a morning satsang, once or twice a month, on a weekend. At the Pacific Palisades apartment where Rob and Robin Vance lived. On those weekend mornings, there would usually be six to nine or ten people, since seating was quite limited at that apartment.

Sunday evening satsangs drew fifteen to twenty people to the house on Ashwood in late 1989 and early 1990. After the Bhakti Sutra Tour of 1990, we would host twenty to thirty enthusiastic people for Sunday evening satsang at the house on Ashwood. In 1992, it was thirty to forty, then eventually forty-five. Which was when we reached a comfortable limit of room for people to lie on the floor.

In those days, our sweet satsang would consist of group practice of pranayama and Sudarshan Kriya, SKY. After SKY, we would have a peaceful, short group meditation in silence. Then we would sing some harmonious bhajans. We would have a vegetarian potluck to conclude. It was common for the kitchen to be crammed full of happy people, chatting away during and after eating.

Potluck Secret of Mr. X

Potluck food after satsang was always vegetarian. In those days, some people were still uncertain about what was or was not vegetarian. Ahead of time, in newsletters, we would specify that meant no meat, no eggs, no fish, and no chicken.

We also chose to follow the guidelines that Gurudev had given for food at Advanced Courses and ashrams. Which meant that we requested that food not contain any garlic or onion. Most people were comfortable with strict vegetarian, onion-free, and garlic-free food. Though someone once brought some garlic bread. They started yelling in anger when they were gently reminded of the food guidelines.

Interestingly, Ayurveda says that onions and garlic contain more fire element and that when consumed, they will increase pitta dosha. An increase in pitta dosha promotes impatience, anger, frustration, and irritation. Garlic and onions are often important digestive aids for people who eat meat and/or live in cold climates. They can also help with certain elevated vata problems.

On the other hand, while garlic and onion are initially stimulating, the aftereffect is dullness. Onion, especially, is sometimes used to bring people down, after they have done too much meditation.

Some of us noticed that food brought by a certain Mr. X would tend to cause an upset stomach. That experience caused a couple of us to make a secret agreement to tell each other which item had been brought by Mr. X.

This was not as easy as it might sound. Mr. X was there regularly, but he never arrived at the same time. His movement was less predictable. Also, Mr. X would sometimes enter through the side gate and come in the side sliding door, or rear kitchen door, to throw us off. Mr. X was clever. He nearly always brought his offering in a brown paper bag. Each item was different than the previous.

"Did you see what he brought for potluck?"

"No, I didn't catch it."

"Oh well, I'll just eat what I cooked."

We realized that the deviously cunning Mr. X would

wait until the kitchen was empty. Then he would slip in, rapidly put his food down, crumple the paper bag, and zip out of the kitchen. This was done before anybody could connect him with a particular food. Most of the time, nobody witnessed his food placement.

One day, I devised what I thought was a good strategy. I eyeballed the food lined up on the big wooden counter. I thought I had the relative locations in mind. When I stepped out of the kitchen, I figured that I could easily tell which item had been added to the lineup. Mr. X zipped in behind me. When I came back just a minute later, I discovered that he had tricked me again.

He had completely rearranged the food lineup. I could not tell what he had added, as I did not entirely memorize the exact name of each thing. It was an odd predicament. It was clear that Mr. X did not want to be associated with whatever random item he brought. The mischief of Mr. X was conducted by him with determination.

Board of Directors

In early years, I sometimes attended board meetings. At the end of the first 1989 Camp Whittier Advanced Course, we had a board meeting with Gurudev. The main topic of discussion was the idea of having our own facility in the US. All of us liked the idea of having an ashram of our own. The California residents were, of course, unanimously in favor of finding a location in California.

A meeting took place without Gurudev after the Camp Whittier course. I did not attend that meeting. I heard about the details later. At that meeting, someone said, "There's a problem with the tapes." He said that cassette tapes cost too much. He didn't think it was fair that Art of Living teachers should have to pay the full price.

Interestingly, by that point, M was editing and selling video tapes of Gurudev lectures for $25. Someone pointed out that since audio cassette tapes sold for $10, $25 for VHS tapes seemed rather expensive. M disagreed. The bottom line was that the board decided that it seemed reasonable to allow teachers to pay half price for audio cassette tapes.

Taking Instructions Only from the Guru

One day, in his characteristic style of addressing things head-on, Gurudev became emphatic with me. He insisted, "You take your instructions from me, and me alone!" I was comfortable with this and felt lucky to be well taken care of by the master. However, once in a while, other people would sometimes think that they knew better and would attempt to give me instructions.

Since I was given the message that the board thought that teachers should be able to buy audio cassette tapes for half price, I made a phone call to Gurudev to check with him. Gurudev agreed that it was okay. Thus, during the late fall of 1989 and early 1990, teachers could buy Art of Living audio cassette tape recordings for half price.

Relationships

At almost every public talk and on every course that Gurudev taught, someone would ask something about relationships. People sometimes say that they want to meet the perfect partner. Or ask a question such as, "When do we know if it is ok to start or end a relationship?" Or, "How do I know my partner is right for me?" Or, "How do we deal with disagreements?"

Many times, when such questions came up, I heard Gurudev say, "Use all your skills and apply your knowledge to work things out." Work on yourself to improve your skills.

Repeated many times, Gurudev famously said, "If you can't row one boat, you can't row any other boat." It took hearing this a few times to feel comfortable with it.

His perspective was that just changing our relationship to a new partner would ultimately not bring us the contentment that we seek. The key is that we need to clear away our own old patterns and work on ourselves.

Real contentment is something we develop inside ourselves, regardless of any relationship. Yoga helps us to develop contentment. Contentment is part of Niyama. Contentment is a fundamental achievement known as *santosha*. Contentment makes it easier to feel your true self.

This is a prime area for applying all the knowledge we have been exposed to in order to help the situation. Sometimes another person's habits bother us, and the best thing is a "so what" attitude with some forbearance. Wisdom says, "Educate and ignore." Style of toothpaste use is not worth a major fight, for example. Obviously, it doesn't mean putting up with harmful, destructive, or criminal behavior.

For the people anxious to be in a relationship, the master will say, "Don't be in a hurry to be in a relationship."

Anger from the Master

Mikneem called me on the telephone and started asking questions about audio cassette tapes.
"How are you editing the audio tapes?"
"On another cassette deck."
"Are you duplicating them all yourself!?" (He already knew the answer to that.)
"I use tape duplication services to make copies."
"What's the average cost for duplicating a tape?"
"The cost is more involved than just the fee charged by the duplication house, since we have to pay for the printing of the inserts, called j-cards, and for sticky labels."

He tried to pin me down to an exact cost per cassette. The cost varied per batch size, and length and quality of tape. I didn't appreciate the direction this was going.

Predictably, the next thing Mikneem said was, "Why should teachers pay half price for a tape? Teachers are donating their time to help the organization, the organization should support the teachers by charging just the cost of the tapes. Or maybe one dollar more than the cost of the tape. Half price for a tape is more than a teacher should pay!"

I did not agree with Mikneem's latest idea. He asked me to ask Gurudev. *This is so disrespectful. He doesn't get it.* Once again, I was in a distasteful position.

Shortly after Gurudev arrived, it was quiet in his room. Gurudev was smiling. I was feeling cozy and relaxed. Gurudev asked about what was new.

Gurudev listened to a statement of Mikneem's request to lower the price of audio tapes to below half price for teachers. Gurudev blew up and started yelling.

"He is trying to make it a business!! It is not a business!! Teachers are doing seva!! We donate our time!

From now on, everyone pays full price for tapes!!!"

As fast as Gurudev's anger arose, that quickly it was gone. It was simple, natural, and impressive. And we were back to everyone paying full price for tapes, $10 per audio cassette.

Newsletters

Over the years, there have been a number of newsletters put out by people in various countries. From my perspective at the time, a good newsletter would have at least one big and one small photo of Gurudev, a complete, transcribed talk, as well as whatever pertinent news items were appropriate to include.

One of the best newsletters ever put out was edited by Bob Brown in Montreal. Bob's Montreal newsletter always had two or three nice photos of Gurudev and at least one full talk, accurately transcribed. Some other newsletters would only transcribe a small segment of a talk.

Sometimes the transcriptions in other newsletters would have errors. Not just misspelled words, but other things such as missing sentences or inserted phrases that Gurudev did not speak. The worst is when a newsletter doesn't quote the master and only paraphrases a little bit of what the master says or quotes other people talking about what the master said. The newsletter put out by Bob Brown had a resonance of purity. I could tell that the transcriptions were accurate, complete, and carefully rendered with respect.

In June of 1990, when Gurudev arrived at the house on

Ashwood in West Los Angeles, a stack of newsletters from Bob Brown had arrived the day before.

The first night, the house was almost empty of visitors by 10:30 p.m. Gurudev asked to see the newsletter. He began to read it while Michele and I watched.

Someone had suggested that it would be good to list people's experiences in the newsletter. This particular issue had a new section with a number of experiences quoted.

Gurudev didn't like one of them. He became serious.

"What is this? Why is this in here? Some lady is complaining. Some lady says that she didn't like something. We can't have this in here. People might get the wrong idea and be put off. We can't give these out."

Gurudev did not like people complaining. He wanted people to focus on gratitude.

"Okay, we could just keep them for devotees. There is some beautiful knowledge in the newsletter."

"Sooner or later, someone gives it to a friend, and someone sees it who has not taken the course. We can't give these out."

"Okay."

"We have to tell Bob not to give them out. They should be put in the trash."

"We could cut out the offensive part and hand out the rest."

"There's some good knowledge there. It's such a nice newsletter."

"They have to be thrown out. Tell Bob."

"Okay." I didn't want to be the one to have to deliver the news. I sat motionless, hoping to be invisible.

Gurudev turned to me. "You can call him."

"Okay Gurudev. Tomorrow might be a better time to call Bob."

I sat, not moving, as it was just a moment before 2:30

a.m. in Montreal. Restraining every muscle, I attempted to become as small and motionless as possible. *If I have to call, it would be best to call the next day.* Apprehensively, I held my breath.

"Go ahead, call him. He has to put all the newsletters in the dumpster."

"It's 2:30 a.m. there, and Bob will be asleep. I can call in the morning."

"Call him now. Where is the phone?" Gurudev turned his head back and forth, looking for the telephone.

Gurudev was serious and focused. "Get the phone."

It was a direct instruction. I had no choice. Dreading making the call, I felt sorry for Bob.

After I dialed the number, a sleepy voice answered, "Hello???"

"Hi Bob, Gurudev was looking at the newsletter and had some feedback about it." I kept my voice as even and neutral as possible.

Looking at Gurudev, I offered him the phone. My guts shrank further as he silently gestured for me to keep talking.

"Gurudev wanted me to deliver a message to you."

"Yeah."

"Gurudev thought that one of the experiences was a bit inappropriate. He says that the newsletters can't go out the way they are."

I paused. Gurudev instructed in a low voice, "Toss them in the dumpster."

"He says that they should all be thrown in the dumpster."

There was a silence of disbelief. Gurudev whispered, "Jai Guru Dev," and mimicked hanging up the phone.

Obediently, I said, "Jai Guru Dev." While hanging up, I felt sick and apprehensive. *This is such an extreme solution.*

I was wishing that it could have been handled

smoothly, differently, with more compassion, and at a more reasonable time during the day when Bob was wide awake.

Imagine what it would be like to have a deep sleep interrupted by a call at 2:30 a.m. from someone you did not know well. Imagine what it would feel like to have that person tell you to throw out a pet project. A project that you had spent your time and money putting together.

It was impressive how skillfully I had been used by the master. Undoubtedly, it was set up by Gurudev to make it possible for me, and especially for Bob, to lose more karma. I felt sad that someone who had done what I thought was a great seva, had to get slapped by my actions. After that phone call, Bob refused to speak with me and was angry whenever we crossed paths in the following years.

I was also disappointed because I had submitted a letter that was printed in that particular newsletter. Gurudev had said to me out of the blue one day that if he "just drank juice," he "would be perfect."

From the context at that moment, it was clear that he was talking about his physical health. When he made that comment, he had cast a scornful eye at the bags of chips and cookies that surrounded him.

Because of that, I wrote a note for the newsletter suggesting that since Gurudev liked carrot juice, it would be nice if some organic carrot juice could be bought right before he arrived in any given city. I did not quote Gurudev; it was just a heartfelt suggestion. After the instruction to dump the newsletter, I felt sad that nobody would see the letter about organic carrot juice.

Often, with true blessings around enlightened masters, bigger karmas shrink and are delivered with reduced intensity. Events happened so that I experienced all this.

It took a few years for me to understand that I had some bad karmas. These karmas necessitated my being judged, disapproved of, ridiculed, looked down upon, scorned, and rejected. I have been aware of key events in my life when people made serious decisions based on lies about me.

My sincere attempts at peaceful diplomacy were not only met with hostility; they were misrepresented and used against me. This resulted in me being vehemently rejected.

These experiences were shocking for me as I lived through them. Some people were eager to help deliver such karmas to me. This was an unthinkable surprise with a sad, bitter aftertaste. Ultimately, this strengthened me. It helped to lead me to being more centered and solid on the path.

Again and again, Gurudev has encouraged us to drop the past and live in the moment with joy. He frequently reminds us that our true nature is joy.

He would tell us to sing, laugh, dance, and meditate. If something we didn't like happened, he encouraged us to say, "So what!" and keep smiling.

The basic formula for success is to build our lives around sadhana, satsang, and seva. I was continuously using this basic formula. Yet it took me years to be able to smile and face the challenges with happy determination.

There was a bad habit of not smiling when I felt serious. Challenging life circumstances had repeatedly beaten me up. I was determined to keep going; that is my nature. Many times, before I met Gurudev, you could have called it a grim determination. Real yoga lightened things up.

Using all the tools Gurudev taught brought me relief and lightness. Later, I understood intellectually and also felt deep inside that I could smile a real smile while being serious. Real yoga helped me become able to view the play of karmas from a bigger perspective. I was even able to feel grateful that I had been relieved of some serious, negative karmas. Gratitude nurtures the blossoming of real yoga.

SECTION FOUR: BHAKTI SUTRAS

Chapter Twelve: Opposite Values

Gurudev Sri Sri has often stated that "opposite values are complementary." This is a basic point. We live in a world of opposites. Hot/cold, light/heavy, soft/hard, and wet/dry are examples of paired opposites that give depth to reality. Ayurveda uses a palette of opposite qualities to analyze situations.

People often wonder why there are bad people or why God allows disasters to happen. Gurudev says that what we view as negative events bring out compassion. If there were no people suffering, where would compassion be? "Without a villain, how can there be a hero?" He told us that "evil glorifies good."

A person will do bad or mean things because of stress or tension. The master told us, "Everyone is a saint in their core."

According to Gurudev, "Every heart is a gem. Do not hurt other hearts with sharp words."

A truly enlightened being will attract all kinds of people. Around a realized master will often come many different types of people. Differences in orientations, beliefs, religion, habits, tendencies, backgrounds, careers, diet, etc. will be thoroughly represented.

The potency of pure consciousness, the magnetism of the big mind, is supremely powerful. People who would never have chosen to hang out with each other, people who are opposites, will show up around a master, around the sages and saints. It can take a little getting used to. This dynamic is certainly part of the mechanism of the dynamic working out of the karmas of groups of people in a sangha.

A saint effortlessly delivers experiences of opposites. Gurudev Sri Sri told us that Brahmananda Saraswati, Maharishi Mahesh Yogi's master, had a saying that if you get hit in the ashram, you won't have to be hit outside. This means that when you are within the saving grace of the master's umbrella of influence, a reduced karma may be delivered to you within the group of followers. This relieves the need to experience the full intensity of it outside the group. The reduced karma will often be much milder than the original karma. A real yoga miracle. There are a number of stories I could tell to illustrate this point.

For the Los Angeles talks and Basic Course that were scheduled for June of 1990, we heard about a good property that had space available to rent. This was a facility on the border of Santa Monica and West Los Angeles. Prior to signing a rental agreement, I went to the property to inspect it.

Mr. Trick had attended various workshops at that facility. He met me there to show me around.

Gurudev had instructed me to record all of his lectures. My routine was to set up my microphone and professional Marantz PMD430 portable tape deck before a talk started.

Mr. Trick repeatedly urged that I would "get a great recording" if I used the facility's built-in sound system. His excitement about the idea of me not using my own equipment and using the facility's equipment went beyond enthusiasm. It was almost like he was intoxicated and trying to get me to eat his favorite dish at his favorite restaurant. Several times, Mr. Trick claimed that I wouldn't even have to set up my own equipment.

It seemed like a good venue for many types of courses. Reviewing the details, I had a calm, pleasant phone conversation with an administrative officer for the building. I signed the contract and paid the rental and security deposit.

At this facility, Gurudev began a six week-long series of talks on Rishi Narada's *Bhakti Sutras,* ancient wisdom about love.

The first *Bhakti Sutra* talk, *The First Thing, Types of Love*, was the introductory talk prior to a Basic Course. Gurudev asserted that everyone has experienced love, and that love is our essential nature. Gurudev stated that when we have a desire, it means that we think that the present moment is not okay. If we desire love, it means that we still have limitations, which can block experiencing love.

During the *Bhakti Sutra* talks, Gurudev gave a technique for managing desires. By directing our energy into action and being 100% fully focused on whatever we are doing, desires will automatically fade away.

To record the first talk in the 1990 *Bhakti Sutra* series, I used the built-in system at the rented facility. I did not even use my own tape deck as a backup. Many times, after that, I wished that I had followed my gut instinct rather than Mr. Trick's suggestion.

Mr. Trick had gleefully tricked me. That first talk had an annoyingly loud buzz all the way through. It was the single worst-quality recording I ever made in my entire life.

That bad recording was a tricky slap in the face. I felt that I had failed my master.

My profound chagrin was compounded by the knowledge that Gurudev intended for this series of talks to be widely duplicated and dispersed around the world. Even after extensive EQ filtering and noise reduction mastering, the noise on the recording was still bad. That one recording made some people question my suitability for working with Gurudev's talks. It made me an object of ridicule, providing an opportunity for me to lose more karma.

On the second night, Gurudev gave the second talk in the *Bhakti Sutra* series, as part of the first evening in an introductory course. I brought my own equipment and was mystified that some buzzing, though much less than the night before, was still coming into my deck. The next day, I found out that there was an electric power station next to the facility, contaminating all the electricity in nearby buildings.

The only way to avoid the buzzing on the recordings was to power the equipment entirely with batteries and not use any of the electric outlets. Fortunately, that experience gave me impetus to be better prepared in order to be able to make decent recordings. After that, I decided to use my own batteries, not rely on electrical outlets, and keep my equipment entirely self-sufficient. It was a good lesson for the long term.

After a full week in West Los Angeles, we proceeded to the mountains next to Santa Barbara to enjoy a week-long, silent Advanced Course retreat with Gurudev. We stayed at the old summer camp called Camp Whittier.

The tapes that I sold before and during the 1990 Bhakti Sutra Tour included the following titles:

> *Dealing with Feelings.*
> *God Loves Fun.*
> *Question and Answer; Inside Edge, Tuesday.*
> *Real Laughter; Inside Edge, Wednesday.*
> *Chant Live; Camp Whittier.*
> *Bhanu Sings.*

When the final invoice arrived for the rental of the facility that we had used for the first five days of the Bhakti Sutra Tour, it conveyed a hostile tone. The accompanying letter demanded that payment had to be received within two weeks, or they would take us to court. The original contract gave us thirty days to pay, yet, in the letter with the invoice, they threatened a lawsuit if we did not pay within two weeks.

We had agreed in the original contract to pay extra if we used the outdoor portable toilets in addition to the indoor restrooms. Since the indoor restrooms were sufficient, we had not touched the outdoor toilets. Yet the facility management was also charging us for the use of the outdoor toilets. The original contract did not contain any harsh language, such as a threat to take us to court. This hostility was surprising and puzzling.

Concerned about the extra, invalid charges and the hostility conveyed by the letter, I called them up to resolve the matter. Calmly, I began to outline the situation.

The guy on the phone interrupted me, and raised his voice. He abruptly insisted, "You have to pay the full amount in two weeks or we will take you to court!"

I was stunned by his antagonistic attitude.

"Why are you acting like this? Why are you breaking your agreement and threatening us?"

"I can't say."

Before Gurudev had arrived, when I was setting up the rental, I had spoken to the same person, and he had been relaxed and friendly. His hostile attitude, out of the blue, was perplexing.

He repeated his assertion, "If we do not receive payment in full within two weeks, we will take you to court!"

"All of our previous conversations were very congenial. What happened to change that?"

The gentleman seemed to relax just a little, and he stated, "It was a direct instruction from the director of the facility."

Still, it does not make sense.

"What could have happened that would make that person so angry? Why would they want to charge more than what we really owe, arbitrarily shorten the grace period for making an on-time payment, and also threaten a lawsuit??"

Reluctantly, the person on the phone confided that a person who had taken our course had said something that upset the director of the rental facility. The gentleman on the phone refused to give any other details.

After discussing the situation with an attorney, I decided to keep the payment dispute as peaceful as possible. I paid the full amount. I didn't want negative publicity. Or the hassle and expense of an unnecessary legal battle.

Using the Land Line Before We Had Cell Phones

When a world master travels from country to country, he needs to be able to communicate with people in various cities in multiple countries. Before we had any laptops or cell phones, things were orchestrated via the use of a landline telephone. It was simple enough and had some distinct issues. The telephone company would charge for every long-distance call. With only one phone line in the house, only one call could be made at a time.

I was happy to have a telephone that Gurudev could use whenever he needed. Usually, people were respectful, and there were not many random requests to use the telephone.

During Gurudev's stay in Los Angeles in the summer of 1990, a guy showed up that I had not seen before. This person was at the house every day, and every day he would ask to use the phone. At first, his calls were respectfully less than five minutes long. Oddly, each time he used the phone, the calls would get longer and longer.

More than once, the stranger was on the phone when Gurudev would want to make a call or receive a call. Gurudev beckoned me to his room and said, "Ha, someone is on the phone? I need to make a call."

When it happened more than once, I began to look at Phone Freak with a more serious eye. I did not appreciate anyone hogging the phone, especially if they were obstructing the business of the master.

No longer were polite requests being made. Phone Freak was helping himself and making calls when he felt like it. I began to take a more serious tone when I would catch Phone Freak hogging the phone in the kitchen.

The day that we were leaving the house to go to Santa Barbara, things came to a peak. As people were packing bags and preparing to leave, Phone Freak was on the phone in the kitchen. Several people left in various cars. Thirty minutes later, Phone Freak was still on the phone!

"We have to leave; please get off the phone." Phone Freak nodded yes and continued talking.

Ten minutes or so later, I was about to lock up. Finding Phone Freak still on the phone, I again asked him to "please get off the phone."

As soon as Gurudev got into a car, people ran to get into other cars. The house was empty and silent, except for a murmur of Phone Freak talking on the phone in the kitchen.

Going from room to room, I made certain that everyone was out of the house. Phone Freak was still there, on the phone. This long phone call had gone on throughout the whole time that people were gathering baggage and leaving the house. I estimated that he had been on the phone for close to an hour. The timing was crazy, and it was worse in that he had just helped himself without asking permission.

Again, asking Phone Freak to get off the phone, I

graciously gave him another minute to wrap up. I walked out of the kitchen and made an extra, unnecessary, final sweep of the house. It struck me that everyone else was long gone. There were not even any gossip sessions on the porch. All the other cars had left. I was going to be the last one out. It was annoying that I had missed my time deadline.

All my bags were packed in the car. I was past ready to go. I went back to the kitchen. Phone Freak was still on the phone!

He even had the audacity to tell me, "You can just leave. I'll hang up when I'm finished."

It seemed like a bad dream.

Finished with politeness, having had no response to several repetitions of please, I raised my voice. "I have to leave! You have to hang up now!"

As unbelievable as it sounds, Phone Freak kept talking! He didn't hang up. He turned his back to me as if to hide his ongoing telephone marathon. He was ignoring me.

That was it. Furious, I explosively grabbed the phone out of his hands and hung it up for him. It was time to shout.

"Hurry up and get out! Stop making me wait!"

Finally realizing that his days of free phone calls were over, Phone Freak slithered out. At last, I was able to lock up the house and start driving to Santa Barbara.

Bedtime Trick by the Master

Gurdev Sri Sri does not need as much sleep as the average person. Sometimes, a few devotees will hang out with Gurudev at night, after everyone else is gone.

Given my persistent, chronic state of fatigue and multiple illnesses during 1988 and 1989, staying up late was not appealing and could leave me wiped out. Even just staying up until 11:00 p.m. could leave me feeling much worse the next day. Attempting to feel better motivated me to be quite brisk about getting to bed after the group was dismissed.

Hearing some tidbits of the previous night's circle with the master sparked a sense of loss and longing in me. I wanted to be there too. I wanted to get that extra time in with Gurudev. For the first year that I knew him, I knew it was not healthy for me to be up late, and I was tired of feeling rotten, so I still did my best to get an early sleep.

The longing to hang out with Gurudev in the evenings, after the majority of people had left, grew more intense as time passed. By this point, in June of 1990, there was competition to get to hang out with Gurudev later at night.

At some point, on my way to Santa Barbara, I made an inward decision that this trip would be the trip when I would not watch the clock. I felt a little stronger and healthier than I had felt in several years. I figured that maybe I could handle staying up, to some extent. I was uncertain, yet determined.

In Santa Barbara, I set up a tent on a wooden deck outside Jeff's house. As I was setting up my sleeping bag, I affirmed my intention to myself. *Tonight will be the night. Tonight, I will not worry about getting to sleep early. I can hang out with the gang until we get sent home!*

Nobody knew about my fresh resolution. I felt a sense of excitement about making a personal breakthrough. I didn't want to spoil it by telling someone who might say it was stupid.

There was a public talk that night. After the talk, Gurudev went to John and Catherine's place on the beach. A handful of people were spread around the house when I arrived. They were happily enjoying the afterglow of the evening lecture while waiting for a more intimate satsang. Then the small group went to the kitchen to have a drink and a snack. A loud gossip session started.

I found Gurudev unpacking his suitcase in the bedroom. By himself. I felt childlike, relaxed, and eager for whatever was on the program. Twice, I offered to help and was disappointed when Gurudev flatly ignored my offer.

Gurudev asked me, "What did you think of the talk?"

I sensed something up Gurudev's sleeve as I gave my response.

"It was a good talk and people seemed to like it."

I thought about how the lecture had created good energy in the room. Then I stumbled over trying to say that out loud. I figured that whatever I thought didn't matter. Also, I sensed this was just a preamble to a completely different topic.

"How are you doing?"

He seemed to enjoy being self-reliant at that moment. The urge to do something for him pressed inside me. I had a brief flash of frustration that Gurudev would not let me help.

Out of the blue, Gurudev said, "Okay, you can go rest."

I was startled. *What? It's not even ten o'clock yet!* I told him, "That's okay; I'm not tired."

"Wouldn't you like to sleep? You can go and sleep."

"No, no, I'm fine."

I was determined to stay up and hang out. When I entered the bedroom, the gray color scheme of the bedspread and towels visible in the bathroom, seemed crisp and clean. The same gray was now hinting towards cold clouds gathering on my horizon. That I was determined not to feel.

"Go now. Go and sleep." He was more serious, and it was an instruction. Amazed and disoriented due to the surreal irony of the situation, I was having a hard time believing what I was hearing. *Why is he doing this?*

Just to be certain and to give Gurudev a chance to change his mind, I asked, "Do you want me to leave?"

He responded with finality, "Go and sleep."

He was standing between the bed and a door to the outside. In wonder, with a pinch of feeling rejected, I bowed down and got up to go. As I turned towards the hallway to the living room, which was on his right side, Gurudev gestured to his left side and instructed, "You can use that door."

He was indicating a side entrance. Nobody had interrupted us during this exchange. Any hope of getting looped back into the scene, even momentarily, by a giddy straggler, for example, evaporated quickly. I saw that he was sending me off through a side door that was dark and quiet. Instinctively, I knew that nobody would see me, and I would be alone again. Gurudev standing there guaranteed that the departure would not be delayed.

Puzzled, I slipped out as instructed. As I closed the door, the distant laughter I heard was like a cosmic comment. I could not see the kitchen windows or the front door. Alone, I walked back to my tent. I wanted to follow all of Gurudev's instructions with enthusiasm, so I avoided focusing on disappointment in that moment. *Okay, he gave me an instruction; that is what my focus is.*

My enthusiasm was confusion and wonder as I walked off. My footsteps seemed to be loud. Divine energy somehow magically kept my path along driveways and dark streets absolutely free of people, so I was kept in silence.

Usually, when I get in bed, I fall asleep quickly. Sometimes I fall asleep so quickly that I don't have time to do more than think one quick sentence in my head. From experience, I have learned it is wise to arrange my body for sleep right away, or I may wake up hours later uncomfortable with my hands on my chest, where I fell asleep pulling up the covers. That night in the tent, I lay awake with a strange inability to fall asleep. Each minute was slow and quiet. I felt entirely alone.

This seemed to go on for hours. Adrift in wondering, I was feeling amazed at how Gurudev had blown my mind. Thinking about the irony of the situation, I felt foolish and useless. Time didn't seem normal. I figured that I had been awake for such a long time that soon I would hear people coming home. Nothing did I hear but a train in the distance.

Eventually, not checking the time, I even thought that maybe everyone else had already gone home and I was oddly still awake while everyone else was asleep. *Am I just going to be awake all night?* Refusing to keep looking at my watch, I finally drifted off. The sunrise woke me up with bright immediacy through the tent walls.

Gurudev knew about the resolution I had stretched myself to make in order to stay up late. Even though I had not told anybody. He then stretched my mind even further by blocking that resolution. It was an advanced technique that worked well. Later on, I realized that Gurudev was helping me to be more surrendered. He was helping me to be more present in the moment. From that day on, staying up with the guru became much less of a source of tension.

Wherever he goes, Gurudev helps people get past personal obstacles. Inner blocks seem to catch his attention, regardless of whether anyone has mentioned the obstacle. This process can yield varying degrees of surprise and/or discomfort.

If your system can handle losing a limitation, circumstances will likely be triggered to give you opportunities to face your own limitation. You may not think that you can handle some of what comes at you. However, divine consciousness knows all your strengths and weaknesses. It is important to keep a positive attitude. Surrender is a valuable support.

Gurudev had said that our growth toward liberation or enlightenment is a movement towards the unknown. This was driven home by my experience. I was not yet at the place he described as "loving the unknown" (as a prerequisite for divine love). Real yoga prepares us for the unknown future.

Gurudev made it clear that liberation doesn't happen by hating anything or running away from society. Trusting Gurudev's assurance that we were growing to be able to experience more joy, I deepened my resolve to be steadfast about facing whatever would come in front of me.

Love and Longing

In the summer of 1990, Gurudev spent five weeks touring along the west coast of North America. He went into great depth talking about the *Bhakti Sutras* of Sage Narada. It was amazing and gratifying to receive such extensive knowledge about love. It felt reassuring that many aspects of love could be analyzed in depth from a perspective of sattva.

The second week of the Bhakti Sutra Tour of 1990, we had an advanced silence program at Camp Whittier. It was impressive that Gurudev could talk about love for weeks at a time and keep coming up with new material. Gurudev's clear explanations brought the ancient sutras of Narada to life. It was easy to be in wonder and appreciation during this deep, prolonged dive into knowledge. *"The Concept of God"* lecture was given at that 1990 Camp Whittier course.

There are different types of love, including love towards children, love toward peers, and love towards elders. We also explored sattvic love, rajasic love, and tamasic love. Love is expressed in different ways. Honor is a sign of love. Unconditional love does not have demands.

Bhakti is devotion. Many people experience attraction. Fewer people experience love. Rarely do people experience devotion.

Gurudev emphasized that for love to last, it is important that love mature into devotion. Until love has matured, it can create bondage. Bhakti is devotion that has blossomed.

On the path, knowledge from the master is valuable. Knowledge helps people avoid making mistakes. It is important to listen to the knowledge, and it is important to think about the knowledge. This is part of real yoga.

Shravana is listening. *Manana* is reviewing the knowledge in your mind. It is important to digest the knowledge. Gurudev discussed Narada's points about this.

A keen desire to listen to the beloved is a sign of devotion, of bhakti. Bhakti can cause a person to keep bringing their mind back to what was said by the beloved. Knowledge will not fully satisfy; it nurtures a thirst for love.

Knowledge, seva, and yoga are all helpful tools to reach bhakti. Ego about achievement on a path can cause a person to stumble and lose the safe haven of bhakti.

"Bhakti itself is not a practice. It is a result. It is the fruit of the practice. The purpose of yoga is to be in bhakti."

Gurudev repeatedly emphasized that love and longing go hand in hand. When you love someone, separation causes longing. If there is no longing, then love lacks depth.

Here is a place where "burn, vanish, and dissolve" has deep meaning. Longing creates a burning. When deeply in love, two vanish and become one. Dissolving in divine love is an ultimate experience. *Govind* is love. *Radhe* is longing.

Gurudev spoke about the desire to be near vs. the desire for respect. It was an aha! moment for me when he articulated that respect requires some distance. People who are close often find after some time that there is less respect in the relationship.

When you love someone, you want to be close to them and spend time together. At first, there is respect. After spending a lot of time together, there is more intimacy, and respect tends to be less. It becomes a paradox of love to balance closeness and respect. With surrender, in divine love, respect and intimacy flourish together.

A valuable point from Gurudev is that being indifferent to whatever is opposing love helps to maintain love.

The last satsang at Camp Whittier was magical. Everyone was focused on singing. Immersed in the chanting, the unification of the group was palpable. It peaked with a Radhe Govind bhajan that rocked everyone for a solid fifteen minutes. It felt timeless. With great enthusiasm, the whole group sang Radhe Govind, and we lost all sense of leading or following. We fulfilled the real depth of bhajan.

Radhe Govind, Radhe Govind, Radhe Govinda bhajo, Radhe Govind

Radhe Govind, Radhe Govind, Radhe Govinda bhajo, Radhe Govind

Radhe Govinda radhe, Radhe Govinda radhe, Radhe Govinda radhe, Radhe Govinda radhe

Radhe Govinda radhe, Radhe Govinda radhe, Radhe Govinda radhe, Radhe Govinda radhe

Radhe radhe radhe, radhe radhe radhe
Radhe radhe radhe, radhe radhe radhe

Radhe Govind, Radhe Govind, Radhe Govinda bhajo, Radhe Govind

Lemon Ginger

People in India had made an herbal digestion supplement that Gurudev enjoyed. He brought some in his suitcase. This was chopped ginger, soaked in lemon juice and salt, that had been dried. It tasted good and quickly relieved upset tummies.

One day, Gurudev was eating some of the lemon ginger. Michael, Michelle, and I were in the room. As he ate it, Gurudev had an absorbed, inward look. We were quietly watching him, happy to be sharing the moment.

Gurudev looked over at Michael and observed, "Oh, you want some." Michael said his stomach was upset. Gurudev laughed like he didn't believe it, yet gave some to Michael. Then Gurudev walked over to Michelle and gave some to her. Gurudev stated, "Now we can digest all the food that we ate."

Gurudev turned to walk back to where he had been standing and looked at me. I noticed how watching him give something to the others stirred a little desire to also have some, even though I didn't honestly want it. He paused, then, with a smile, observed, "Oh, but if I give some to Daren, he will be hungry immediately!"

They all found that amusing and laughed. In that moment, I was not quite in a state of detachment and was feeling a little left out. I did appreciate Gurudev's wisdom in not producing hunger in me right after I had eaten a full meal. Then I quickly dropped the desire, feeling gratitude for the master's wise choice.

The Third North American Teacher Training Course

The third week of the 1990 Bhakti Sutra Tour coincided with the first week of the third North American Teacher Training Course, TTC, with Gurudev Sri Sri. I was already a teacher, but there was no way I would pass up an opportunity to spend quality time with Gurudev. We stayed for that week at a house in Pacific Grove. We took over the property. Gurudev enjoyed the apartment, above the garage. A number of people stayed in the various rooms of the front house.

I was camping, in just a sleeping bag, on the uncovered wooden deck of the back porch of the house. It was the only level spot in the tiny backyard, other than where someone already had a tent. There was a small water heater on the porch that looked like it was left over from the 1940s.

A lady who slept in the house was always the first person into the bathroom. At 5 a.m., when she would start her shower, the ancient water heater would make loud popping and cracking sounds. The popping water heater would wake me up even when I wore ear plugs. The first morning, it came as a surprising jolt. Subsequent mornings, I would hear the sound and tell myself to keep sleeping. It was of no use. Too many pops and bangs woke me up earlier than I was ready.

I tried to talk to that lady in an effort to convince her to delay her shower for just half an hour. She wouldn't budge. She had to take a long, comfortable hot shower from 5 a.m. until 5:30 a.m. She was worried that other people would come into the bathroom while she was in it.

I was in charge of cooking lunch for the group. I would rush to get vegetables washed and cut and pots set up on the stove, so I would not miss any precious time with Gurudev.

A couple of times, it happened that I was still working in the kitchen when Gurudev came and sat in his chair. The chair in which he sat for our meetings was on the other side of the door to the kitchen. Before the meetings, we often kept that door open. It brought a wave of alertness to look up from the stove and see Gurudev sitting, looking over his right shoulder at me. We smiled at each other.

I worked as fast as possible to avoid missing any points. With much-appreciated graciousness, Gurudev waited for me to join the group before he stopped the idle chitchat and started the TTC meeting.

It was an eclectic group of people of many ages and nationalities. Gurudev wanted to hear each one of us say something about why we wanted to be teachers.

Each day, we would sit with Gurudev for two to four hours in the morning and then again in the afternoon. In the evenings, Gurudev gave lectures at various venues in the area. Over the weekend, there was an Introductory Course, which was the new name for the Basic Course.

Many of us participated in helping Gurudev teach the Introductory Course. It felt like the group of us attending that TTC were all in a space of doing our best to be instruments of pure knowledge. Gurudev led the sessions of the course, including the Sudarshan Kriya, in person.

In the TTC, Gurudev put a lot of emphasis on our ability to accept people and situations. He wanted us to decide that we would accept every person and every situation that would come in front of us. If we slip and do not accept, then it is important to surrender that to get back into the space of acceptance. Gurudev emphasized that it was important that we integrate this into our lives.

Gurudev asserted that it is critical that we not hate anyone. It is okay to avoid certain people, but we must do so without any hatred. Gurudev stated that we have to be resolved to accept everyone, or we will not find success as teachers. We must not hate anyone no matter what they do.

As teachers, we understand that we are not the doers. Grace is what brings about transformation. To be a channel for grace, we have to be hollow and empty.

Collectively and individually, it seemed clear that we all understood that the correct use of techniques is important. Gurudev likes to give the analogy of using a spoon to eat soup. He has used this analogy many times. If you hold your spoon upside down, you will not be able to transfer soup to your mouth. The cup also has to be right-side up to hold the soup.

Doing our part and doing our sadhana on a daily basis is the foundation. We must have a commitment to flow with the knowledge. On top of that, we grow into a hollow and empty space of devotion and surrender. Seva, satsang, and the daily practices, with devotion and surrender, are the means to keep the spoon and cup in the proper position. Then we can catch the grace when it flows.

Gurudev strongly encouraged us to accept people as they are. The present situation must be seen as inevitable. Hatred binds us to those we hate.

At one point during the TTC, a man and a woman got into a dispute over who was the most experienced teacher. From a bigger perspective, the argument was surely a test to see if all of us could accept that situation. On a petty, mundane level, the argument seemed bound to happen sooner or later. Given the negative attitudes that man and woman had been holding and expressing about each other.

Watching them argue with each other consumed a surreal chunk of time. At least ten plus minutes. At first, it was rapid, going back and forth. They seemed like brother and sister as they both used nearly identical arguments against each other with a virtually identical demeanor.

After a while, the pace of the argument slowed down. They would pause to think about what to say next. Silent gaps began to come between statements. The silence between sentences grew longer and longer as they had to think harder and harder to find the next cutting remark. Each time it seemed like finally it would be over, one of them would say something else. Neither of them seemed comfortable letting the other have the last word.

At first, I felt sorry for them. After a while, I was annoyed that they were wasting our time putting their gigantic ego trips on display. I was sitting right beside Gurudev. I was amazed that he did not intervene.

I had a desire to end the argument with an attempt to redirect back to the discussion of the knowledge. But I sat on it and dropped that desire. The rest of us also took our cue from the master and sat silently.

I kept looking at Gurudev and then looking back at the arguing people. Gurudev sat there with a blank face, just watching the show. It was all the more bizarre, since a number of people in the group were usually quite vocal and habitually more than happy and eager to blurt out their opinions. Yet we all sat there watching the argument.

I gazed at Gurudev, soaking in as much of his benevolent gracefulness as I could. His dispassion inspired all of us to bear with the disrespectful disturbance.

At some point, I finally realized that Gurudev was modeling perfect acceptance. We had resolved to accept people and situations, and we were going with the flow. There we were, accepting the pathetic situation.

He essentially promised us that situation after situation would be thrown into our faces. "How do you deal with them?"

That scenario was certainly part of our training to develop a "yes mind." Gurudev explained that enlightened beings say "yes" to what is happening. He told us that his body is designed to say "yes." It is harder for him to say "no."

The purpose of a master will be different for different people. Gurudev stated that the knowledge and the path, especially teacher training, are working to help us develop a "yes mind."

People have different buttons. Gurudev let us know that our experiences were carefully calibrated. "The master will not serve the same exact soup to everyone. Yet on the level of being, it is all based on oneness in the big mind."

This was the TTC at which we worked out a specific outline for the four days of the Introductory Course. Before this, the sequence of topics in a course had a little more variability. The exact sequence of course points and which points to give on which day became set there in Pacific Grove. The majority of the main points used in most Art of Living courses over the next 24 years were covered in that week in 1990.

We decided that the name should be changed to the Introductory Course. For shorthand, many of us later referred to it as the "Intro Course." The name of the course changed several times during the next 26 years, from the Introductory Course, to the Art of Living Course, to the Healing Breath Workshop, to the Part One Course, to the Happiness Program.

Several sessions during that TTC time with Gurudev ended up being talks on the *Bhakti Sutras*. Gurudev instructed that one of these should not be duplicated. Most of the talks I ended up editing and duplicating for the first 1990 release of the *Bhakti Sutra* series of talks on cassette tapes.

In Pacific Grove, Gurudev spoke about the importance

of the thirst for truth. It is important to continue on the path with a thirst for truth, for love, and for the divine. Unfortunately, many people hear or see something and think they own it when they have not had any experience with the truth. Thirst for truth, thirst for the divine feeds real yoga.

Making it more interesting and, for some people, more confusing, Gurudev insisted that truth contains opposites. Opposites can make the truth seem illogical, especially when you don't see the big picture. Knowledge can deepen the mystery of love, but it can never fully explain it. One has to keep going until they are fully established in divine love. In divine love, surrender is maintained, and respect and love coexist. In surrender, one wants the other to be happy.

Years later, Gurudev gave new talks on the *Bhakti Sutras,* which were recorded on digital video equipment. He gave new, revised commentary on those sutras whose commentary was left out of the original series, and these were part of the new *Bhakti Sutra* collection.

One morning, in 1990, I was in Gurudev's room with him quite early. It was just the two of us. He said that he wanted to wash his hair and that he needed some oil.

Ayurveda makes extensive use of oil on the head in order to nourish the brain, enhance all mental functions, sooth emotions, balance elements and doshas, and protect the hair. He looked at me and asked, "You have some oil?"

At the time, I just shook my head. It seemed like such an odd request. *Why would I be carrying around bottles of oil?* Perhaps his awareness was sensing the future, six or more years later, when I would be building the collection of the many oils that I work with now.

When Gurudev realized that he wouldn't get oil from me, he muttered something about having some oil from Liz Luedemann. In those days, Liz Luedemann had a skincare line in Germany. She made a high-quality oil that was healing for the skin. It had a distinctive, appealing, and exotic aroma. Liz brought some of the oil to California with her and gave a bottle to Gurudev. Gurudev showed me the bottle.

Gurudev poured at least two tablespoons of that oil on top of his head. He patted it and rubbed it extremely minimally with his hand. I was laughing to see this unexpected minimalistic oil treatment on the head. Gurudev had an air of innocence and straightforward simplicity. Gurudev said he was going to bathe and that we would talk later, which was my cue to leave.

For the second week of the 1990 TTC course (the fourth week of the Bhakti Sutra Tour), we stayed in the Oakland Hills in the San Francisco Bay Area. The Goodrum household was taken over by the course. Gurudev stayed in a downstairs room. I slept in the open air outside his room on a wooden deck, which overlooked an empty swimming pool. One night, we sat right beside the pool for a seven- or eight-person satsang with Gurudev. A single candle provided light.

In Oakland, we went over puja pronunciation and some fine points about Sudarshan Kriya. Gurudev emphasized that the breath during Sudarshan Kriya was long and smooth. He made the point that people should not be doing kapalabhati-style snapping of the diaphragm during Sudarshan Kriya.

During the fourth week of the Bhakti Sutra Tour, Gurudev gave a talk at a church in Berkeley. The main point of that talk was that the people you spend time with have a strong effect on how you think and feel. You become like the people you spend time with.

It is wise and important to avoid bad company. We were encouraged to spend time with good people who uphold sattva, harmony, truth, and wisdom. This talk was later given the title *The Company One Keeps*.

In the first half of 1990, I sang an adaptation of a Ganesh bhajan. I would sometimes chant it at satsang. I had chosen it because it was easy, with a sense of playfulness. In the early years, most of the bhajans we sang in Art of Living were still simple, such as *OM namah shivaya, Krishna Govinda Gopala, OM namo bhagavate vasudevaya, bhajamana ma,* and *OM guru deva deva.*

At the end of *The Company One Keeps* talk, we had a session of bhajan chanting. I was sitting on a side of the stage by myself. Chris Reed joined me. Chris was in a super giddy mood. He was giggling, grinning, laughing and literally flopping his body against wall and floor.

I started leading the Ganesh bhajan that I had been practicing. Chris kept laughing louder and louder. Chris moved closer to me and nearly bumped me, which was profoundly distracting. The playful energy was too much. I was near the edge of the stage leading the bhajan. I didn't think it was a good idea to try to move across the stage, in front of the master, to get away from Chris.

The laughter was strong and contagious. I started laughing while I was still leading the bhajan, lost the rhythm, and had to end it prematurely. It was an odd set of circumstances. I felt embarrassed, but I figured everyone would hopefully just forget about it.

That night, after the satsang was over, I got back to the Goodrum house shortly after Gurudev. I went down to his room. As I walked in, greeting him, he was sitting, looking serious. He gave me a frown and asserted, "Don't lead that bhajan anymore." Right away, I simply agreed, "Okay." I wanted to accept the instruction fully and immediately. The seriousness was evident.

Feeling small and sad, I was deflated. That was the last of that bhajan. It hurt to feel that I had let down Gurudev and Ganesh too. Inside myself, I felt in that moment that I wanted to make it up to them. I resolved that I would learn more Ganesh chants and sing them respectfully.

Part of me wanted to hide, but I wanted to stay with Gurudev as long as he would let me be in the room. Feeling embarrassed, I don't know if I managed to speak another word that night. I observed the sensations bubbling inside me as I sat with acceptance of what was happening.

Gurudev taught a course at a Zen center in Berkeley, near Oakland. The Zen monk who was in charge of the center liked Gurudev. After meeting with Gurudev, the monk wanted to take the course with Gurudev. Gurudev thought that the monk had a good master. Gurudev wanted the monk to stay with his Zen master. Gurudev told that monk that he would only agree to teach him if the monk would promise to stay with his master. The monk agreed and took the course.

At the end of the TTC, we had a flight scheduled to Vancouver, Canada. At the Oakland airport, there were just a few devotees waiting with Gurudev to catch the plane. Many of us were on our way to Vancouver. It seemed like we had our own little wing, just our own small group in an alcove in the terminal that had comfortable seats. The seats had royal blue cushioned upholstery that looked new.

Only one seat was beside Gurudev. I was sitting right next to Gurudev in that single seat on his right side. Most people were avoiding the other, farther seats in order to stand close to Gurudev. In short order, Gurudev turned to me and requested, "Ha, Daren, let someone else have the seat." I got up and joined the people standing.

Gurudev suggested that we could start producing our own newsletter. Some ideas were tossed around. Then someone asked, "What else could we put in the newsletter?"

Gurudev got a little grin and said, "We could have some Daren and Michael stories." Gurudev was chuckling.

I'm not sure if anyone else found it funny. Most people were not aware of the various things that had happened to make such stories. The idea did not appeal to me. It made me feel a little queasy.

The first night in Vancouver, Gurudev gave a public talk in a more modern building. I slept in a tent in a local backyard. We had a transitional day in Vancouver. Before we headed out to the gorgeous, secluded forest location of Loon Lake for the week-long advanced intensive.

Loon Lake Guru Purnima 1990

We had the Loon Lake facility to ourselves. The closest major road was miles away. The final approach was a long, dirt road. It was a remote, peaceful, and beautiful setting. The Loon Lake facility had rustic wooden cabins on the edge of an isolated lake surrounded by hundreds of trees in an evergreen forest. Our meeting hall was a giant log cabin. Some of the cabins were essentially dorm rooms.

Since I was depending on a ride with a local resident, I had to wait till that person was finished with work before they could drive to the facility. We ended up arriving late, after the evening meal had already started.

My assigned room was identified by some barely perceptible markings on the door. It was tight against the side of a big tree. I stared at it for a moment. *It's too small on the outside to have a bedroom in there.*

When I opened the door, I experienced a brief moment of surprise, as it was actually a tool storage shed, with many tools hanging on the walls. I noticed that the tiny floor space was quite uneven. Then I noticed that it was not a real floor; it was just oil-soaked dirt. Standing there, holding a bag, it seemed that I was occupying all the free space in the shed. It smelled strongly of dirt, gasoline, tools, gardening equipment, sawdust, engines, and oil. There was no clear space to put my luggage and sleep. The shed was just wood attached to the side of a tree.

I had very little time to get to dinner before it was over. Some people had already finished dinner and were gathering for the evening meeting. I had to figure something out quickly. I knew that if I went to try to find someone to help me with housing, I might not find them before the meeting. And there was a chance of not getting another space. I didn't want to engage in a wild goose chase. Missing dinner or the meeting with Gurudev was not an option for me. I figured that I had better just make do and hurry up about it. It was a good thing that I made that choice, since I later was told that there was no other available space. It was a strong test of acceptance.

I cleared a space on the work bench, which was the only level surface. Some pieces of wood, including doors without hinges or knobs, were leaning against the wall. Taking a piece of plywood, I put it on the workbench, and that became my bed. I put up two sawhorses with a smaller, unfinished door on them to support my luggage and keep it out of the dirt. There was no floor space left. I sat on my bed to change clothes. Entering and exiting the room required careful maneuvering in order not to run into anything, especially the many sharp and/or dirty tools hanging all over the walls. Putting on shoes and removing them required focused precision to avoid contact with the dirty, greasy, oily ground and the many tools hemming me in.

The only advantage of sleeping in the tool shed was

that I had a private space with no roommates.

Strikingly, on the night that Gurudev had us woken up at 2:30 a.m. for a session in the main hall, someone, perhaps accidentally, woke me. Loud banging on various doors, other than mine, got most of the course participants up. Alerting all the rooms in the area, someone between my tree and the buildings across the path yelled in a loud voice, "Gurudev wants everyone in the hall now!"

For the 2:30 a.m. meeting, as we gathered in the main hall, Gurudev had us keep the lights off. Many of us were in a daze. For a while, we simply sat in silence. You could tell that there was some discomfort in the air, while I'm sure that I was not the only one experiencing a big state of wonder.

Someone asked why we were there. Gurudev became serious and told us to turn around. Many of us were confused. *Did he mean that we should stand up and rotate, spin our bodies?* I was trying to figure out what kind of turn he wanted.

He wanted us to sit facing away from him. "Turn around. Turn around, and if your neighbor does not turn around, give them a hit."

Just this simple instruction and minimal activity, sitting in a dark room with our backs toward Gurudev's chair, was enough to make some people very uncomfortable. Some people wanted to keep facing toward Gurudev. Again, he repeated the instruction to turn around and hit anyone who did not turn around. He was serious.

It seemed strange and unusual, yet it was a great opportunity to observe one's own mind and limitations. Why should we always expect predictable things to happen? He encouraged us to be comfortable with uncertainty.

Gurudev's cabin was on the edge of the lake. The square of land it sat on was a small corner projecting out from the shore into the lake. Two sides of the cabin were right on the water. There was a wooden deck walkway that went all the way around the cabin.

One day, people were standing on the land next to the cabin, in between meetings. Most were just hanging out, hoping to catch a glimpse of Gurudev. Some people were by themselves, and there were a small number of clusters of two or three people. We were being respectful and staying off the wooden deck going around the cabin, except for right by the front porch. I was feeling relaxed and peaceful.

Swiftly, there was a change and pause as Gurudev came out of a side door that faced the lake. People shifted their attention to him. The calmness was poised for a moment then shattered when Gurudev burst into running. He ran over to one side of the deck and disappeared. The scattered group abruptly followed him. We ended up chasing Gurudev around the cabin. There was wild laughter, especially as Gurudev ended up running behind the back of the group that was chasing him. The master then chased the devotees.

After things had settled, some of us were standing around him. One lady asked, "Why did you run?" Gurudev ignored the question. When Gurudev next spoke on the *Bhakti Sutras,* he talked about the devotees chasing the divine and the divine chasing the devotees. The knowledge resonated all the more deeply after having had the physical, playful experience of chasing Gurudev around his cabin.

One afternoon, a couple of us were sitting with Gurudev on the deck outside his room, overlooking the lake. Gurudev and I sat in small chairs at a little round table. It was a truly beautiful day, with clear blue skies punctuated by a few puffy, white clouds above the many green trees. A lady was standing at the railing, looking out across the lake. She did not speak English. She spoke to Gurudev, gesturing excitedly as she stood in front of him. Then she swiveled her broad body and remained gazing out at the lake.

Gurudev laughs and says in English that she is telling him what a beautiful view it is. "But she is standing right in front of me, blocking the view!"

He thought it was funny. We were all laughing, and the lady blocking the view was quite happy as well. Being included in such a joyful, innocent moment felt magical.

The first time Gurudev walked into the meeting hall, he didn't like the stale air and the used fireplace odor. He had us move his chair further away from the smelly fireplace. He instructed, "These doors and the windows should be kept open all the time." There were several people standing around him when he said that. Unfortunately, many groups have people who like to be contrary and do the opposite.

One morning, we had an unstructured period of time to do sadhana on our own. Enjoying my personal silence amidst the silence of nature, I walked to the hall by myself. My typical deliberation for the Loon Lake course venue, as with many others, was where to leave my shoes outside the hall.

I had already had the experience of someone walking off in my shoes while leaving their own behind at the course in Lennoxville in 1989. That person was truly oblivious, spaced out, and out of touch, as they did not recognize the different feeling of wearing my shoes instead of their own. It was only when I chased around searching for them and luckily found them that the reality of the situation registered with the other person. After an experience like that, one becomes much more careful about shoe placement.

At our main hall in Loon Lake, there was a small, rounded slope on the side of the building with the main entrance. Steep stairs transitioned from the path or fire road that led past the building. There was a small concrete entryway outside the double doors. A few feet away from the concrete entryway, there was a piece of pavement leading to the edge of the stairs. Around the stairs were dirt and grass.

Many people already had their shoes tucked into the spaces under and along the wooden stairs. I preferred to have my shoes a little closer to the door. After a session, one hopes to find their shoes in roughly the same spot they were left in. To minimize the chance of them getting kicked aside, I looked for a grassy spot that was dry and off the concrete, down along the side of the building.

That morning, I wore a simple, short-sleeved t-shirt, enjoying a beautiful summer day. It was perfect, sunny weather for short sleeves, yet the doors to the hall were closed. That surprised me since it was mid-summer and many people were already there.

I opened both doors and was hit in the face by a warm blast of stench. A bunch of bad smells. It was like an ancient locker room reeking of sweat and archaic toilets. It also smelled like a fireplace, bad breath, and other foul things.

People were at many different stages of practice. Some were doing asanas. Multiple types of pranayama were being done. Some people were meditating. Oddly, no windows were open, hence the grungy odor. It was hard to believe people would do breathing practices without caring whether they got the benefits.

Concerned about the health and safety of everyone in the group, I was determined to follow Gurudev's instructions to keep the windows open. I went along the side and opened the three windows. I turned back and saw that the front doors were again closed. It was still smelly and stuffy, so I went back and opened the doors. There was a hefty French-Canadian gentleman named Robert (pronounced "Row-Bear," with a silent "t" and an accent on the "b"). Robert was sitting on a chair near the door, doing some pranayama.

After I opened the doors, Robert said, "No. The doors must be closed." He jumped up and closed the doors.

Keeping my silence, I just looked at him blankly. My personal identity mysteriously vanished. My consciousness was altered. I was there, but I was not there. I was not the doer. I felt like a rag doll.

With a sense of divine vastness, I felt Gurudev's presence with an inner resolve to protect the entire group by keeping the doors open. Again, I opened the doors.

Robert was getting increasingly agitated. It didn't make any sense at all. He started yelling. "The doors have to be closed!" He grabbed the doors to close them. Calmly, I watched and then quietly opened them. Then I stepped away.

As I moved aside, I had my back to the outside stairwell. Robert erupted. His face was bright red, and his body was visibly shaking. This explosion astonished me. My big mind remained peaceful and watchful. Robert roared and charged at me with both fists raised in front of his hefty body.

I tried to step further back to give him room, and I found that I was in an even more profoundly altered state of consciousness than I had realized. I was watching things happen as an observer. My body was relaxed and frozen stiff. My arms were simply hanging rigid at my sides. It was clear to me that I no longer had control of my body. *This is strange. What happened to me?*

On a previous occasion, when someone had charged at me with both fists raised to hit me, I had gone automatically into martial arts mode. I flipped that person easily over my head without needing to think about it. Calmly, watching without moving, I was surprised to find myself being passive and relaxed as Robert charged me. His heavy weight hit me hard, and I flew backward, like a stiff, airborne statue.

I was witnessing the experience in slow motion from the moment that he hit me. I felt my body airborne, parallel to the ground, facing the sky. As I was airborne, my mind reminded me that falling backward down the stairs could be seriously damaging. Especially for someone like myself, who already had multiple musculoskeletal injuries.

Yet I was still in a calm, passive state of witnessing. I watched my fall in slow motion, feeling light and insignificant in stillness. It was about an eight- to ten-foot drop from the top of my trajectory to the lower steps my head landed on. There was no way out but to let it happen.

As I landed, miraculously, the rough, wooden stairs with splinters and sharp edges felt like pillows. Sliding backwards down the stairs, I ended up completely on my backside, with my head at the bottom of the stairs and my feet aimed toward the top of the stairs. It was amazing that I felt no pain. My mind was blank. My body was essentially frozen in the same position that I had been standing in, with legs straight and arms at my sides. I felt like a rigid mannequin in a store. What an amazing miracle!

I was upside down and in a state of wonder. It was real, not a dream, but it seemed quite like a dream. From a fall like that, it would make sense to experience a lot of pain, yet I was quite pain-free, a genuine miracle. The grace of the master saved me from serious damage.

The feeling of being frozen in stillness faded as I remained motionless at the end of the fall. As I regained control of my body, the force of gravity made my legs start to move over my head, as if to go into a plow pose. At last, I was able to move on my own. I deliberately bent my knees and started twisting sideways to avoid falling any further.

After getting up and dusting myself off, I walked to the hall. From an experience like that, it would be typical to feel a lot of pain. Astonishingly, I had no splinters and did not feel any bruises or pain. One of the double doors was again closed. I silently opened it and walked into the room.

A woman inside the hall had begun sobbing after Robert had yelled at me. Robert was also crying now, and someone was holding him.

A tiny bit of shock was in me as I floated back to my spot and began to do some asanas. My focus was inward. I inhaled and exhaled consciously, willing the shock to leave. I watched it leave my body. I was grateful that I had been able to keep my silence in spite of the aggression against me. The doors and windows remained open, and gradually some freshness from the forest was available in the room. It was uplifting that everyone could do their pranayama safely now, with the benefit of the warm, mid-summer air.

A friend of mine came over to me and squatted down beside me. Terence asked me if I was okay, and I nodded positively. He was sincerely complimentary, saying, "Look how calm you are. Most people would be totally upset."

I was grateful, yet I was wondering about the play of karma that I had just gone through. As if reading my mind, Terence finished with a big grin, saying, "Now you don't have to get mugged!"

After that morning session, I entered the crowded dining hall. That building looked like an abandoned railroad car that had stopped as it was going up a hill. And it remained stuck there. The dining hall was the size of a large train car, with a narrow central aisle and tables and benches along both sides. The tables were like the wooden picnic table/bench assembly found in many parks and playgrounds. They may have been assembled inside the railway car. As I began walking uphill in the aisle toward the serving station, Robert suddenly materialized in front of me. He seemed like a completely different person.

With a big smile, he grabbed my hands. Startled, I was amazed by his profuse apologies. "I hope you are okay. I'm really sorry! You fell down but didn't get hurt, did you? You don't look like you got hurt. I'm sorry; please forgive me."

Smiling at him, I did my best to remain silent and still reassure him. He seemed reluctant to let go. He left right before I reached the food.

After I had some food and was eating quietly, Robert sat down across from me, on the other side of my table. He wanted to make sure that I was not hurt or upset. I was in a peaceful state and gave him a smile and a silent affirmative.

Over the years after that, our paths crossed many times. Robert was always cheerful, positive, and friendly towards me. We would greet each other cordially, without tension.

The Guru Purnima 1990, Loon Lake course, was where the puzzling and profoundly experiential talk, *2+1=0,* was given. It was part of our training to be able to move from a question to a wonder. To many questions, Gurudev repeatedly responded, "What is the answer?" One lady asked several times, "What is the question?" I enjoyed figuring out the meaning of $2+1=0$.

Gurudev said that in ignorance, people say, "I don't know." And they get stuck with questions. As we grow towards divine love, the question mark changes to "a wonder mark," an exclamation point. Then we get into what Gurudev calls "the beautiful 'I don't know!'." He said that "the beautiful 'I don't know'" is a basis for divine love. If we can love the unknown, then bhakti can blossom.

Gurudev Enjoys a Canoe Ride

One afternoon, a lady wanted Gurudev to have a canoe ride. She was talking about it as people gathered around Gurudev's cabin. Sometimes, people attempt to recruit support for their ideas when they want to make plans about doing things for a master.

It struck me that perhaps Gurudev had not been consulted about this canoe ride. This lady was clearly feverish for it to happen, which made it less likely that it would happen.

I stood there and thought that maybe hanging out there was just a waste of time. Then I figured that if Gurudev came out of his room, even for just a moment, it would not be a waste, so let me see what happens.

There was still a lot of uncertainty about whether Gurudev would actually come out of his cabin, let alone go out for a ride in the canoe.

Some people were debating about waiting or going elsewhere, as Gurudev was still in his cabin. Since I was in silence, I kept quiet.

Ignoring us, Gurudev quietly came out and stood on the deck. At first, he seemed otherwise occupied. He was gazing down, pausing, and seemingly deliberating. Then he looked up, and he gave a big smile to the people around him.

Then he seemed to notice the lady, S.W., who kept talking, saying, "The canoe is ready. You can go out on the lake." Slowly, Gurudev moved away from the door to his room. Gurudev glanced around and smiled at a few people. The group was quiet, standing, and watching.

S.W. said a few more things to encourage Gurudev to get in the canoe. By this point, we were only a few feet away from the canoe. Taking a slow step closer to the canoe, Gurudev looked down at it and paused. He then slowly responded, prolonging each syllable, "Oohkaay."

There was a group of people behind me. Everyone seemed frozen in place as Gurudev paused.

Gurudev then took a step to get into the canoe.

Realizing that the canoe was unstable for a person stepping into it, I thought that someone should hold it steady. Unless held in place, it could tip over. I quickly hopped to the edge of the deck, bent down low, and held the canoe steady for Gurudev to get in.

The canoe only had two seats. *Who is going to paddle for Gurudev?* We were all in a state of pause, observing Gurudev as he slowly and carefully got in and sat down.

In disbelief, I realized that nobody was in a position to paddle for Gurudev. I jumped in with delight and grabbed the snow shovel that was used as a paddle.

S.W. got upset because she was hoping that someone else would paddle. When she yelled at me, Gurudev laughed, and we took off.

As I was paddling the canoe with the snow shovel, Claire jumped into the lake and started swimming behind us. Claire swam along behind us for a while and then headed back to shore. We had a relaxing, peaceful ride. Gurudev waved at people waiting on the deck while we went along the opposite side of the lake.

On the last night of the course, after satsang, four of us, all men, took the canoe out under a full moon. Philip played his flute as we floated along. We took turns paddling with the snow shovel. That snow shovel was high-octane fuel compared to a regular, wooden oar.

Raft Tied to the Shore

There was a wooden raft next to the shore. An old rope attached it to another rope that was strung between some metal pipes stuck in the ground. The raft was topsy-turvy since the empty flotation containers underneath the raft were not evenly distributed or firmly in place. If two people stood on the raft in the same corner, it would tilt. Supporting three or more people required keeping the people spread out so the raft would stay more or less level. By pulling on the rope that secured the raft to the shore, the raft could move a few feet. Taking the raft out on the lake, away from the shore, was a bad idea since it was difficult to maneuver.

Gurudev got on the raft, and two or three people would join him. The group of people had to stay spread out around the edges so the raft would not tilt precariously. Naturally, someone would go closer to Gurudev, the raft would start to tilt, and Gurudev would tell them to move back. There were more people on the shore who wanted to get on, but the group with Gurudev discouraged it because the top of the raft was getting close to being submerged.

Special Tears on Guru Purnima

On the day of Guru Purnima, we had a small table set up near the entrance to the meeting hall. A puja set was placed on the table for Gurudev to use to perform Guru Puja.

I was one of the first to arrive at the hall. While waiting for Gurudev, I helped set up the puja articles. A solid group of people, shoulder-to-shoulder, ended up gathering between the entrance and the table before Gurudev himself arrived.

Often, when Gurudev arrives at a venue, everyone will stand up as he enters. Some people will rush to the front to grab seats while everyone is standing, in complete disrespect and disregard for those already situated.

Gurudev floated in and stood in front of the puja table. The crowd pushed me until I was beyond the table. As I faced the table, I was now looking at the back of the table. The whole area between Gurudev and the door was packed with people.

I wanted to be next to him for the puja, but I was not willing to push and shove to get back in place to be able to face the same direction as Gurudev. I felt a little sad and uncertain. From the table to the entrance of the hall and beyond, it was filled with people standing side by side.

Not knowing what else to do, I stayed just beyond the table. I figured that if Gurudev wanted me to move, he would say something.

Gurudev was drawn inward, silently focused. He was ignoring the group that had followed him into the room.

The entire group behind Gurudev was facing towards me, with a wide variety of expressions on their faces. I turned so that my back was against the wall on Gurudev's right side. I was facing Gurudev. I was determined to focus only on Gurudev and the puja and ignore everything else.

The room was quiet as he began to sing the puja. We were all standing, and I was looking directly at his face. In front of my chest, I was holding my hands, palms together, in a prayer position.

At first, I felt awkward being on the other side of the table from Gurudev. Then I got swept away in the puja. Other concerns faded out. I felt a sense of celestial reality.

As Gurudev placed the final offering and bowed down, I was directly facing him. I bowed down at the same time.

As we rose up, I saw a single tear fall from his eye and land on the puja table. His face showed a tender intensity that vanished as he got up from bowing down.

I felt deeply moved and profoundly blessed to witness

this delicate expressiveness from Gurudev. My good luck astonished me when I realized that nobody else could see the one tear from Gurudev.

That strange sequence of losing my place and having an awkward standing position was actually a tremendous blessing, as I was the only one who had been allowed to witness this precious tear.

Gurudev did not wipe his eye. His face was surprisingly dry as he got up and walked over to his seat. Nobody suspected that he had wept. I was in a state of awe and wonder. My physical body felt light and insignificant.

Even the Master

Even the master
has cried for his beloved master!
I have seen with my own eyes,
this rare blessing of an event,
a moment I glimpsed.
He has pushed me,
and pulled me,
into the middle
of an invisible sacred fire.
I watch as it burns.

We sat for a while in a warm atmosphere of profound feeling. Gurudev spoke about devotion and Guru Purnima. Then he started talking about Krishna's final moments with his devotee, Uddhava, before Krishna's death.

Gurudev told us that Krishna had told Uddhava that the love of the Gopis was impressively strong. As Gurudev spoke, the intensity of feeling in the room increased.

Gurudev continued describing the scene with Krishna and Uddhava. Krishna told Uddhava that he could feel the love of the Gopis.

Krishna told Uddhava, "I'm not in the temples. I'm not in heaven. Where my devotees sing, I'm right there."

As Gurudev said, "I'm right there," quoting Krishna, he choked up and could not continue speaking.

He put his hands in front of his face in prayer position, and tears sprang into the eyes of most of us in the room. Many people were sobbing out loud. Every time I think of that moment, I feel it in my heart. It was surprisingly powerful.

We were swept up in divine devotion. There was no possible way for me to be in that moment other than to weep with the master, invoking that precious moment with Krishna and Uddhava.

We were absorbed in a profound experience that, from the inside, seemed impossible to measure. As Gurudev dried his eyes, there was a lot of blowing of noses and the use of tissues. The atmosphere shifted as we chuckled together.

As commentary on things other than the profusion of weeping, Gurudev said, "Love can melt even the rocks." Then a wave of laughter rippled through the group.

I watched carefully and noted how Gurudev tucked inside his empty drinking cup the tissues he had used to wipe his eyes. As he walked away from his seat, I picked up that cup and held it close to my heart.

It is noteworthy that Gurudev spoke a couple of times about an unusual saint named Shandilya. Shandilya was known for doing things in unpredictable, unexpected ways.

Some thought Shandilya was anti-social since Shandilya would go against norms. Shandilya taught Bhakti Sutras. Narada mentioned Shandilya in the Narada Bhakti Sutras.

After we had left Loon Lake, at the end of the 1990 Guru Purnima Advanced Silence Course, there was one more evening satsang in Vancouver. We started that satsang with just two people with Gurudev. I was surprised that only three other people joined us. It ended up that way because a lot of people caught earlier flights to Nova Scotia.

Not Move at All During Sudarshan Kriya

From Vancouver, Gurudev flew to Halifax, where he concluded the 1990 North American Bhakti Sutra Tour. An Advanced Silence Course, as well as a TTC, were offered in Halifax.

During the satsangs in Halifax, Gurudev taught the *Shri Radhe Radhe Radhe Shyam* bhajan. This bhajan became a mainstay of the Art of Living.

> *Shri radhe radhe radhe shyam Govinda radhe*
> *Shri radhe radhe radhe shyam Govinda radhe*
> *Shri radhe*
> *Govinda radhe radhe shyam*
> *Gopala radhe radhe shyam*
> *Govinda radhe radhe shyam*
> *Gopala radhe radhe shyam*
> *Shri radhe radhe radhe shyam Govinda radhe*

During these Halifax courses, Gurudev gave the instruction that it is better not to move at all during Sudarshan Kriya breathing (also known as SKY). This was interesting given that I had developed a habit of holding yoga poses during SKY breathing.

It was helpful to understand what was happening during my first year of doing SKY. Inevitably, my physical pain would increase while I was sitting and breathing. It would reach a point of burning intensity where I had to change my position so I could continue the technique.

In the first year, I would hold each position until the pain forced me to move. The first position that I started in could last for about fifteen to twenty minutes maximum. In the second position, my maximum was eight to twelve minutes. Subsequent positions in a session might last four to eight minutes.

Over the weeks and months, during my second year of doing the SKY, I started holding various yoga positions in anticipation of avoiding the pain. The time in each pose got shorter as the weeks and months went by.

Somehow, I fooled myself into thinking that the movement was uncontrived. Shortchanging myself, I was doing asanas during SKY.

As soon as I heard the instruction that it is better not to move during SKY breathing, I was able to sit all the way through without moving.

I was grateful for that instruction and how it magically eliminated both my self-deception as well as the need for my body to move or change position during SKY.

In the Pavilion of Joy

Here,

In the pavilion of Joy

    I have met integrity.

        It is You.

        It is All You.

In the storehouse of Strength

    I have met gentleness.

        It is You.

        It is All You.

Over the threshold of Wisdom

    I have met simplicity.

        It is You.

        It is All You.

In the basket of Fullness

I have seen the Empty Space

It is You.

It is All You.

At the home of Beauty

I have seen Your face.

It is You.

It is All You.

It is Only You.

    One day, the lines from the poem above kept hovering in my mind. I quickly wrote some of the lines on the back of a business card.

    Miraculously, that business card managed to survive a lot of travel. It drifted from pocket to pocket in different pairs of pants of mine, sometimes hanging in the closet, sometimes being worn. It was buried in a book for many months.

    I guess Gurudev wanted something to happen with that poem, because a few months after I wrote it, I saw that he said a few of the same words in a similar way. It gave me a tingly sensation to see that synchronicity. At first, I felt briefly disoriented. There was a pinch of possessiveness, which I then felt ashamed of. Thankfully, it passed quickly, and I was able to expand in wonder.

It connected the dots for me to see that nice words written in a charming way come from one big mind. Being an embodiment of the big mind, Gurudev could feel those words before, during, or after I thought them.

When you haven't been the recent focus of any ridicule, judgment, or harassment, it is easier to feel detached. When you have assimilated what the master says, it is much easier to feel detached. Real yoga brings healthy detachment that stays with us through ups and downs.

I was getting into longer periods of detachment. Sometimes, I was able to sustain detachment for most of the day. One time detachment percolated deeply into my system, and the following poem came up.

It was as if a message not only to myself but also to many others, from big mind to small mind. The flavor of it lasted for several days deep within.

Everyone is on Fire

Everyone is on fire.

Who among us knows it?

Life is smoldering!

How much ash

have you left behind?

Forget about your collections!

They are dead!

Just a bit of distraction.

The light of knowledge beckons.

Chapter Thirteen: The First Temescal Canyon Advanced Course

The fall of 1990 passed quickly for me. Gurudev had said that he would come and lead a week-long, silent Advanced Course in December. He said that I would be in charge of setting it up for him. We were in luck; the Temescal Canyon Retreat Center was available for rent.

Gurudev specified that everyone had to apply ahead of time for the course. This was important because we had limited capacity for participants. We ended up overflowing with applicants. Impressively, the first Temescal Canyon Advanced Course was sold out more than three weeks before the course.

The Temescal Canyon Park Management had a strict limit of 139 people maximum for programs, with participants receiving food in the dining hall. Therefore, we could only have 139 maximum course participants. Three weeks before the course started, we had a waiting list of seven people. Some people who attempted to rush into the course at the last minute had to be turned away.

After I had the maximum number of applications, I spoke with Gurudev on the phone to go over details about the course. Gurudev was planning to teach an Advanced Course on the East Coast, in Connecticut, right before the West Coast Temescal Canyon Advanced Course.

In order to accommodate more people for Temescal, Gurudev wanted me to ask applicants from Fairfield, Iowa, to attend the course on the East Coast. Only a few were willing and able to attend the East Coast course. We felt successful at having filled the Temescal course to maximum capacity, with no room to spare. There was a lot of excitement for this course. It was full of devotion.

Typically, I would drive to the course site immediately after eating breakfast. One such morning, I arrived at Gurudev's room and had a moment to sit with him.

Gurudev pulled out from his bag a couple of jars with Indian labels. He became animated and said that they were fantastic rasayanas, made somewhere near Bangalore. He ate a spoonful from each of a couple of different jars. As I watched him, I was salivating and getting excited about the herb formulas. Gurudev's eyes were big and bright as he praised the rasayanas. He enthused that they were exceptionally good and that some other famous preparations were "nothing next to this!" Then, in a neutral tone, he said,

"They are for an empty stomach." Shifting to an expression of surprise, "Oh, your tummy is full!"

It was the perfect setup for me on several levels. I saw myself getting excited about the herbal formulas. I felt myself dying to taste them. The disappointment over not having any was a real letdown. I realized that I had reacted in a predictable way. Gurudev had set me up, and I had fallen right into the trap. I was becoming aware of it. Yet I still ached for a taste of the herbal rasayana. Dispassion was not there. Then I felt regret for my own reactions.

Dancing with the Master Under a Full Moon

On the last night of the course, there was a full moon. We all went outside and gathered in a meadow. The moonlight was filtered by some clouds and the branches of gigantic, old sycamore trees. At Gurudev's suggestion, all the course participants made a big circle. Gurudev asked us to stay in place in the circle. He said he would move around the circle.

Full of joy, Gurudev was magically in front of me, and we danced together. Then he moved on to the next person. Once he had danced with me, I felt like a cloud. Peacefully floating in the sky. Time became meaningless.

Gurudev danced with every person in the circle. Murmurs of delight and laughter punctuated the stillness. There was a sense of creating brand new magic. Also, a sense of ancient times. Moments stretched and lingered. What a wonderful way to end a course!

Be a Tree

During April 1991, I was feeling a lot of emotional upset. It was challenging in those days, as I would often feel like I was a smoking fire. I was burning inside, sometimes for days on end.

One day I reached a point where yoga, pranayama, meditation, breathing, and focusing on work or seva were not enough. All my enthusiasm was gone, and I felt discouraged. Floundering hopelessly, it was as if I were lost in billows of smoke. *Maybe I should go ahead and call Gurudev on the telephone.*

It is often quite difficult to reach Gurudev by phone. Masters are often super adept at avoiding phone calls. Many people have had the experience of trying to reach Gurudev unsuccessfully.

Sometimes I would call and be told that he was giving a lecture or traveling to another location.

Near-misses were common when people only had a landline phone and did not know his exact location. Ironically, sometimes you might hear Gurudev talking in the background while you are being told that you can't speak with him.

Luck was with me, as I reached Gurudev on my first try. In most cases, phone calls with Gurudev typically end up being extremely short. Adding another miracle to the miracle of reaching him, the master spoke with me for an incredibly long time that day.

I did not feel any sense that he was in a hurry to hang up. I just heard him understanding me and supporting me, giving me gentle, loving encouragement. Gradually, with the sound of his soothing voice, I started to relax and feel better.

The only words I remember from that call were that

Gurudev told me to live like a tree.

"A tree provides shade for whomever is there. If someone is enjoying the shade, the tree is happy. When a person goes away, the tree does not cry, 'Please come back.' If a crowd is there, the tree is happy. When nobody is there, the tree is happy."

This is a captivating description of an experience associated with a profound level of consciousness. Something to aim for. Feeling soothed and inspired, part of me wondered if I could ever fulfill the essence and be like a tree.

The phone call was so uncharacteristically long that some people in the room with Gurudev noticed. It is rare that a call will exceed five, ten or fifteen minutes. Having a call last more than forty-five minutes is seriously improbable.

The identity of the upset person on the phone was a mystery for some time. The master kept it secret.

Some months later, a person who had been in the room with Gurudev during the phone call found out that I had had that surprisingly long phone call with Gurudev. The man who had been in Gurudev's room during the long phone call exclaimed, "Was that you? I was there, and his voice was so soft and soothing, I thought he was talking to a woman. I thought he was talking to a woman!"

Refuge and Solace

Refuge and solace

You have been for me,

holding my heart

and setting it free.

Nurturing and kind,

thoughtful and loving.

Caring beyond

what any could imagine was coming.

Wiping out lifetimes

of struggle and stress.

You are the reason.

You are the best!

SECTION FIVE: INDIA, 1991

Chapter Fourteen: First Trip to India

Flying to India, I discovered that it was impossible for me to sleep on the plane. While reading on the flight, I would feel sleepy, put down the book, and close my eyes. Whether my eyes were closed for twenty minutes or an hour, I remained alert, except for a couple of brief moments. Meditation on the plane felt barely refreshing.

The large time zone change of 12.5 hours, no sleep on the plane (well, maybe thirty minutes of sleep), and not drinking enough water combined to give me intense jet lag. My mind was a dull fog, and it was difficult to stay awake during the day. I discovered on subsequent trips to India that if I drink water multiple times every hour during a flight as well as after landing, I will have less jet lag. Walking outside for a couple of hours during daylight each day without sunglasses is also crucial. Then I barely feel any jet lag.

In July 1991, the plan was for all course participants to go first to the Bangalore city ashram/center, Gyan Mandir, and spend a night there. Arriving at the city ashram, I felt a serious need to rest. As I walked through Gyan Mandir, I discovered that every room was occupied. The entry room had people receiving visitors and people making phone calls. People were even cutting vegetables in the hallway. People were bathing or washing clothes in the bathrooms. Even the stairwell landings had people huddled, chatting intensely, chanting, or playing musical instruments softly.

In one small bedroom sat a fellow American I recognized from a previous course. I had not seen him in many months. When I stuck my head in the door, it appeared that I was interrupting his agitated state of mind.

Forcefully, he asked me some random question that had nothing to do with me. "Should I go to Japan?"

I figured that the only way someone in that house would consider going to another country would be if they had already spent a big chunk of time with Gurudev. I asked him, "How long have you been here?"

When he replied, "Just a couple of days," I felt sorry for him. He shared that he got sick right after he arrived in India. I suggested that he wait and let himself get strong and healthy before making any decision. As I stood there, he seemed to submerge back into his fog of confusion; his passionate outburst ended in silence. I excused myself and resumed my search for a peaceful spot to rest.

The instruction was that the master wanted all the arriving foreigners to spend a night at Gyan Mandir before making the journey to the ashram on Kanakapura Road. I felt a sense of despair as I realized that every decent sleeping spot was more than well accounted for.

I finally gave up looking for empty spaces by the wall. I sat down in the remaining empty space in the middle of the floor of the large meeting room. One side of the space had doors to several small rooms along one wall. The other walls were lined with people in many different states of activity or rest. Old friends were being greeted. New friends were being made. Clothing was being sorted. People with various looks of focus or seriousness would cross the room on this or that errand. A nap or a meditation would be happening here or there, in between suitcases.

A German lady was sitting against the wall with her eyes closed. For a while, she would make a long, drawn-out sound every couple of minutes that made it sound like she was breathing extremely slowly. Softly, Michael joked that she was doing super big circles, and a couple of us laughed.

After a few hours, there was a shift of energy and a

flurry of motion as Gurudev emerged from his small private room that was immediately adjacent to the meeting room. He walked into the big room and greeted several people.

Word spread that the small bus was ready to make a trip to the ashram. I felt sad that I would have to stay while Gurudev left without me. Following Gurudev downstairs, I then stopped in the doorway and watched from a distance as a couple more people boarded the already crowded bus. It was not much of a bus. It was more like a large van with bus-style seating. I wondered what I should do next.

Someone rushed from the van called "bus" and called my name. I was being told to hurry and grab my luggage because Gurudev said I could go! I was grateful that I had not unpacked my bags. I ran back upstairs and brought my two suitcases to the bus. As I stood just inside the van/bus door on the entry steps, I could see that every single seat was occupied. The luggage was jammed into the back of the bus and in the aisle. The only empty seat was the driver's seat.

I was uncertain how to place my bags, and it looked like there might be room only for me or my luggage. We had been told that the van called "bus" could hold sixty children.

I realized that if they put skinny, tiny, four- or five-year-old kids, three on each seat, with school bags on their laps, they could hold sixty small kids. Two adults filled the seats generously, and in many cases, much too generously.

Every seat had its own conversation going on. With Gurudev already in the front seat next to Reiner, a German gentleman, it sounded like a party was well under way.

Amazing Journey in the Tiny School Bus

Seeing my predicament, Gurudev told Reiner to scoot in as much as possible. Gurudev told me I could sit there with them. We packed in tightly, side-by-side.

I filled the remaining aisle space with my bags and felt such relief at having a seat. Not only a seat, but a seat shared with the master! *Thank goodness, what a blessing!*

It didn't matter that there was only room for one half of my body. I felt such a huge sense of relief to be riding on that bus with Gurudev.

As the bus began to move, I had to press my left foot firmly into the floor to keep my right side perched on the bus bench. My entire left side was in the air over the aisle. I also had to grip the bar in front of us with my right hand to keep myself in place.

There were lots of ruts, holes, and ditches in the road. The abrupt and continued lurching of the bus provided plenty of challenge for my efforts to remain perched in the seat.

Everyone was adjusting to the unpredictable motion. During a brief, quiet moment, Gurudev leaned over with a big grin on his face and said, loudly and clearly, "Where is your seat, Daren? Is your seat in imagination or reality?" Most of the bus burst into laughter as I used my arms and legs to keep the right half of my body in the seat.

Forcefully, it hit me. "Imagination or reality?"

I realized that with a small joke, he was imparting knowledge.

Tingles went up my spine as my mind expanded in wonder. One's seat is wherever you decide that you are and the position you take. If you are nursing anger or sadness, that is your seat. If you think that more people need to think a certain way about you, that is your seat. If you are immersed in knowledge, that is your seat. Gurudev had put me into an experience of huge awareness in a flash.

I was stunned into speechlessness and filled with great wonder. Not a word of the conversations around me mattered. I was lost in pondering whether I was living in imagination or reality.

What is reality?
What part of life is imagination?
Am I actually here right now?
How much of my life has been just a fantasy?

The squeaking bus, grinding gears, growling engine, and honking horns, interspersed with giddy laughter and multiple conversations, wove around me like a complex tapestry.

Reiner had a lot to say. Reiner talked on and on and on with Gurudev, and not a word registered.

Lost in following the thread of reality vs. imagination, the next forty minutes seemed like a blur.

I was grateful for the genuine care that Gurudev expressed very effortlessly. I felt blessed by Gurudev's joke, which had become, for me, some powerful magical nectar of teaching. My mind expanded in wonder.

Is this imaginary?
How does one best determine what is true or false?
What is reality?

I was perched, literally, on both the edge of my seat and within a fantastic experience of wonder. Awestruck, I felt small and insignificant.

Awareness of my sitting position shrank to a minimum and disappeared.

What about my life?
How much of what a person thinks is imaginary?

Nobody else spoke to me. I was in deep silence.

"*When can I be sure about reality?*

I was attempting to expand my discernment. I wanted it to yield only truth. This alternated with floating in a state of hyper-awareness. I was immersed for a solid forty minutes in long stretches of inner silence punctuated by focused words. Gurudev set this up so effortlessly.

How much of my experience is real?
Is my thinking accurate?
Is this thought process part of reality or imagination?
Does it have any deeper meaning?
Does it make a difference?

The laughter and words floated around me as the sun began to set and the sky gradually grew darker.

Various colors of lights at the ashram twinkled and greeted us as we came near.

Waves of gratitude and wonder made my skin tingle.

On the One Hand

On the one hand,

infinite space,

the ultimate depth of experience.

On the other hand,

a dazzling carousel of life,

so vast and intricate.

Too many directions and choices

for one life to experience.

How can it all be contained

within the glorious Oneness?

The ocean may be an answer.

It is also part of the tapestry,

which was decorated for our play.

My first night at the ashram was spent in a dorm-style transition room. Housing arrangements for subsequent nights had to be specified later. An influx of people was expected for Guru Purnima celebrations.

The following day, I started feeling ill. All day, I waited for my room assignment. The suspense and illness distracted me from the hunger that raged after having only one tiny meal. Close to sunset, I was given my next room assignment. I managed to move my luggage into my next room in the Vasishtha building. The four beds were already taken. I found a spot on the floor under a window. My energy was dwindling rapidly.

It seemed to take forever to spread my sleeping pad and bag on the floor. Fever was building in my system. I felt weak, hot, and delirious.

There were a number of elder Indian gentlemen in the room. As the darkness of the night thickened, another group of men arrived. Unable to converse, I was overcome with exhaustion. As I lay down to sleep, there was a commotion of eight people in a room made to house four adults at maximum. Multiple conversations bounced off the walls.

When I awoke from a deep, dull sleep, my head was turned to my left. I opened my eyes to find an Indian gentleman lying right next to me, only inches away.

This was inconceivable to me. First, that someone would choose to sleep very close to a stranger. Second, that I was so out of it that I was not awakened by their presence.

Ordinarily, my sleep disturbances were such that slight noise and movement in the bedroom would wake me. I raised my head and counted eleven people packed tightly into our little room. All the floor space between the real beds was covered with bodies and luggage.

That day, I was too sick to leave the room. It took all my energy just to wobble my way to the toilet and drift back to collapse into my floor space. Luckily, a bathroom adjoined the bedroom. I was glad that the sickness had knocked me down only after I was situated at the ashram.

Guru Purnima Blessings

I was told that Gurudev had given assurance that those who were too ill to attend the Guru Purnima celebration would still get the benefit of the chanting if we sat up while it was happening. Part of me wished that I could actually be in attendance, but it took a lot of effort just to sit up. In my vague fog of fever and sickness, I sat and felt gratitude for this blessing. Even though I was sick for several days, it felt like the blessings of Guru Purnima helped me to recover more quickly than I would have otherwise.

Public Talk Given by Gurudev in India

One evening, Gurudev gave a public talk near the ashram. The venue was a small meeting room at a Hindu temple somewhere between the ashram and Bangalore city. The simple concrete building was off the main road, near undeveloped land, close to the ashram. All the women sat on the left side of the room as you walked in, facing toward the stage area. A central walkway kept men on the right side, away from the women. I sat in the front row with the men.

Eberhard, one of the first Art of Living teachers in

Europe, sat on my right. Eberhard seemed comfortable being in India. We all sat on the concrete floor. Gurudev happily sat on a tiny, child's-sized chair, facing the audience.

Gurudev began the talk by saying, "There is no such thing as a perfect action. But there can be a perfect actor."

All action on this planet is part of material reality, where the three gunas rule. Perfection is only found in the big mind, known as the true self, or divine consciousness. That seemed to be the key point.

Meeting a Shankaracharya

One day, while in silence, we took a short bus trip, in a larger bus, to what looked like a small, abandoned school.

Sitting in miniscule, hard, uncomfortable chairs, we waited in the school for Gurudev and some special guests. There were a few Americans and Canadians. Most of the group were from Europe, including people from Germany and a large group of women from Poland.

While we were waiting for the dignitaries to arrive, Eberhard led the group in pranayama practice. Eberhard sat in a vajrasan position on the stage at the front of the room.

Eberhard's enthusiastic bhastrika was so energetic that his elbows actually made a clearly audible sound when they contacted his ribcage as he brought his arms down. When he straightened his arms above his head, his reach was so vigorous that he actually became slightly airborne as his slim body responded to the arm movement. Eberhard was visibly moving in little hops on the stage. Witnessing this, some of the ladies sitting near the front started giggling. As often happens around the master; once the giggling started, it became contagious and hard to stop.

Gurudev came in with a couple of men in orange robes. The eldest gentleman was a *Shankaracharya*. Adi Shankara started the sacred post of spiritual authority known as Shankaracharya. Adi Shankara was a brilliant young saint who revitalized spirituality in India during his brief lifetime, many hundreds of years ago.

We met the Shankaracharya, who seemed to be in silence. His glasses were so thick that I could not see what his eyes looked like. He had a gentle, kind demeanor. Gurudev praised this Shankaracharya. Our planned endeavor of silent, Advanced Courses was praised. Gurudev was pleased to share that the Shankaracharya was happy that we had come from many countries to spend time in knowledge, silence, and meditation.

When we left the venue, the large school bus that had delivered the group of us was not there. There were a variety of smaller vehicles to take us back to the ashram. In the dark of the night, with a dozen others, I managed to get into the back of a small truck. The cargo area was enclosed on the sides and covered with a roof. We loaded in like cattle, and the back gate was closed. It was difficult to see anything at all. As the truck started to move, it lurched to the side, and we were tossed around, bumping into each other. Fortunately, nobody was seriously hurt. Luckily, there were slats of wood on the sides, which we quickly grabbed. We silently journeyed with new friends and held on tight to avoid falling.

Early Morning Meditation with the Master

My recovery from my initial illness at the Bangalore ashram seemed to coincide with settling into a daily rhythm that happened for the ashram as a whole. This was after the departure of the guests who had come just for the 1991 Guru Purnima celebration.

We would enjoy a thirty-minute-long meditation with Gurudev from 6 a.m. to 6:30 a.m. Then there would be an hour of asanas. I enjoyed doing asanas on the smooth concrete without a mat. For a while, we had no leader. Everyone did asanas on their own. Some people had a thin grass mat, or a blanket, on top of the concrete for the yoga. Most days, I put a thin cotton cloth on the concrete in order to keep myself clean.

One morning, while we were meditating before sunrise, the atmosphere was typically quiet and peaceful. After about twenty minutes of meditation, our group of about forty people was deep in stillness. Freakishly, sounds started coming from the speakers. We heard the words, "Are you recording me?" Then some silly laughter began.

A recording of Carla's distinctive voice was playing. When Carla laughs, she literally makes a sequence of sounds that go something like, "Aaah ha ha ha hoo hoo hoo hoo hohoho heeehee heee heee aaaah ha ha ha ha hooo haaaaaa hee hayhayhoho." It is some of the wackiest laughter ever heard. When Carla starts laughing, she can easily laugh non-stop for five or ten minutes.

Our mischievous master had surprised the whole group. Everyone was laughing. People dissolved into laughter. Even the most serious people there laughed wholeheartedly. The highlight for me was to see two female psychotherapists, who were both generally fairly serious and sometimes skeptical, literally rolling on the floor near each other. Those two ladies were able to laugh in a record-breaking way. They were still giggling on the floor long after many others had stopped laughing. It probably helped that they were sitting quite close to the Guru.

The previous day, Gurudev had been enthusiastic when he told me that Carla had sent a laughter tape. He even played the beginning of the tape for me. In spite of the Guru privately sharing the tape the day before the meditation, it still took me by surprise to hear it being played during the morning meditation. I could not help but laugh along with everyone else, even though I recognized the recording. I figured that it must have been a superlative blast of a surprise for everyone else who was hearing it for the first time.

The Original Incense

During a break between courses, one morning there were few people at the ashram. The sky was gray. I did not see anyone else as I walked to Gurudev's room after breakfast. After I knocked on Gurudev's door and entered, I was surprised to see the floor covered with big gunny sacks.

Radiating enthusiasm, Gurudev explained, "We are making incense!"

Each sack was filled with a type of flower, bark, leaf, plant, or resin. The incense makers would bring the sacks to Gurudev, and Gurudev would pick out which items to use and determine the proportions. The ingredients would be mixed and ground to make incense.

Dhoop means incense. Gurudev had a big grin as he

declared, "This is dhoop. This is the original incense!"

Gurudev filled a smaller sack with a variety of these substances. He urged that since many people on the last course had been sick, we should burn incense in all the empty rooms.

He gave me the small sack and pointed at an old-fashioned metal censer. The censer was a box, like a miniature house with a roof. It had lots of holes and a chain that had four smaller chains attached to each corner of its roof. Gurudev wanted me to be the official bearer of incense. My job that day was to "dhoop the rooms" that were vacant.

I would go into each empty room, light the incense, and leave the room. When the room was filled with smoke, I would take the dhoop to the next room.

I hoped to finish quickly since there were not many buildings on the ashram at that time. It took me all day to get to every room, and I felt overly saturated with smoke.

How Gurudev Sri Sri Made Me More Ahimsa

Since the ashram was at that time quite isolated, with a lot of fields spreading into the distance in multiple directions, it was usually quite peaceful and easy to stay in silence. There were no cell phones or computers.

During the first month of my stay, there was only one pay phone in a small shack available for just a few hours on a certain day of the week. When I first found out about it, it may have only been available on Tuesdays. Then, after a while, maybe Tuesdays and Thursdays. Later, sometimes

Saturdays, if the worker showed up. For a while, availability was difficult to predict. In hopes of making a phone call, one day I waited outside the empty phone shack for two hours. This was during "open" hours. I didn't see anyone nearby.

I was glad that I generally did not need to make phone calls. As the weeks went by, more hours were made available, and an inscrutable sign was posted with hours of service. Sometimes the phone shack was empty during the hours of service listed on the crude sign. The longer I stayed at the ashram, the more sophisticated the telephone service became. More hours of phone service became available, especially after more than one phone was on site.

Shortly after Guru Purnima, we had a person who was leading asanas mostly silently. Later, the leader of yoga changed. The new leader took a lot of time explaining each posture, so we did very few poses.

My enthusiasm to continue to join the group yoga class fizzled out when I realized that I did not enjoy the minimal asanas or the style in which the asanas were being taught. Some yoga teachers think that they have to keep talking about random stuff throughout the class. This makes it harder to go deep into transcendence in each pose. During silence courses, I wanted less talking during the asanas. I decided to go find a secluded place to do my own thing.

As I wandered around the ashram, looking for a place to do my asanas, I was getting frustrated with the lack of flat, level ground and the absence of privacy. The ashram was still very primitive in 1991. I didn't want to spend all morning looking for a venue.

The first meditation hall was under construction and seemed to have the only reasonable space. There was no roof at that point; there were just partial outer walls and stacks of building materials. The area of the building that would end up being the stage was not clear from a quick glance.

Frustratingly, the floor was just sand. I gave up on the idea of doing yoga asanas and started practicing Tai Chi.

For a couple of months before traveling to India, I had been practicing a style of Tai Chi that included both slow and fast moves. It was known as a Yang form as opposed to the slow Yin style that most people are familiar with.

As long as I practiced it regularly, I could remember the Tai Chi sequence, but I was still learning it.

Slowly, I walked around the construction site to get a sense of all of it. Instinctively, I stayed off the area that ended up being used as Gurudev's seating area, simply because it felt wrong to do the Tai Chi right there, even though it was the most level and the best surface to stand on. When I found out eight weeks later that that was where Gurudev would sit, I was grateful for my instinct to avoid exercising there.

After three days of performing Tai Chi in the morning by myself, Gurudev called me to his room. He gave me new instructions. "When you wake up, come to my room. As soon as you wake up, you come to my room."

This was a special adventure that had many interesting components. Having moved down the hill from the Vasishtha building, I was staying in a square, concrete block, single-story building called Parashara. It had no bathroom. There was a simple, minimalistic bathroom in a small building nearby.

In a mirror at the ashram, I never saw myself. Mirrors were rare items at the ashram in those days. Of course, some people must have carried small mirrors with them. Not once did I see my face in a mirror at the ashram.

There was no mirror in the bathroom. A small scrap of shiny metal pretended to be a mirror, but with no success. Standing in front of the piece of warped, dull metal, you could tell there was light in the room and not much else.

Sometimes you would catch a fleeting glimpse of a dull reminder of something vaguely different than the color of the room. No facial features, ears, hair details, or bodily outlines were ever visible in our fake mirror. Shaving happened strictly by feel, with a bit of luck.

Most days, my roommates remained asleep as I woke, dressed, went to the neighboring building to use the bathroom, and then made final preparations to leave the room. This worked out well, as I was not to tell anyone what I was doing. Most people stayed asleep and had no idea that I left. I did my best to be quiet. One morning, I found Philip awake, sitting on his bed, when I came back from the bathroom. On another morning, Bryan was awake before I left. As time went on, after several weeks, sometimes I would find someone meditating before I left the room.

Many mornings, it was still dark as I began my walk to Gurudev's *kutir*, a small hut. (Wherever Gurudev stays, devotees often refer to his room as "the *kuti*.") Some mornings, Gurudev opened the door to his room right as I arrived, without me knocking. Some days, the door opened right after I knocked. Sometimes he looked at me and said, "Not today." There were times the door never opened, and other days Gurudev left the door ajar for me to walk in. Each morning was precious and special.

There were times we did asanas together, but Gurudev preferred to relax, be passive, and have me hold his limbs so that I was essentially moving his body for him, doing his asanas for him. Some mornings, he would just want some massage.

Weeks later, I realized I no longer remembered the Tai Chi sequence. I also realized that it was better at that point in my life that I was not practicing that form. Tai Chi does not, in and of itself, promote violence. The practice of a form does not necessarily cultivate violence. There was something in me. The seed of violence was in my own mind-body system. Real yoga helps flush violent tendencies out of us.

It was clear to me that there were memories of battles and fighting in my system. Maybe from multiple past lives on ancient battlefields. Even just a few kicks and punches at that time were enough to stir up fierce warrior energies with ego, which was counterproductive to my unfolding of divine awareness. As a yogi, I needed to be fully *ahimsa*, nonviolent.

Grateful for the generosity of Gurudev, I knew that he had skillfully offered me a sweet, desirable alternative to that punching and kicking form of Tai Chi practice. The skill of a master lifts us out of situations that are not the best for us. Sometimes this happens without the master making any emphatic declaration or even a slight comment. It can be mysterious and graceful or abrupt and challenging, depending on the needs and karmas of the people involved.

Observing Emotional Discomfort

One day, at the Bangalore Ashram in 1991, I was upset when I arrived at Gurudev's room. Inside myself, I was churning. Gurudev looked at me, seemed thoughtful, and motioned with a hand for me to come in. He indicated a space along the wall and said, "Be seated; I have something to attend to." He left the room as I sat down. I figured that I should close my eyes and be with the sensations.

Feeling emotional, there was physical discomfort clearly in my abdomen. I sat and watched the uncomfortable show inside my body as whatever emotions were processing.

Just as the last bit of it was fully fading away, Gurudev walked back into the room. I realized that he had wanted me to process the emotions on my own. He wanted it done before we started interacting. It was definitely empowering.

Many people avoid feeling things and then carry the same set of feelings for years, even an entire lifetime. Undoubtedly, this is one reason why classic Ayurveda says that most illnesses have emotional roots.

Many times, I have heard Gurudev speak about observing sensations and not analyzing any feelings. If a person analyzes and tries to figure out all the causes of a feeling, that tends to prolong bad feelings. When you simply observe, positive feelings last longer, and negative emotions dissolve and fade away. It can happen fairly quickly, too.

It is such a revelation to actually do the observing and feel the intense feelings fade away. One set of fresh feelings might only require one intense sitting to actually dissolve. When you observe, your sensations will change sooner or later. This is part of real yoga.

Gurudev said succinctly, "You are not the slave of your feelings. You are the master of your feelings." I wanted to live this truth.

Whenever Gurudev dismissed me, I left his room. Sometimes it was during the breakfast period. It happened a few times that I was dismissed after breakfast was finished and my seva team was standing, waiting for me.

There I was, running to try and grab some food, and people were looking at me with disapproval.

"Where were you?"

"What have you been doing?"

"We were looking for you and couldn't find you!"

They were often skeptical when I told them that I had been doing some seva for Gurudev. It was awkward since I wasn't supposed to tell them the complete truth.

Some people thought that I was just an airhead or a loser. Another opportunity to lose some karma, as people would judge and disapprove.

In one instance, a seva team of ten or more people had already dispersed since they assumed I would not show up. This was frustrating to me. I was dedicated to planting trees around the ashram landscape. Gurudev was giving me more opportunities not to be a football of the opinions of others. And to drop expectations while burning through karma.

Gardening Seva

Various options were available for seva at the ashram. It was expected that everyone would do some seva after breakfast until just before lunch. Gurudev asked me to be in charge of gardening, leading groups of people to do some planting of trees, watering, and minimalistic landscaping.

At that time, in 1991, the Bangalore ashram was primitive, mostly barren, with a lot of rocky terrain. The red dirt would stain clothing, especially when we were gardening.

Planting trees was a significantly important activity for the ashram at that time. The planting of trees is inherently satisfying and promotes joy for me.

Flowers, such as marigolds with yellow or orange blossoms, were growing in a few small patches scattered across the ashram. When I noticed such flowers had dried blossoms, I would gather the flower heads and keep them in my pocket. Marigolds grow fairly easily. As I walked back and forth across the ashram, I would scatter the seeds along the edges of pathways. After some rainy days, it was satisfying to observe new flowers coming up from seeds that I had scattered.

The group of people on the gardening seva teams changed at the end of each course. Some people would leave the ashram to return home. New people would show up for the next course. I found that I was repeating instructions a lot.

Some people were quite happy to be gardening. One day, some ladies even started dancing as we scattered grass seed.

Sometimes a few people did not want to be there. I would do my best to ignore the random, hostile attitudes. It was challenging to keep my silence and give instructions to guide the teams to take care of various areas. I would carry a pen and paper and write notes.

Some days, it seemed like definite progress was being made. Some days I spent the entire seva period running back and forth trying to make sure that each group had what it needed and that they understood what needed to be done.

Around the middle of my four-month stay at the ashram, there was a person who seemed quite agitated much of the time. One day, in anger, he forcefully dumped an entire bucket on a baby tree. As we stood there looking at the tree, I wrote a note about pouring the water slowly.

I had not gotten to describing the importance of protecting the small tree when that man started yelling at me, saying, "What difference does it make?" I tried to write another note to keep my silence, and that guy burst out again. I spoke to him to explain that we were attempting not to waste water and also to protect the baby trees from uprooting. We needed to give them enough water so they would not dry out and die before the next water delivery.

That same man was much calmer a few days later. He explained that he had been taking malaria medication that made him both lose a lot of weight and get upset easily. He finally realized that it had seriously undermined his physical and mental health. He stopped that medication, and then he was perceivably much more relaxed, and easy to talk to.

After I had been at the Bangalore ashram for about three months, Gurudev said, "Seva is the only work done without *vasana* (latent tendencies), without selfish cravings."

"When you take action without vasana, you become an embodiment of enthusiasm."

Chapter Fifteen: Saving My Life Again

With the warm weather, it was comfortable for me to wear a t-shirt and shorts for gardening seva. There I was, the guy from California, walking through waist-high weeds in shorts. I was fascinated by the insect life, from the turquoise-blue spider with gold stripes on its leg joints to the centipedes that hid under my meditation pillow.

I failed to put two and two together. Even though there were only a few sections with tall weeds where water collected, I was getting lots of insect bites all over my legs each day.

Our first three weeks in the Parashara building were spent without any screens on the windows. We had clotheslines made of rope crossing inside the room in multiple places. Mud wasps would build nests in my t-shirts while the t-shirts were hanging on the indoor clothesline.

We also had a nest of fire ants outside that I got too close to since I was impatient to get more gardening done.

The fire ant bites happened like magic and hurt instantly. Those fire ants moved like lightning. It was incredible.

When I was growing up, I was registered with Medic Alert as having allergies to insect stings. (Medic Alert is an organization in the USA that provides medical personnel with critical medical information about patients who have life-threatening conditions.) As an adult, I forgot about my allergies to insect stings.

Each day, during most of the first three months of my four-month 1991 ashram stay, there were more bumps from numerous insect stings on my legs. Foolishly, I was ignoring (having forgotten) my own vulnerability. My focus was on doing as much as I could to improve the ashram. Unaware of my own recklessness, I ignored minor itching that repeatedly came and went as my allergies to insect stings worsened.

For several weeks, all the gardening tools were kept locked in my dorm building, Parashara. I had to wait for every tool to be returned before I could wash up and change. Which meant that I was generally the last person to finish.

Midway through my four-month stay at the ashram, we were having small satsangs with Gurudev after seva, before lunch, in the Devi platform meeting area with thatched roof.

One day my skin started itching like crazy, worse than ever, during the seva time. Eager to beautify the ashram, I ignored it and kept working. By the time all the tools were turned in, I was hot, sweaty, and itchy all over. Ignoring the insect bites all over my legs, I thought that maybe something on my skin was the irritant. My scalp was especially maddeningly itchy. I washed all over with some iodine soap.

After bathing in cold water, the itching subsided. I thought that I was in the clear.

The next day, the same thing happened. As I waited for the last tools to be returned, I felt like the itching would cause me to explode. My whole body felt extremely odd and itchy.

Again, I lathered all over with the iodine soap, including my head, and rinsed over and over with the cold water.

Nothing helped. I was still itching like crazy. Getting dressed was strangely awkward. Plus, after getting dressed, I felt like I was underwater. Physical movement was becoming more difficult. My head felt strange, with increasingly greater pressure all over. Mentally, I was out of touch with my body's intense allergic reaction to the insect stings.

If we had had a decent mirror, I would have been shocked by my appearance. I was by myself, trying to get to the meeting. Vaguely, I had the thought that I was more tired than I should be before lunch. My inner determination to get to the satsang was the only thing keeping me going.

With unaccustomed difficulty, I slowly climbed up the hill to the meeting area. Thoughts were becoming more muddled. Each step was challenging since my joints did not like bending. I forced myself to keep moving. The allergic reaction intensified with every step.

The rocks and dirt were the same as they had been earlier, but I was starting to feel like I was on another planet. It was hard to move, and the thought of lying down made the dirt look softer than it was. I talked myself out of attempting a brief rest. *One step after another, just a little further.*

After I passed the top of the hill and the meditation hall, I slowly approached the meeting area. From about fifty feet away, I could see the whole side of the building. Since there was no wall on that side, nothing was hidden. Everyone was already seated, and Gurudev was talking to them. I was heading directly toward them. Gurudev's right side was toward me, and the audience had their left side towards me. There was no wall, only open space between us. On previous days, Gurudev had continued talking as I approached and entered the room. His routine was to ignore my legitimately late entry.

Curiously, Gurudev stopped talking and looked at me. His eyes popped open wider than I have ever seen. The master kept staring at me as I slowly approached. The whole group was silently looking at me for the last twenty feet of ground that I covered before I reached the hall.

I felt like my body was a big container of weird liquid in a pressure cooker, and the pressure inside was increasing. He kept staring, his eyes opening enormously wide.

There was a brief flash of self-consciousness since I was the center of attention. Gurudev remained silent and never dropped his gaze.

Part of me was drowning in the overload of venom in my veins. Part of me was noticing and thinking it was odd that Gurudev would keep staring. My cognitive abilities had decreased and were fading.

As I came within about six feet of Gurudev, full of concern and urgency, he asked me, "What happened?"

Miserably, I barely managed to reply, "I don't know."

I had not connected the dots that I was full of insect venom and verging towards a fatal allergic reaction.

My body felt like it would burst; the swelling was becoming severe.

"What should I do?" I asked, feeling desperate and with a vague awareness of being trapped and exhausted.

Gurudev pointed at a spot on the ground, just 3 feet away from where he sat. He gave an abrupt, serious command: "Sit in *vajrasan*. Do *ujjayi* breath." Vajrasan is a simple, basic, kneeling pose that many people sit in while doing pranayama. Ujjayi breath is a simple pranayama that involves a slight closure in the upper back of the throat, also known as victory breath or sounding breath.

As I sat, I closed my eyes and started ujjayi breathing. Ujjayi breath in vajrasan was quite familiar since I had been doing it daily for more than three years.

I felt a sense of safety for having reached the master, though it hurt to bend my legs. Gurudev resumed his talk. Unable to focus, I have no idea what the topic of discussion was.

At first, it was difficult just to sit and breathe. Gradually, I began to feel the pressure inside my body begin to decrease. Gurudev gave me a miracle of healing. It was such an incredible relief. I don't know how long I sat there.

Gurudev did not stop the discussion until I felt much more like my usual self. I was only mildly dazed after Gurudev got up and walked away.

Right after Gurudev walked away, Pierre, one of my roommates in Parashara, came up to me and exclaimed, with his distinctive French-Canadian accent, "My friend, I did not recognize you! Your face was swollen! You looked like a clown! You looked like a clown!"

With that, I realized that I had been way too careless. After that, I remembered my allergies and made an effort to avoid being an easy target for insect bites and stings. When we ignore nature tapping on our shoulder, it sometimes takes a strong shaking to get us to wake up to a reality we chose to be blind to.

Gurudev effortlessly providing a miracle of healing was just a small moment in his day and a huge turning point in my life. I am deeply grateful for that profound miracle of rapid healing.

Real yoga makes it easier for miracles to happen. Feeling gratitude for what we have received makes it easier for more good things to come to us. Real yoga facilitates the experience of gratitude.

Components of Exhalation

Most of the ashram areas for group sadhana were open-air venues. There was a thatched roof overhead and a concrete wall on one side, behind the audience, for the meeting hall that we sat in for the first three months of my time at the ashram. There were no glass windows, just open space on the other three sides of the room. Two sides had low, decorative, minimal, and partial walls. With no barriers, birds could fly in and out if they wished. Fresh air was continuously abundant all day long. Having had this experience made me even more aware of the types of rooms used for sessions in our so-called modern world.

When the exhalation of humans is analyzed, amazingly, over 3000 different substances can be found. This is a deliberate understatement of the reality of what is in an exhalation. If you start with fresh air containing about 21 percent oxygen, each human exhalation will end up with approximately 16 percent oxygen. It makes sense that, whenever people are breathing deeply in an effort to imbibe more energy and life force, they would want to have the freshest air possible.

Keeping windows closed promotes the growth of mold and fungus. Even the US government agency known as the Environmental Protection Agency says that indoor air quality is a major health issue, in many cases due mainly to people keeping windows closed.

The average person consumes about 420-480 liters or 111-126 gallons of air per hour, more while exerting or doing pranayama. During pranayama and other types of yogic breathing, stress goes out of the body along with waste gases. Thus, the trend of keeping windows closed during pranayama and yoga classes is not just unhealthy; its effect is completely opposite to the goals of Yoga.

Properly executed, with abundant fresh air containing lots of oxygen and fresh prana, pranayama and yoga slow down the aging process. In stuffy rooms with closed windows, as a group of bodies are exerting themselves, oxygen and prana reduce drastically, waste gases increase rapidly, the mind loses clarity, and aging accelerates. Most of the components in each exhalation are not life-supportive for humans.

As yoga and meditation have grown in popularity, attendance at gatherings has increased. Workshops with spiritual leaders have widely variable sizes of groups of people. Hotels and convention centers provide convenient space for larger groups. Just because a group resorted to holding gatherings in buildings with canned AC air does not mean it is good to use canned air spaces on a regular, daily, or weekly basis for yoga classes and pranayama practice.

On the other hand, in 2006 and 2016, Art of Living hosted two extremely large events in India. Literally 2.5 million people were in attendance in 2006, and 3.75 million people attended in 2016. Such massive gatherings were held outdoors, under the open sky.

Darshan with an enlightened master is often only available for brief periods of time. It is worth having darshan even in an enclosed, air-conditioned arena.

Most people want to get some benefit from their actions. If you are going to invest time and energy in doing yogic practices, it is worth making a little effort to ensure fresh air flow to get healthy results. The same holds true for weekly or monthly gatherings for groups. You can set up conditions to get beneficial results from your practices.

Anyone who wants to be good at yoga and pranayama would be well advised to maintain fresh air flow as much as possible, wherever they are, throughout the day. A person who is used to breathing fresh air will notice quickly when the air in a room becomes stale. Unlike someone who lives mostly in canned, AC, and heated environments and doesn't notice if the air is stale, low in oxygen, or low in prana.

Teachers of yoga and pranayama especially need to pay attention to the air quality in a room. Powerful experiences of higher states of awareness can be more easily attained when one is in a place with fresh air. Prana is associated with oxygen, though oxygen alone is not prana.

Gurudev talked about obstacles to yoga as detailed in Patanjali's *Yoga Sutras*. Illness is an obstacle. Stale air promotes illness. Since freshness in the environment is a part of cleanliness, having windows open could be said to be a part of the component of Raj Yoga known as Niyama, or how to manage oneself. (See page 70.)

Cobra Cave Adventure

In between silent Advanced Courses, there were often times when the ashram was quite empty. One day, in between courses, about five of us who were staying at the ashram were standing together. We stood by a Ganesh statue near the ashram entrance, deciding what to do. Walking briskly, Gurudev appeared and asked us if we would like to go on an adventure. Of course, we all agreed with big smiles.

Gurudev had us get into a small car that drove us for just about seven minutes, not far north of the ashram. The land on both sides of Kanakapura Road was still mostly undeveloped.

We parked in a dirt lot that had only a few large rocks

and small bushes and trees nearby. As we got out of the car, a skeletal man dressed in tattered, worn clothing appeared and greeted Gurudev. Gurudev said something, and the man just wiggled his head and moved away from us.

Very nonchalantly, Gurudev announced that there was a cave we could visit. Gurudev started walking and took us to the entrance of the cave on the other side of the boulders. As we walked up to the cave, Gurudev calmly and quietly revealed that there was a cobra who lived in the cave. A slight ripple of shock passed through the group.

Gurudev reported that the cobra's home was a temple and that people would perform puja to the cobra every day. Gurudev told us that the cobra was a yogi who had decided to incarnate as a cobra. Gurudev also stated that he had lived there for hundreds of years.

The quiet group was now silent. Some eyes were open wider. Probably some of us felt a bit squeamish about going to visit a cobra, whether or not he had been a yogi in a previous life.

We figured that since Gurudev was with us, we would keep going. The cave was cool and quiet. Some minimal Sanskrit writing in red paint decorated the pale brown rock.

Gurudev invited us to sit against the wall. He said that we would meditate.

I wanted to sit next to Gurudev. Since everyone else was on his right-hand side, I sat on his left.

With growing alertness, I realized that the small hole at ground level in the back of the cave was where the cobra came out. I was the closest person to the cobra's doorway. For a moment, I felt a slight hint of queasiness, then I thought that Gurudev would not put us in danger. I urged myself to go back to feeling relaxed.

The situation contributed to my being in a state of alertness. I watched my thoughts and failed to find a definite state of calm. *How does one greet a cobra? What is proper behavior with a cobra of exalted status? What might the cobra do? What would Gurudev do?*

I grew determined to return to simply enjoying being with Gurudev. I wanted to drop that thought as well. After observing myself and breathing deeply, I finally started to settle into meditation.

The cobra decided not to visit us. Our meditation ended peacefully and quietly. I felt an odd mixture of relief and disappointment in not seeing the cobra.

Marriage

Gurudev has stated that the purpose of marriage is to nurture your partner. Marriage is an opportunity to develop unconditional love. Marriage is a place for us to grow and live with acceptance.

Gurudev told us that, often, in many cultures, we live a life that is based on fantasies and fairy tales. It is important to accept some discomfort as part of life and not expect that we are always going to be completely comfortable. We have to live with reality instead of fantasy. Gurudev pointed out that love requires courage.

Many try to find an ideal partner who is perfect. This is not realistic. Gurudev emphasized that it is natural that the charm one finds initially will fade with time. It is important to accept this and not be in a hurry to change partners. Whatever karmas we have, they follow us wherever we go.

"Marriage is so that you can complement your partner if you see that they are deficient in some area."

Marriage is a form of relationship that can cultivate devotion. When you come from a space of giving, then you will find success. Then you start to make it possible to reach divine love. Real yoga supports this process.

Judgment interferes with love. Gurudev revealed, "When you are not aware of judging, you are more attached to it."

"Love includes anger. Nothing is excluded in love."

He made it clear that it is your job to help your partner if you see that they are lacking in some area. Honor is a sign of love. A person or thing that is loved will be treated with honor.

Many people have unrealistic expectations about love. Gurudev stated the reality that an expectation is just a creation of our imagination. On a number of occasions, Gurudev has insisted that hurt is part of love. Rather than running away from hurt, he says we should embrace it. Meaning that when it happens, we face it instead of rejecting it. Which does not mean becoming a masochist looking for a sadist to hurt us. It is wise to stay away from deliberately hurtful situations.

Even with the best, most loving intentions, sometimes people cause loved ones to feel hurt. The hurt that came accidentally from a place of loving intention should be accepted and observed. Gurudev taught that unintentional hurt makes our love more unconditional.

"You can love a person as God. Can love as wife or as God. Can love as husband or as God."

"Love void of any demand whatsoever is true love." Gurudev said mature love, divine love, and unconditional love are the same thing. In true love, we totally relax.

Real yoga helps us to develop the ability to experience unconditional love. It is really a matter of cleaning out the blockages so we can experience our true self.

Ancient Wisdom of Ashtavakra

It was my great fortune to be present at the Bangalore Ashram in 1991 for Gurudev Sri Sri's original presentation of talks on the *Ashtavakra Samhita*. Also known as the *Ashtavakra Gita*, this text is quite ancient. Ashtavakra was a saint who lived during King Janaka's time. King Janaka was the father of Sita, who wed Rama. Thousands of years before Krishna. Ashtavakra had eight physical deformities in his body and thus acquired the name Ashtavakra, which means "eight bends."

The days of lectures on Ashtavakra were magical, powerful times. Gurudev's evening lecture impressively included references to the experiences of multiple people. Our experiences were somehow related to the knowledge contained in Ashtavakra. Gurudev declared that *Ashtavakra* was happening for us every day.

One day I overheard two ladies talking at a meal. Skeptance complained to Artile that a certain man had told her that he found her attractive. Skeptance was bothered that this man had told Skeptance that he had frequent sexual thoughts about her. Showing frustration and anger, Skeptance then got emphatic and, leaning towards Artile, surprised her by heatedly proclaiming, "I never give off sexual vibes! Have you ever seen me put out a sexual vibe? Ever!?" Pulling back a little in surprise, Artile softly replied, "Well, no."

That night in the talk on *Ashtavakra*, Gurudev asserted, "If you are against sex, you are stuck to it like glue." He emphasized that such people are in the same boat as those who are obsessed with sex. We are being encouraged to "walk the middle golden path," free of craving and aversion. The best way to handle unwanted cravings is to wonder about them. Observe without indulging, and do not get upset.

Gurudev nailed me one night in *Ashtavakra* when I was burning with anger. Some people did something to me that day that I repeatedly asked them not to do. Having been treated with carelessness, disregard, and disrespect, I felt angry about it. I was so upset that I did not want to look at them or acknowledge them. Satsang started while I was feeling the anger.

Close to the beginning of the talk, Gurudev started talking about anger and forgiveness.

"So, you are angry. So what."

"When will you forgive? Next lifetime?!? Forgive right now!" He was vigorously emphatic.

I was sitting a few feet from his right side. He was not looking at me, but I instantly got the message. There was a brief moment of reluctance. I thought the people needed to learn a lesson. Then I just let it go and physically bowed down. I forgave them right then and there.

Ashtavakra is jam-packed with potent, pertinent knowledge. It seemed like the perfect text for Gurudev to comment on since it says some things quite bluntly. *Ashtavakra* gets right in your face with the truth.

Expounding on *Ashtavakra*, Gurudev confirmed, "Your feelings and worries arise in your own mind. You are totally responsible. For all that you feel and think, you are responsible." Real yoga includes taking responsibility.

Sometime during *Ashtavakra*, the master addressed many situations when he observed that "your concept that things should be a certain way causes pain in the mind."

In the Bhakti Sutras, Gurudev said that love for the unknown helps us blossom in bhakti, or devotion. In Ashtavakra, Gurudev revealed more about love for the unknown, equating faith with love for the unknown.

"Spirituality honors the secret, and the honoring of the

secret is called *shraddha*. Shraddha means not knowing what it is but being willing to know with love something that is unknown. Loving the unknown is shraddha."

Shraddha is usually translated to mean faith. Faith gives strength, while doubt weakens a person.

Skill of Handling Silk at the Waterfall

Many of the course participants who were staying at the ashram managed to fit into a large bus. The bus drove south from the ashram to a large waterfall. This picturesque waterfall is impressive for its size and beauty.

Some of us were standing on the bluff, overlooking the falls. Gurudev was walking by himself. I stood to one side, just outside the frame of the camera, as someone took a photo. That photo, with Gurudev facing the camera, ended up on the cover of a truly beautiful book called *The Way of Grace* (Art of Living Foundation). Many people said that Gurudev looked a lot like Jesus in that photo.

At the top of the waterfall, Gurudev was in a silent frame of mind. He just smiled. He turned around. We looked at each other without speaking. With a bright twinkle in his eye, he moved on. His silk cloth billowed in the wind as he walked past me. The thin, fine silk caught on a thorn behind Gurudev's back and out of his line of vision. As I jumped forward and held the cloth carefully to prevent the wind from tearing it further, Gurudev stopped walking. He did not turn his head or look at me. Gently, I pulled the silk off the thorn. Gurudev paused as he remained silently facing away until the silk was freed. Without looking at me or what

I was doing, Gurudev knew exactly when the silk was free of the thorn. As soon as the silk was free of the thorn, Gurudev immediately started walking away. After releasing the silk, I simply stood there and watched him walk toward the edge of the cliff by the waterfall.

Near the edge of the cliff, Gurudev slowly lifted his arms and then slowly lowered them to his side, as if he were embracing or blessing the whole area. Just as he did this, someone took another photo from directly behind Gurudev. This photo of Gurudev, taken from the rear, was duplicated and sold in the ashram a couple of weeks later.

That night, during his commentary on Ashtavakra, Gurudev spoke about skillfulness in life. He mentioned that it takes a particular skill to remove a silk that has caught on a thorn. He used it as an example. He made the point that just as it takes a particular skill to remove a piece of fine silk cloth from a thorn without ripping the cloth, it takes some skill to manage one's own mind. Real yoga gives this skill.

Typing a Letter for the Guru

One day, Gurudev asked me to type a letter for him. He dictated the letter to me in the morning.

"Do you have a typewriter?" I asked.

Making a vague gesture, he replied, "Look around."

It made sense to me that the easiest place for me to find a spare typewriter would be the classroom for village women, where Gurudev's father, Pittaji, taught classes. I walked over and saw that the door was open. As I walked up to the door, I could see old-fashioned typewriters on desks. Sticking my head in, I called out. Pittaji came over. Pittaji did not know me or show any recognition of me.

"Yes, what is it?"

"Gurudev asked me to type a letter for him, and I was hoping to use one of your typewriters."

"No."

The terse refusal took me by surprise. "Gurudev wants this letter typed today. I don't know where else to type it. Please, may I use one of these typewriters?"

"No."

"But nobody is using them right now; it's for Gurudev. I can be very quick."

"This is a school; you have to leave now."

Perhaps he thought I was an imposter. It was an unexpected, surreal moment. *Is he afraid someone would see me? A white man in a room for women?* "Do you know of any other typewriters? Where can I type this letter?"

"I don't know. Goodbye."

With that, he closed the door. I was left in a personal puddle of bewilderment.

Where am I going to find a typewriter? At that time, there were no offices on the ashram with a typewriter. Laptops did not exist.

I asked each person I saw if they had a typewriter or if they knew someone who had a typewriter. This became time-consuming. There were not many people at the ashram that day. Someone suggested I would have more luck at lunchtime when more people were gathered. Lunchtime arrived. After asking a few people, someone suggested that they thought some lady named M had a typewriter. Then I searched for Lady M.

When I finally found Lady M, she hesitated. Reluctantly, she agreed that I could use her typewriter, only because it was to type a letter for the master. She stipulated that I would have to get it from her room by myself since she did not want to walk back to her room with me.

Once I managed to find the room where Lady M kept her typewriter, I discovered two ladies sitting on the bed. These ladies were having a quiet, intense discussion in a language that I did not understand. As soon as I stuck my head in the door, they clammed up. When I said hello, they did not answer. *Do they live in this room? Or not?*

When I explained the reason for my being there, the two ladies still did not say anything. They watched me intently, yet refused to meet my eyes. The two ladies were watching my every move closely the entire time I was there. When I looked at them, they quickly looked away. *Weird.*

One wall beside the bed was covered by piles of stuff. I figured that hopefully the typewriter was in one of the stacks, which went from the floor to above my head. Since most things did not look like typewriters or a typewriter case, my choices were narrowed down. A couple of small suitcases tricked me into pulling them out, but no typewriter was inside. There was a wooden box that had a nice finish. When I pulled it out, the heavy typewriter was revealed.

It took another ten minutes to find a place to sit and set up. Then it took more time to figure out the quirks of that machine. It was a memory typewriter. I had used memory typewriters but not that particular model. At first, it refused to respond to any coaxing of the keys. Finally, hours after the dictation, I was typing the letter.

When I was done, I ran to Gurudev's kutir. He took the letter and read it.

"You forgot 'Jai Guru Dev'! We always say 'Jai Guru Dev'. You didn't even put 'Jai Guru Dev'."

I was embarrassed and surprised by my omission. In my rush to type the letter, I had omitted a crucial detail.

"Jai Guru Dev" was assumed and not explicitly stated in the original dictation. I ran back to the machine, feeling deeply grateful that I had one more, clean sheet of paper. Quickly, I typed the corrected letter.

Once I gave the final letter to Gurudev, he glanced at it and then dismissed me. A huge chunk of the day was consumed by that simple task.

Trip to Mysore and Miracle Photo

During a break in between silence courses when there were only about fifty people staying at the Bangalore ashram, a small group of about forty of us made a bus trip with Gurudev. We drove South from the ashram to the city of Mysore. This was a carefree, surprise interruption of the evening discourses on the *Ashtavakra Gita*.

On the way to Mysore, we stopped at a river and lake area that had rowboats for rent. Someone burst out, "There are crocodiles out there! It's too dangerous to go out in a rowboat!"

Gurudev was not bothered and walked right up to a boat that some devotees were holding for him. I wanted to be on the boat with Gurudev, but I could see that the boat was full. Amazingly, a kind gentleman who lived long-term at the ashram got out and let me have his space. Some of the group stayed back on the shore, while a few went out into the crocodile-infested waters with Gurudev. The crocodiles ignored us and kept their distance as we paddled around.

After the boat ride, we continued riding in the bus. Before we got to Mysore, we made another stop beside a river. Only part of the group went to the riverbank with Gurudev. With a lot of trees in the area, it was easy to find a peaceful spot. A simple concrete entry to the river, called a *ghat*, had steps starting on the dry riverbank and continuing down under the water. The border of the ghat was a concrete wall that projected out into the river. Gurudev walked out on this wall and stood there by himself, silently gazing off into the distance. It was a beautiful, tranquil moment.

Some people in the group started taking photos of Gurudev. Several others went running to get their cameras. I had been enjoying the scene, feeling quite relaxed, when I noticed that I was getting the urge to take a photo myself. Generally, I am not a photographer. People who know me know that I hardly ever take photos.

It was odd. I knew that I was feeling the desires of the people around me. Yet I still thought that I should also take a photo. On the other hand, I had a feeling that it would be best to ignore the desire. When nobody had a cell phone, cameras were less common. Over the years, I observed Gurudev sometimes disapproving of people who would lose their centeredness for the sake of a photo.

I was still witnessing multiple cameras clicking away. Gurudev had turned around and was beaming a loving smile. Abruptly, I gave in to the desire and went over to a friend and asked to use their camera. As I turned back to Gurudev with the camera in my hand, he looked right at the camera. Gurudev's smile disappeared as he looked into my eyes. He looked even less happy as I took a picture.

Realizing that I had ignored my higher wisdom and given in to the group fever of camera frenzy, I still felt sad that I had missed the nice smiles. Gurudev looked more serious and annoyed as he approached and walked by me. I half-heartedly snapped another photo. Then I felt stupid for getting photos with a serious look and without the big smile.

Gurudev kept walking. It was clear that he didn't like how easily we had gotten feverish about getting a photo.

Sometime later, my friend gave me the photos I had taken. I was puzzled because there was an extra photo. This photo was between the two photos that I had taken. In it, Gurudev was standing in front of a tree, facing toward the camera, with a kind, loving smile on his face. I knew that when he had walked by that tree, he had not turned and looked at me. It was clear that I had not taken that photo and that it would not have been possible to get that shot. When I had been holding the camera in front of that tree, Gurudev had his right side facing me. He was frowning and not looking at me as he walked past the tree.

Only divine grace could insert a photo onto a film negative. When I realized that this miracle had happened, I got goosebumps all over. I was stunned. Gurudev had made me heed the lesson by being stern as he walked past me. He didn't want us to get into idle feverishness. On the other hand, he fulfilled my desire by giving me not only a photo of a beautiful smile but also a photo of a moment that none of us who were at the scene had witnessed!

During my first trip to India in 1991, I was moved to write about my thoughts, feelings, and experiences in a way that was new to me. Prior to this, much of my writing had reflected a lot of pain and sadness. What was emerging in India was much more in alignment with the divine wisdom that I was fortunate to be swimming in on a daily basis. For a number of years, drops of poetry expressed through my pores were few and rare. This changed abruptly in Mysore.

While we were parked in Mysore, a friend of mine gave me a copy of an English translation of the *Ashtavakra Samhita*. In the front of the book was a handwritten inscription that included a long version of the meaning of the word "namaste." "*In India, when we meet or part, we often say, 'Namaste,' which means: I honor that place in you where the whole universe resides. I honor that place in you of love, of light, of truth, and of peace. I honor that place where, if you are in that place in you and I am in that place in me, there is only one of us."*

When I read this, I felt a physical sensation in my heart and chest. I sat on the bus, unable to speak. I watched people outside the bus hanging out amongst some handicraft vendors. I felt a sense of disorientation. Gurudev was looking at a wood carving that depicted Krishna driving Arjuna's chariot. Through the bus window, I could clearly see what was happening. It felt like the presence of Krishna was somehow touching and containing the moment in the present as well as in the ancient past. The carving was purchased for Gurudev by a member of the group.

I did not want to miss out on the action with Gurudev. After waiting some time till I felt a little more solid, I got up and climbed off the bus. A moment later, somebody yelled to get on the bus as we were about to leave. Since most people had left the bus before me, when I turned around, I was one of the first ones to get back on the bus.

People continued walking over to the bus. I finished climbing on the bus and getting seated when someone else yelled, "Gurudev is going for a walk! Get off the bus!"

It was as if I were caught in the churning of a cosmic washing machine. I felt vulnerable. I walked up the aisle of the bus. I was behind a line of people waiting to get off.

A number of people had not even climbed back on the bus. It was a densely packed group. I got off the bus behind many people. Yet without planning or thinking about it, I somehow managed, amazingly and blessedly, to wind up right behind Gurudev. My sense of identity was vague. I felt a sense of safety being close to Gurudev. With his presence, it was easier to deal with the disorientation and vulnerability.

Most of my focus was on his feet as they moved back and forth below the edge of his simple white cotton dhoti cloth. We started walking across a street and then along a typically uneven sidewalk on the edge of a road.

As soon as I stepped up onto the curb after crossing the street, there was a surprising sense of the pressure of words, which I felt I must write down at once.

Quickly, I grabbed a used, torn envelope out of one pocket and a pen out of my belt pouch and started scribbling hastily. I kept my walking pace aligned with that of Gurudev in front of me. I had to walk carefully so that I would not step on the back of his sandals.

Magically, words bubbled up to describe a tender, delicate, personal, inner experience that I had not yet even articulated to myself. Seeing the words, I felt both contentment and peacefulness, yet surprise and vulnerability. At that moment, I could not imagine letting anyone see this poem.

No sooner had I penned the last line of the poem when Gurudev stopped abruptly, immediately in front of me. I was grateful that I stopped at once and didn't run into him.

He turned around and walked directly back to the bus. We hadn't even gone a full block.

I felt distinctly that the walk was a way of jolting the poem out. Once it was out, the purpose of the walk was complete for me. *Is that why Gurudev turned back? How could it be? How did Gurudev know?*

That poem on the back of an envelope amazingly survived six more weeks in India, the journey back to the US, and long months and years of storage in random spots. Years later, it was typed onto a computer. A definite miracle.

On the next page you may read that surprising poem.

To My Dearest Lord Sri Sri Parameshwari Gurudev

You are the temple

at which I worship.

You are the heart

with which I pray.

Each day, let me give

thanks for your blessings,

and another chance to play.

The eternal moment is now

and You are always here.

(Written hastily by Daren, September 1991, on a used envelope, while walking behind Gurudev Sri Sri.)

Washing Dishes in Noisy Silence

At the ashram, food was served on rectangular metal trays. Each tray had multiple sections that could hold several more servings than we usually received. Each diner was supposed to rinse the majority of food remnants off their own tray. The setup for washing dishes would change from time to time.

During a particular, ten-day silence course, the arrangement was to wash the metal trays on a little hill, about a two-minute walk from the dining area. There were large metal tubs that held approximately ten gallons. We had one tub full of suds, then two tubs of hot water. Once a tray was rubbed with the suds, it would go through two hot water rinses before being placed in a drying rack.

Groups of four people were assigned to do the washing after each meal. If we worked quickly and efficiently as a team, the whole process could be finished in less than an hour. In my group, three out of the four men were thoroughly committed to keeping strict silence throughout the day. The fourth member of the team disregarded the commitment to keeping silence. Harold complained about washing dishes.

"Why are we doing it this way? This is ridiculous! I hate this!"

"How can the dishes really get clean?

"We're supposed to eat off these trays? This is disgusting!"

Every minute, Harold gave out another criticism or complaint. As the disheartening tirade continued, I could see everyone else's face tighten up. Eventually, I felt my own jaw clamp tighter. The atmosphere became more strained as Harold kept up a stream of stupid complaints that rained into our faces like mud from splashing gutters.

"Why are we doing this? There should be machines

doing this! This is stupid! I don't believe this."

"Are these even clean? We shouldn't be doing this! This is ridiculous! This is disgusting!"

Amazingly, the remaining three of us kept our silence in spite of Harold's noise. Harold was essentially saying the same things over and over, sometimes varying the words slightly. After a while, I tuned him out.

There was an ethereal, collective sigh of relief when our group seva was finished that first day. We rapidly went our separate ways, drifting like silent clouds in different directions.

The next day, when we gathered to wash the trays, only the silent team of three showed up. Harold abandoned us. All the subsequent days of that course were the same: three guys in silence, harmoniously washing trays without Harold.

It was a bittersweet experience. On the one hand, we had a more pleasant, peaceful silence without the turbulence of Harold's agitation and the noise of his complaints. On the other hand, it took longer to finish washing the trays.

I wondered about Harold's nasty strategy of making himself an irritant. That way, when he skipped out on us, we would feel an ironic sense of relief that he wasn't there. At first, I was reluctant to get into a space of acceptance. I was angry at Harold for being lazy, pathetic, and unreliable. I thought he needed a stern talking too. *He avoids real seva. He disrespected the team. He disrespected Gurudev.* Eventually, I was able to drop it. After a few days, acceptance grew into a sense of peacefulness.

Gurudev has said that when someone does something wrong, you can see it as though they are showing you a hole in the ground by falling into the hole. Then you don't have to fall in.

Real yoga requires acceptance and dispassion.

Keep Your Smile

Many times, Gurudev has advised people to keep their own smile at any cost. Most people are quick to anger, making their anger inexpensive. Many people rarely smile. Gurudev says that we should make our anger expensive and our smile inexpensive. Happiness and contentment are both fundamental in real yoga.

My years of receiving abuse and living in survival mode, combined with my serious nature, made smiles less familiar to my face. In 1991, I was still learning how to make my smile dominant. It was gradually getting easier for me to smile.

One day our master asked me to lead the group at the ashram in the long, slow OM Namah Shivaya chant. This powerful chant soon put a big smile on my face.

More Gardening Seva

The 21-kilometer South Kanakapura Road ashram, in 1991, was a rocky, barren place. This was broken up by just a few scraggly weeds and small bushes here and there. Clusters of small trees were minimal.

Around the outer edges of the ashram property, there were a couple of buildings that had been started but never finished. Since there were no large trees, these shells were easy to see. One day, as we passed by the shell of an unfinished building, Gurudev reported that there was a saying in the local area: "When you try to build a home or make a family, then you will see how hard that it is."

In 1991, I was eager to get as many plants planted on the ashram as possible. Donated plants would arrive in tiny plastic bags. Carrying baby plants around and nestling them into freshly dug homes in the ground was the start of the profusion of plants that grow there now. Planting trees was important and timely.

Some of us were enthusiastic and vigorous about planting as much as possible in the short time available. Yet some people who showed up for seva did not share that enthusiasm. There were even a few who could not stand being involved and refused to come back after a single, two-hour session. Much of this happened during ten-day silence courses that happened almost back-to-back. Imagine attempting to lead people and instruct them while in silence. Imagine "leading" people who can't stand to be there.

One such person was a man, Mr. Handle, who had an intense dislike for me. He once complained to me that many of his photos of Gurudev were ruined. I was surprised and, with concern, asked, "How were they ruined?"

As if it were obvious, Handle replied, "Because you were either sitting or standing right next to Gurudev." It surprised me that he was insulting me. I didn't know what to say.

Mr. Handle gathered with my team once, when we were carrying rocks in metal buckets to improve dirt pathways. These metal buckets would hold roughly 1.5 gallons. Filled with rocks, they were quite heavy. The bottom of each bucket had a thin metal rim, the thickness of a knife, which extended about 1/2 inch below the bucket floor.

At one point, I was standing near Mr. Handle, who usually avoided me. We were on a fairly flat concrete surface. When all the other people were further away and not looking at us, and I was looking away from him, Mr. Handle dropped his bucket full of rocks. The edge of the bucket nearly cut the small toe off of my foot. It was lucky that I was wearing new rubber flip-flop sandals, as the rubber had some spring. Mr. Handle continued to keep silent as he watched me writhing in pain on the ground.

In spite of the intense pain that caused me to fall down and flop around, I managed to keep silent. Since my toe was still attached to my foot and there were yet more projects to be done, once the writhing had stopped, I limped away to check on the team's progress. I knew there was no point in confronting Mr. Handle. Much later I had some awareness of the karma of the situation. If I had retaliated against him, I would have taken back the intense karma that I had been freed from. Accepting and swallowing the sharp pain, I successfully kept my silence.

This was an extremely painful experience. One of the worst that I have had since meeting Gurudev. Accepting it contributed to my development of dispassion and further depth of silence within. That toe hurt for many months, for about two years afterward.

The years with Gurudev promoted inner expansion. From an expanded space within, new poems sprouted forth. My "Beware the Exploding Heart" poem (see below) describes some flavors of experiences with the guru.

Next to Gurudev's chair, there will usually be a basket into which people place questions and notes. I put a copy of "Beware the Exploding Heart" in the basket.

Some irony prevailed on a later day. Mr. Handle read my "Beware the Exploding Heart" poem to the group. I thought that he might stop, since my name was at the bottom. Given that Gurudev had handed it to him, he was obligated to read it. He read the whole poem in an attentive, feeling manner. He did not mention my name. It is nice to see that, years later, Mr. Handle and I have had peaceful interactions.

FINDING REAL YOGA

Beware the Exploding Heart

Beware the exploding heart,

it sets you on fire,

and tears you apart.

Nothing is left

but that seed essence;

a start.

Beware the exploding heart,

it leaves you flaming,

and the sky is your home.

The sensations go turning,

and you can never part,

always being everywhere.

Beware the exploding heart,

it grabs your awareness;

taking you deeper in,

and further out.

You get stretched

so far in each direction,

the edges are beyond detection.

Beware the exploding heart,

it seizes your eyes,

and opens them forever!

Gazing, gazing,

endlessly gazing.

Beware the exploding heart,

it bursts into pieces

and sets you free.

Birthing One Smile

After we had been immersed in talks on Ashtavakra for several weeks, it happened that I was eager to speak with Gurudev about some personal matters. Every attempt to meet with the master for any purpose was entirely thwarted for at least a week. After that, I was able to sit with him only in groups and not privately.

In his kutir one day, I was sitting with Gurudev along with a group of people. I asked again when I could talk to him. With twinkling eyes, he laughed. While making movements with his hands as if kneading dough, Gurudev's eyes widened. He declared to the others, "Ahh, cooking, cooking!"

Everyone else laughed. Gurudev thought it was hilarious. I sat with my bafflement and embarrassment. He cranked up the heat even more by saying we could talk during a walk to the lake. I knew that would not work since people crowded, surged, and pressed close around him during any walk.

Of course, that was all the answer that I got that day! I felt humiliated, tortured, bursting, and aching. *What should I do if I can't get answers?*

Unbelievably, another two whole weeks went by without Gurudev even looking at me or acknowledging me. We were well into the Ashtavakra series, and there I was, feeling that the most important thing of all was to be able to communicate with Gurudev. Gurudev was completely ignoring me.

Satsang would begin after dinner with the chanting of bhajans. One night, we were chanting for a solid forty minutes before Gurudev arrived. He gracefully swept over to his chair, sat, and scanned the room, moving his head from his left side to his right.

I was sitting in front, just off the center of his chair, on his right-hand side. He kept turning his head until he looked right into my eyes. He gave me a huge smile! Wow! It was like taking off in a jet! Astoundingly, everything felt fantastic, and I no longer felt a need to talk with my Gurudev.

After a moment, words were magically coming into my

head in English while I was still chanting in Sanskrit. It was at once both magical and natural.

The words were powerful and attention-grabbing. I knew I had to write them down. I wrote the poem *One Smile* in one swoop while continuing to keep the beat and simultaneously chant the bhajan in Sanskrit.

We chanted for another twenty minutes. then Gurudev spoke on Ashtavakra for ninety minutes. He concluded by comparing the Ashtavakra Gita with the Bhagavad Gita. He said that with Krishna and Arjuna, it took 500 verses for Arjuna to say he would do what Krishna suggested, whereas with Ashtavakra and Janaka, "all it took was one look, one touch."

Then I remembered the poem. My mouth dropped open. Astonished, I looked up at Gurudev and back down to the poem. I mumbled, "That's what the poem is about."

Gurudev reached out to me, and I handed the scrap of paper to him. He read it in silence and handed it back to me. Then he asked me to read it out loud and commented, "It's good to share your experience."

When a person makes real yoga a fundamental part of their life, miraculous synchronicities happen more often.

One Smile

One smile,

enough to blow away years of misery.

One smile,

and I melt at your feet.

One smile,

and my heart bursts with fullness.

One smile,

and I feel so near to you.

One smile,

and all I can do is thank you.

One smile,

and I know I'm taken care of.

One smile!

Chapter Sixteen: Navaratri, 1991

Navaratri is considered by many to be the most powerful series of events one can attend with Gurudev. Multiple ceremonies with sacred fire, known as *yagyas* or *homas*, are performed during Navaratri. The number of people attending Navaratri at the Bangalore ashram increased every year. By 2009, the size of the crowd was over 5000 people. Finding one's shoes after attending a yagya became an event in itself.

In 1991, the first puja for Navaratri was the initiation of the then-new Meditation Hall.

That first puja in 1991 started at about 10 p.m. at night. There were about 19 to 25 people present (the group fluctuated as people arrived late or left early). Many were devotees from the USA and Europe. The next couple of days, we had about 45 people in the audience. Each successive day usually brought a few more people into the audience.

Each day brought new yagyas, generating waves of powerful, positive energy. Our Gurudev was presiding while keeping strict silence. His silence was awe-inspiring. When Gurudev walked, it was like a quiet wave of infinity passing.

Just to gaze at Gurudev when he was keeping silence was inspiring and transformative. I made an effort to respect his silence by avoiding staring at him.

Chandi Homa

The Chandi Homa is the peak of Navaratri. It takes more time than the other homas. In 1991, at the 21-kilometer South Kanakapura Road ashram, there was more than one fire pit for the Chandi Homa. Between multiple fire pits, plenty of smoke was generated.

When Gurudev arrived, he was dressed in his usual all-white outfit, along with a small, bright-orange shawl draped over his shoulders. The orange shawl seemed like a gauzy, lightweight fabric.

An elder priest was initially at the main fire pit, telling a young priest to put wood on the fire. The older priest kept indicating to the younger priest to continue putting more wood in the main fire pit. The fire pit was stuffed tight. It overflowed with wood. It looked like a supply pile for many homas yet to be performed. *Is this real or some bizarre parody?* Thick clouds of smoke from that clogged fire pit filled the room and oozed out the windows and doors.

I was sitting next to Eberhard, close to the main fire pit. We looked at each other and shook our heads in mutual astonishment over the craziness of the thick smoke. My body was desperate for some air.

Gurudev didn't seem concerned about the smoke. *If he is staying here, then I should be here. I will stay as long as he does.*

Luckily, no more wood was added to that big fire pit, and the flames eventually eliminated most of the smoke.

Taken just a few minutes before a final offering into the big fire pit, Eberhard's photo of Gurudev standing, gazing lovingly down toward some flower arrangements, is a famous picture known to many Art of Living teachers. Right after the photo was taken, Gurudev walked over to stand with his parents as they held the tray for the final offering into the big fire pit.

Attending the Chandi Homa were participants from a silence course that was ending, as well as some people who had arrived early for the next silence course. There were about 175 people staying at the ashram. At the time, it felt like a lot of people. In the next few days, the ashram population decreased. We settled into a new rhythm.

Time moved on with the next silence course beginning, going deep, and then ending. Meetings felt more intimate with fewer people on hand.

Losing Track of Time

At the completion of a yagya that had started in the morning and ended in the early afternoon, Gurudev personally gave *prasad* to each and every one of us. Prasad is a portion of edible items that have been offered to the divine. In this case, it was a sweet, juicy mix.

There were roughly 53 people there. Looking at the tiny cup in Gurudev's hand, I hoped that there would be enough prasad for each of us. I figured we would each have to have only a tiny bit, so there would be enough for everyone to have some. Impressively, Gurudev filled the spoon to the brim every time. Thanks to another minor miracle, everyone got to have a big spoonful.

One by one, we approached Gurudev, who sat on the edge of the stage. Pundits, surrounding Gurudev on the rear and sides, chanted continuously as Gurudev gave out the prasad.

As I approached, Gurudev's eyes stared unblinkingly into mine. His gaze was both lovingly open and unbelievably powerful. The intensity filled me, and I burst into tears. I could barely see to accept the prasad with my right hand and slowly shuffle my way back to my seat.

Sitting down by myself, the yummy prasad melted in

my mouth. I felt delicate. I needed to be with the moment. I closed my eyes and took a breath.

There was nothing to think about or do. I let go and dissolved. Meditation began on its own.

The time was not noticeable. No thoughts came, and there was a long space of emptiness.

The sounds faded away, and I was completely unaware of the surroundings.

After what felt like both no time as well as an eternally long time, I started to sense words being spoken. At first, they slipped past without any recognition.

The words were repeating. As I began to feel that I should pay attention to them, I felt that Gurudev was speaking directly to me.

The words filled my awareness.

There was a sense of importance as well as intensity.

Gurudev's face filled my mind, and he was talking to me without moving a muscle. I heard each word clearly inside my mind.

This was a huge experience, both personal and unexpected. I felt small next to the magnitude of this.

Feeling grateful and like a vague mist of energy, I was all the more astonished when I opened my eyes.

When I wrote down what Gurudev had said to me in my mind, it was a stunningly profound poem.

Know Only Me

Know only me,

for I am the One.

See only me,

for I am the light.

Touch only me,

I am everything.

Feel only me,

I am everywhere.

Know only me,

for I am you.

Know only me,

for you are me.

Know only me.

Know only me!

Surprisingly, no other people were in the room with me. Being entirely alone in the hall made it feel like I had been transported to another dimension.

It was hard to imagine not noticing the group leaving to go get lunch. Usually, hunger would drive me to hurry to line up in the queue as soon as possible, at the beginning of a meal. Generally, there would be a few stragglers hanging out in the meeting hall and having conversations for quite a while after any meeting or gathering. Zero people were in sight, which seemed inconceivable. *When did they leave?*

The silence seemed mysteriously thick. I felt a sense of time extending back for inconceivable eons. The thought of reconnecting with the current time became part of my motivation to leave. Even the nearby pathways were empty, which increased the sense that I was not yet back in my "normal" three-dimensional reality. I walked faster until I was jogging. It was a while before I caught sight of some other people. Only then did I slow down.

Another Opportunity to Be Nobody

At the end of my four months in India, Gurudev was due to leave the ashram a few days before my departure. He was scheduled to travel around India and then on to some other countries.

During the last week of Gurudev's stay at the ashram, he had an organizational meeting with some people who had recently arrived. Gurudev wanted to have a meeting about seva projects, including gardening, and invited me to attend.

As we started the meeting, Gurudev revealed that the

top of the hill was going to be level. He announced that the Sumeru Mantap would be placed there.

Gurudev had already appointed a man from the US to be in charge of gardening projects. At the meeting, the new head of gardening was sitting next to me. Gurudev asked that person if he had any ideas for projects. This discussion went back and forth, right over me, as if I weren't there. While I literally sat in between the two parties.

Gurudev knew exactly what he was doing. By not acknowledging my contribution as the previous head of gardening, he set me up to see if any buttons would get pushed. He kept asking the new person what ideas he had. I could feel the pressure inside myself as I was carefully ignored. It was clear to me that this was a set-up to push my buttons, so I played along as an observer for a while.

There were some projects that Gurudev had suggested and discussed with me that had not been completed. It became clear that no mention was being made about several things that had not been finished. The pressure inside me became too much. I finally felt that I had to say something. Gurudev was gracious and agreeable. He heard me, but then switched right back to focusing on what the new person had to say. Even though it was valid to bring up unfinished projects, I felt foolish when I realized that the tricky master and the button inside me had won.

Creating Advanced Course Teachers

Prior to this time in November 1991, all over the world, Gurudev had conducted all the silent Advanced

Courses himself. Since the Art of Living organization was expanding rapidly, there were more groups growing in multiple countries. Gurudev said that he was making some of the Introductory Course teachers into Advanced Course teachers. He mentioned this earlier in the day, on his last day at the ashram.

I felt a little envy about other people teaching Advanced Courses. The more times that I heard Gurudev announce his decision to different people, the stronger became my desire to be one of those Advanced Course teachers. I felt that teaching an Advanced Course seemed like an absolutely wonderful, fun thing to do.

I was walking with Gurudev while he was making his final tour of the ashram. I gathered my nerve and said that I would like to become an Advanced Course teacher.

The response was prompt: "Teach more Basic Courses. You should be teaching more Basic Courses." After a brief pause, Gurudev continued emphatically, "Anyway, you have enough jobs to do!"

I had no idea how busy I would become in just a few years. Gurudev's assignments for me would end up requiring more of my time than a full-time job.

Hard to Say Goodbye

I knew that Gurudev's last afternoon at the ashram would be my final chance to have a few moments to be with him. I met him outside his kutir, and we walked to his door together. He ushered me into his room. His bags were already packed and loaded. There was little left to be done.

I sat on the floor. The enormity of the transformations that I had undergone in those precious months with Gurudev hit me. The gratitude was powerful. I was speechless.

The intensity of gratitude surged. My life had been tremendously transformed while living at the ashram. I felt different from myself. I barely knew who I was anymore. Being able to see Gurudev and be around him every day had been challenging, rewarding, and immensely precious. Sadness about the physical separation that was about to occur hit me seconds later. *How can I possibly say goodbye?*

My Heart Is Soaked

My heart is soaked
with the joy
of your essence.

This is real.
This is worthwhile.
This is it!

It comes from
deep inside.
Your treasure of Being
flows sweetly,
softly,
and accurately
enters my heart.

What a comfort!

Sitting in vajrasan, I wept intensely. Another person came into the room, but I remained lost in weeping. I was surprised at the tears.

My vision was narrowed down to a small slice of the circular room that was in front of me. I saw Gurudev's feet as he stood beside me, observing. Without moving my head, I could see the beginning of his movement as he walked away to my right. Then he returned and handed me a box of tissues.

He actually stood in front of me, for a moment, holding the box of tissues. Then he dropped the box, and it fell perfectly, landing directly in front of me. It seemed funny. I laughed at what was happening, and then more tears came pouring out.

Another Lump in my Throat

Another lump in my throat
as I say yet another goodbye.

Even though it's only on paper,
as a memory,
it cuts deeply.
I feel the longing.
Looking back,
was there any wonder?
My uncertain words:
what use are they to you?

An attempt to wrap up
the inexpressible.
To share a moment
that was so brief.
It doesn't exist
anymore anyway.
Attempts to connect
across time and space,
don't fully satisfy.

When the internal connection
is faster and deeper.
More silent.
Overflowingly full.
Soaked with mystery and completion.

I had mixed feelings about leaving the ashram and returning to California. The ashram had been my home, a safe haven for me to dive deep on an amazing journey into my true nature. So much change had happened in the span of four months. I felt more at home with myself. It was becoming easier to live up to the noble qualities that I had felt were buried inside me my whole life.

The energy at the ashram was very powerful. For those who were fully committed and who followed Gurudev's instructions, the ashram was a cooking pot for the rapid processing of personal growth. For some people, sticking with the program and doing all the sadhana and seva was too much. Some people couldn't handle being in the energy of the ashram continuously. Those kinds of people arranged frequent trips to town. Telling themselves that they needed another shopping trip. Or saying that they at least deserved a full belly from a decent meal. Best found at a five-star hotel.

Most days, I had not stepped foot outside the ashram. I was very comfortable being in the sacred space. I also felt a responsibility to plant as many trees as possible. I wanted to make the ashram as nice as possible for years to come.

On one hand, I saw that I had many responsibilities waiting in Los Angeles. I knew that I would enjoy taking a warm shower with water under pressure while standing up straight. It was clear that I needed to eat much more food than was served at the ashram. And food of significantly better quality than what had been available. During the middle of my stay, I made one of my few trips to town to get a pair of pants for daily wear. I didn't recognize my emaciated self in a mirror. I stepped into a room with mirrors on the walls and, seeing my thin, unrecognized profile, thought a stranger was in the room with me.

On the other hand, I was uncertain about what was waiting for me. How would it feel to be back in Los Angeles?

SECTION SIX: MOVING FORWARD

Chapter Seventeen: Back in California

After four months at the ashram in India, returning to Los Angeles proved to be a challenging experience. Driving, especially at high speeds in dense traffic, took getting used to. Daily asanas, pranayama, meditation, work, hikes in nature, and seva were my grounding points. Every day, I felt myself trying to come up with meaning and answers.

I realized that I had been, and was still, in the process of becoming less judgmental and more accepting. It hurt to feel that I was not able to embody the knowledge every moment. It hurt to judge or doubt myself or other people.

During the commentary on *Ashtavakra*, Gurudev emphasized the true means of eliminating doubt. This went through my mind again and again.

"Answers cannot satisfy doubt. Hearing and seeing cannot eliminate doubt. Only prana can eliminate doubt!"

Many times, I had no words to describe what I was experiencing. There was a lot of aching intensity inside me. I jumped back into managing a full workload. With numerous phone calls required to juggle a packed schedule.

"Reality transcends logic and the rational mind."

The overall gist, of the first few weeks back in Los Angeles, felt like variations on several questions.

Who am I?
What am I doing?
Why am I here?
What's the point?

I was attempting to calibrate myself. Bhajans, seva, and weekly satsang were a saving grace. Seeking clarity, I made attempts to express the process of figuring things out.

Where Is True Value?

Where is true value?

After survival issues are taken care of,

where does the attention go?

What is most important?

What will inspire reliably?

What endures with longevity?

What gives meaning to life?

What is particularly meaningful

in a special way?

What gives comfort and solace

day after day?

What is truly memorable,

after everything is done?

As I applied myself over the months, I began to feel more centered. I felt invigorated with fresh clarity and purpose. Determined to make a positive impact, I felt grateful for opportunities to teach and learn and to overcome my own limitations. Self-doubt was less than before. Eventually, I noticed that I was able to face challenges with less irritation. Even with plenty of room for growth, it was beginning to get easier for me to smile. Real yoga gives many rewards.

Ganesh, Remover of Obstacles

Gurudev has spoken on many occasions about Ganesh. In the universe, there are many groups of things and different types of groups. Ganesh is the ruler of all groups. Ganesh is considered to be a guardian of the path, a remover of obstacles, and a storehouse of wisdom. Ganesh is the name of the natural energies that accomplish these things. Ganesh mantras will promote these energies. Ganesh is often invoked at the beginning of events, journeys, yagyas, moving into a building, etc.

When Gurudev spoke on the *Yoga Sutras of Patanjali*, he also mentioned that obstacles get removed when a person starts having more witness consciousness. Witness consciousness dawns when we imbibe the totality of consciousness which is unconditional love. When a person gets in touch with the core of existence, clarity in thinking and feeling expands.

Gurudev observed, "Just the memory of the Lordship, the divine, can remove obstacles from your way."

The symbolism of Ganesh is ancient and charming. The big belly signifies acceptance and joy, and the snake, used as a belt for Ganesh, symbolizes alertness.

Gurudev has mentioned many times that when people get happy, they get spaced out. On the other hand, when people have a lot of alertness, they tend to get angry more easily.

Ganesh gives an indication that it is possible to have both profound awareness and alertness combined with a fullness of joy and bliss. Real yoga promotes joyful alertness.

Another interesting component of the symbolism around Ganesh is that Ganesh rides on a rodent. How can a huge elephant ride on a mouse or a rat?!?

When Gurudev explains symbols that have been replicated for eons, they seem simple and understandable.

The rat symbolizes the mantra. Just as rats and mice will chew through barriers, the mantra cuts through the stress and gives us a way out. Real yoga skillfully and appropriately uses mantras to benefit many different types of situations and problems.

Mantras can be amazingly powerful. Mantras can help resolve massive and complex difficulties. For these reasons, when depicting Ganesh, a tiny rat is shown to be able to carry an elephant.

Throughout history, many people have felt uplifted when sitting with the chanting of mantras. Many people have experienced the resolution of serious issues when I have helped them by chanting mantras.

If you are wondering if a mantra could be useful for you, please ask me. If you would like to have a mantra to help you deal with a certain issue, please contact me at PracticalAyurveda.com.

In appreciation of Ganesh, one might imagine what it would be like to be a little rat or mouse carrying the divine.

Lord, Let Me Be

*Lord, let me be
the tiny innocent mouse,
who carries you
far and wide.
Chasing dullness,
cutting through obstacles.*

*Let me rest in your presence
with all that gentle gracefulness.*

*Let me be free.
Free of the stench of greed and vanity.
Free to soar to the heights.
Free to rejoice in the sky.
Let me be blessed to know the clouds
that drifted past your fingertips.*

*Let me be that sparkling part of creation,
overlooked by all,
except those who live the truth.*

*When I am swallowed by time,
let me dissolve
into the infinite magnificence.*

Gratitude

The reason I am still alive is because I was rescued by a genuine yogi. I was rescued by the divine grace of real yoga.

The reason that I can do something worthwhile is because I was uplifted. The master lifted me up and made an abundance of knowledge and techniques available.

Through diligent use of these tools, my own life has been transformed beyond what I could have imagined. Repeatedly, I have lifted myself up. I keep moving forward.

True empowerment came from Gurudev Sri Sri, the real yogi. That is the main reason that I am able to offer significant help to others. It is gratifying to realize that I am here to help others uplift themselves.

How can one truly and adequately express thanks? Words are used in an attempt.

My Heart Holds You Softly

My heart holds you softly,

like the softest feather.

My heart holds you sweetly,

like a river of honey.

My heart holds you tenderly,

as you would hold the smallest baby.

My heart holds you with great strength,

like a deeply rooted, giant tree.

My heart holds you in beauty,

like the crisp, deep blue sky.

My heart holds you repeatedly,

like waves splashing on the shore.

My heart holds you endlessly,

like vast space sprinkled with stars.

My heart holds you blissfully,

in singing oceans of ecstasy.

My heart holds you in awe,

beyond the reach of words.

Treasured Quotes of Gurudev Sri Sri

"Uniting with the time, that is Yoga."

"Yoga is part of life. Yoga is that which rejuvenates. By Yoga, I don't mean just the asanas or exercise. Yoga means the entire spiritual practice."

"Yoga is important because it helps you see things as they really are."

"Everything, every moment in life, pleasant and unpleasant, good and bad, is making you grow."

"One who rests in the inner happiness, in the inner space, immersed; that yogi attains the highest."

"True love is total relaxation."

"When there is balance in your body, then your mind is calm, even and free from sorrow."

"The mind of a person who habitually complains has made complaining their mantra. In order to be happy and pleasant, we have to practice being full of joy."

"Anger is a sign of weakness."

"Doubt is a disease."

"Misery is a narrow vision. Yoga is expanding your vision – taking your eyes to the higher truth."

"The purpose of yoga is to put a smile on your face"

"Every crisis reminds you to smile and makes you aware of the impermanence of everything, even ourselves."

"Success in life can be counted by the amount of tears of gratitude we have had."

"Knowledge is like a life jacket. It will always lift you and save you."

"One who is free from craving and aversion becomes eligible to receive the grace and become an instrument of the Divine."

"Abiding in the nature of the seer is yoga."

"You are responsible for creating your own world."

"All praise goes to the Divine."

"It is your choice whether you want to feel good or bad."

"The purpose of yoga is to bring integrity in you and complete you, make you whole."

"If you put your attention on the real and the authentic, you will doubt the fake. Nevertheless, if all your attention is on the fake, you will start doubting the authentic."

"With the power of yoga many abilities will dawn in you."

"Know that what you see in others, other people see the same in you."

"Some karmas prefer to come out in the form of illness."

"Channel your energy into doing something, or you will get restless. Restlessness is also an activity. If you do not channel your energy into some activity, physical, mental, or emotional, that same energy is going to turn inward and turn into restlessness, agitation, and dejection in you."

"Greed is a stress."

"In ignorance, you project your emotions onto others. You are angry at everybody, and you think others are angry at you. You are negative, and you think others are negative. You don't respect people, and you think others don't respect you. You don't love others, and you think others don't love you. You are projecting your mind onto others."

"Divided mind is misery. A one-pointed mind is joy."

"Take the past as your destiny and the future as free will. What was meant to happen has happened."

"Who creates your life? You create it."

"Don't be a football of others' opinions. Let anybody say anything, it doesn't matter."

"Stop wanting love. That is how you become love. As long as the want is there, it takes you further from love."

"A baby is a yoga teacher, a yogi."

"When you have control over your mind, when you train your mind, that mind becomes a very good friend. The mind that you lose control of behaves like an enemy."

"Who leads you in your life? It is your *viveka*, your discrimination."

"Not only misfortune but also fortune, both come to you by divine will."

"When you are confused, you can take a pillow and go to bed."

"See the positivity everywhere and in everyone, and hold the mind steadfast in the self. That is a sign of yoga and it will bring skill in action, success in endeavors and happiness in one's being.

"In deep rest, divinity dawns."

"A real path is to put you onto yourself, into your center."

"Know that everybody is my agent. Everyone is going to push our buttons. See everyone as rag dolls. This is the opportunity for you."

"Only people who accept defeat can be brave!"

"When you gain respect, you often do it at the cost of your freedom."

"Wonder is the basis of yoga."

"Self-hatred brings hatred for others."

"Fear is like salt."

"*Agni* is not the material fire that you sit in front of. The fire in you, the fire of consciousness, is really the *Agni* that moves you forward."

"Your body is offered in the flames of time."

"The goal is in every moment. Yet, the path is long."

"Healthy people must be responsible for taking care of the sick. So also, good people must take care of the bad.

The one called a bad person; their action is sick."

"There is a joy in grabbing, and there is a joy in giving. Unless we move from the joy of grabbing to the joy of contributing, we cannot be satisfied."

"The very awareness that you are part of a whole and that the whole is part of you is a gift. The very fact that you are able to even hear that there is a *Brahman*, meaning the universe is made up of only one thing, is a gift."

"Enlightenment is being in a state of love all the time."

"An enlightened person doesn't crave for people's attention."

"Respecting and honoring your breath is pranayama."

"Karma Yoga is putting in your 100% even though you are not attached."

"Like the self-realized person who takes responsibility for the whole planet yet is not attached. He is not holding on to his actions or the fruit of his actions."

"When you see injustice, you must stand up to it. And stand up with skill; don't be foolish."

"We need to stand in a group. Stand against whatever you feel is wrong."

"Steadiness is dignity. Steadiness is <u>the</u> strength; steadiness is dispassion."

"Truth is that which remains constant and unchanging through the three phases of time."

"Your own body ... is the result of karma. The mind is a result of karma. Your emotions are a result of karma."

"Excess caution creates a weakness."

"Putting oneself totally in the present moment is dharma."

"Yoga brings that inner peace which in turn establishes non-violence."

"Yoga means skill in life."

Jai Guru Dev

More Poetry by Daren

Celebrate the Exploding Heart

Notice the exploding heart,
it sets you on fire,
and tears you apart.
Nothing is left
but that seed essence,
a start.
Appreciate the exploding heart,
it leaves you flaming,
and the sky is your home.
The sensations go turning,
and you can never part
always being everywhere.
Surrender to the exploding heart.
It grabs your awareness;
taking you deeper in,
and further out.
You get stretched
so far in each direction,
the edges are beyond detection.
Explore the exploding heart,
it seizes your eyes,
and opens them forever!
Gazing, gazing,
endlessly gazing.
Celebrate the exploding heart,
it bursts into pieces,
and sets you free.

My Life Burst into Fullness

My life burst into fullness

with your glory.

Like a lightning flash,

a tremendous stroke of grace

lifts us higher.

A thunderbolt

shatters the shackles of the past.

Free we stand,

at last.

Through your grace,

free we stand,

at last.

Bibliography: Books and Lectures

Desikachar, T.K.V. *The Heart of Yoga, Developing a Personal Practice*. Vermont: Inner Traditions, 1995.

Frawley, Dr. David. *Ayurvedic Healing*. Salt Lake City: Passage Press, 1992.

Hari, D.K., & Hari, D.K. Hema. *Historical Rama*. Bangalore: Sri Sri Publications Trust, 2010.

Hawking, Stephen. *The Illustrated a Brief History of Time*. New York: Bantam Dell, 2018.

Hawking, Stephen. *The Universe in a Nutshell*. New York: Bantam Dell, 2018.

Iyengar, B.K.S. *Light on the Yoga Sutras of Patanjali*. London: Thorsons, 2002.

Lad, Dr. Vasant. *Ayurveda The Science of Self-Healing*. Twin Lakes, Wisconsin: Lotus Press, 1985.

Lad, Vasant. *Textbook of Ayurveda Fundamental Principles of Ayurveda Vol. I*. Albuquerque, New Mexico: The Ayurvedic Press, 2002.

Mason, Paul. *Roots of TM*. United Kingdom: Premanand, 2016.

Shankar, Sri Sri Ravi. *God Loves Fun*. Eastern Press: India, 1994.

Shankar, Sri Sri Ravi. Numerous talks on a multitude of subjects in multiple cities attended in person by the author. 1988 – 2019.

Shankar, Sri Sri Ravi. *Patanjali Yoga Sutras, A Commentary*. Bangalore: Sri Sri Publications Trust, 2013.

Svoboda, Dr. Robert E. *Prakriti, Your Ayurvedic Constitution*. Twin Lakes, Wisconsin: Lotus Press, 2011.

Venkatesananda, Swami (translator). *The Supreme Yoga, Yoga Vasishtha*. Delhi: Motilal Banarsidass, 2006.

Yogananda, Paramahansa. *Autobiography of a Yogi.* USA: Self-Realization Fellowship, 2005.

Bibliography: Articles and Websites

Avitzur, M.D., Orly. "3 Hidden Dangers of Hot Yoga and Other Exercise Fads." Consumer Reports, (2014) https://www.consumerreports.org/cro/2014/02/dangers-of-hot-yoga/index.htm

Blackwood, RN, Michelle. "Fresh Air Benefits" https://healthiersteps.com/fresh-air-benefits/#:~:text=Regardless%20of%20the%20time%20of%20the%20year%2C%20having,...%208%208.%20It%20can%20prolong%20your%20lifespan.

Communications Workers of America. https://cwa-union.org/national-issues/health-and-safety/health-and-safety-fact-sheets/indoor-air-quality-and-workplace

Dillbeck, M. C., & Orme-Johnson, D. W. "Physiological differences between transcendental meditation and rest." American Psychologist (1987)

Heid, Markham. https://elemental.medium.com/the-germ-cleaning-power-of-an-open-window-a0ea832934ce

Hoover, N.D., Jerry. "Health – Fresh Air" https://www.stepstolife.org/article/health-fresh-air/

https://www.bridgesbyepoch.com/2019/06/17/florence-nightingales-wonder-drug-benefits-fresh-air-seniors/

https://britplas.com/the-importance-of-natural-ventilation-in-schools/

https://www.ncbi.nlm.nih.gov/pmc/articles/PMC8672270.

https://todayshomeowner.com/hvac/guides/benefits-breathing-fresh-air/

https://yogapodcommunity.com/the-effects-of-air-pollution-on-how-you-practice-yoga

Johnson, Doug. https://sciencing.com/chemical-composition-exhaled-air-human-lungs-11795.html

Kwaku. https://airandwaterexpert.com/is-it-good-to-leave-your-windows-open/

Mike, Gita. https://yogigo.com/can-you-do-yoga-in-a-closed-room/ November (2021)

Rekus, John. https://www.ehstoday.com/safety-leadership/article/21917274/confined-spaces-is-19.5-percent-oxygen-really-safe

Travis, F., & Shear, J. "Focused attention, open monitoring and automatic self-transcending: categories to organize meditations from Vedic, Buddhist and Chinese traditions." Consciousness and cognition, (2010).

Travis, Frederick & Wallace, R. Keith. "Autonomic and EEG Patterns during Eyes-Closed Rest and Transcendental Meditation (TM) Practice: The Basis for a Neural Model of TM Practice." Consciousness and Cognition, (1999).

U.S. Consumer Product Safety Commission. https://www.cpsc.gov/Safety-Education/Safety-Guides/Home/The-Inside-Story-A-Guide-to-Indoor-Air-Quality

U.S. Department of Labor, Occupational Safety and Health Administration. https://www.osha.gov/indoor-air-quality/faqs

Vaszily, Brian. https://theartofantiaging.com/invisible-dangers-of-indoor-air-pollutants/ December (2021).

Wallace, R. K. "Physiological Effects of Transcendental Meditation." Science, (1970).

Wise, Abigail. https://www.huffpost.com/entry/tk-ways-fresh-air-impacts_n_5648164

Thank you for reading
FINDING REAL YOGA!

Hopefully you found this book enjoyable, entertaining, educational, and/or eye-opening!
I hope you loved this book!

Please leave a 5-star review!

Please help yourself to a free report on how to improve your life with Real Yoga practices and tips:

https://finding-real-yoga.kit.com/efd0729b06

Be Your Best
Free Report

If you would like support for your personal journey, I am here to help you. Visit PracticalAyurveda.com to learn more. Help is available whether your need is casual or urgent.

If you need guidance to make a breakthrough, please ask. Visit PracticalAyurveda.com and reach out.

Resources

ArtofLiving.org
FindingRealYoga.com
Gurudev.ArtofLiving.org
Iahv.org
PracticalAyurveda.com
SriSriRaviShankar.org

About the Author

Like a bold rubber band, Daren Black leaped into practicing yoga and meditation in the 1970s.

Multiple vehicle accidents left Daren with chronic injuries, which he did his best to ignore. Life took Daren through a deadly gauntlet of tragedies, heartbreak and homelessness. Fighting simultaneous illnesses, including severe digestive issues, chronic fatigue, allergies, parasitic infections, etc., Daren spiraled down. Daren's life was saved by Gurudev Sri Sri. Intensive breathing practices, mantras, herbs, oils, and large doses of divine grace transformed Daren's life.

Encouraged and inspired by Gurudev Sri Sri, Daren developed PracticalAyurveda.com to make Ayurveda more user-friendly. See PracticalAyurveda.com for health, beauty, and personal empowerment programs.

www.ingramcontent.com/pod-product-compliance
Lightning Source LLC
Chambersburg PA
CBHW030540080526
44585CB00012B/209